INDIA AND REGIONAL DEVELOPMENTS
Through the Prism of Indo-Pak Relations

INDIA AND REGIONAL DEVELOPMENTS

Through the Prism of Indo-Pak Relations

J. N. Dixit

GYAN

GYAN PUBLISHING HOUSE

NEW DELHI—110002

INDIA AND REGIONAL DEVELOPMENTS
Through the Prism of Indo-Pak Relations

Rs. 540

ISBN : 81-212-0785-1

Published in 2004 in India by
Gyan Publishing House
5, Ansari Road, Darya Ganj, New Delhi-110002
Phones : 23282060, 23261060, Fax : 011-23285914
E—mail : gyanbook@vsnl.com
Website : http://www/gyanbooks.com
Laser Typesetting at : Shree Vaishnavi Creations, Delhi
Printed at : Delux Offset Press, Delhi

Contents

Preface

This is the third book containing a collection of my articles and analyses on contemporary trends in and concerns of India's foreign policy being brought out by Gyan Publishing House. The first two books were on "India and its neighbours" and India's meeting the challenge of terrorism.

This book contains articles and papers written by me since March 2002. The attention in this volume is focussed mainly on India's important neighbours, Afghanistan and Pakistan, and on latest developments in Jammu and Kashmir. There are also commentaries on the second Gulf War, Indo-US relations and more recent developments in Iraq.

Many of the presumptions and predications of analyses and commentaries in my previous two volumes mentioned above stand invalidated because of radical new developments in international power equations and regional developments particularly in Asia.

International terrorism has not abated significantly despite the firm and extensive military action taken by the United States against the phenomenon. The United States has become more of an assertive and unilateral player in managing critical events in different parts of the world. United Nations stands comparatively marginalised as an instrumentality to bring about a new world order. While Indo-US relations have improved in range and content, there is disappointment in India about US pressure on Pakistan to cease cross-border terrorism not being as successful as India would have wished. India has also shown reticences about becoming full participant in US operations in Iraq to stabilise that country after the second Gulf War.

The political situation in Afghanistan remains disturbed and unstable even two years after the removal of Taliban from the country. While, of course, India is actively engaged in stabilising Afghanistan. India is subject to critical pressure from Pakistan not to become too influential in Afghanistan.

There have been significantly important developments within Jammu and Kashmir. Free and fair elections being held in the Indian State late in 2002. While Pakistani intrusive activities continue, Prime Minister Vajpayee launched a new peace initiative to restore dialogue with Pakistan in March 2003. The process is still continuing though it is slow. India and Pakistan have restored Ambassadorial level relations after a gap of nearly two years, in the summer of 2003. There has also been a visible increase in interaction between India and Pakistan at the level of people to people contacts through journalists, through members of Parliament, academics and so on.

While Musharraf continues to remain in control of the situation in Pakistan, undercurrents of dissent and criticism about his being supportive of US policies in West Asia is gaining some momentum.

Parallel to this is the remarkable political conundrum of the leader of the Islamic Party of Pakistan Maulana Fazlur Rehman visiting India in June 2003, conveying surprisingly rational messages for peace and normalcy in relations between India and Pakistan.

For the first time perhaps after the Second World War, the harmony among NATO countries stood disrupted in March/April 2003 on the issue of American military intervention against Iraq. Two major European powers France and Germany, opposed the US initiative. Attempts are being made to resolve this contradiction a phenomenon which could affect the international strategic and security environment.

Levels of Islamic extremist terrorism have palpably increased in South East Asian countries. Prime Minister Vajpayee's visit to the Russian Federation and France in April, Deputy Prime Minister L.K. Advani's visit to the USA in June and again Mr.Vajpayee's visit to Beijing in June have had an impact in the nuances and orientations of India's foreign policy and regional assessments.

The analysis in this volume touches upon all these events through the prism of a contemporaneous perspective. The views in the volume will certainly be subject to modification with the benefit of the hindsight resulting from the passage of time. The relevance of this volume perhaps is that it is an attempt at understanding existentialist realities in international politics as they emerge and at visualising their implications.

I convey my thanks to Gyan Publishing House for bringing out this volume. My appreciation is also due to my Secretary, Shri R.N. Sharma who remains of valuable assistance to me in my writings.

The responsibility for the contents of this book in terms of their validity or otherwise remains entirely mine.

J.N. Dixit

INDIAN OPTIMISM IN FOREIGN POLICY

1
The Agra Summit

Fiasco at Agra—Pre-Planned by Pervez Musharraf

One is disappointed, yes. But one is not surprised at all at the abrupt conclusion and termination of Pervez Musharraf-Vajpayee summit at Agra. There was a brief period of about two or three hours on the evening of Sunday, the 15th, when optimistic expectations surged high because of indications about a joint statement being issued at the end of the summit and remarks by President Musharraf that the talks were useful and were going 'Alright'. The minutiae of events in the chronological sequence of discussions at various levels and the exchange of draft documents have all been covered in detail both by the print and audio-visual media. The media coverage in fact distorted the objective perspective in which the summit discussions were held. The dubious virtues of the coverage were political illiteracy and an inclination towards hyperbole. But that is not the purpose of this article. The purpose is to bring out in precise and objective terms, to the maximum extent possible, the fact that the summit failed because Pervez Musharraf had decided in advance that it should fail if India does not accept his demands in toto.

Lest one is accused of a jingoistic approach or of starting a "blame-game". In this context worthwhile re-counting the pronouncements and also orientations of President Musharraf and the Pakistani Government, particularly after he received Prime Minister Vajpayee's invitation on the 24th of May, 2001. In fact, it would be pertinent to go further back to Pervez Musharraf's repeated announcements that he is willing to meet Mr. Vajpayee at any time, on any date, at any place, to discuss Indo-Pakistan relations and to bring them back on track. His lengthy interview to M.J. Akbar, published in the *Asian Age*, was the first detailed articulation by him of his India policies. The second instance is an equally lengthy interview given to Dileep Padgaonkar, the Executive Editor of the *Times of*

India, just a week before he came to Delhi and Agra. In both these interviews he clearly underlined the following points. His primary and over-arching objective to have a meeting with Mr. Vajpayee was to discuss the Kashmir issue from his point of view. He clarified that while he is willing to discuss other issues, affecting Indo-Pakistan relations, he will be willing to discuss these other issues in a substantive and meaningful manner only after a solution satisfactory to him is achieved on Kashmir. When queried about his views on terrorist violence and secessionism, his response was that he was opposed to violence and terrorism but that he does not consider the secessionist violence in Jammu and Kashmir as terrorism. In his view it was a violent struggle for self-determination. That the Jehad in Kashmir was justified. That it was a freedom struggle which Pakistan supports, politically, morally and diplomatically. At the same time he indulged in obfuscation stating that Pakistan was not planning any role in the violence in Jammu and Kashmir and that this was an entirely indigenous phenomenon. He flatly denied Pakistan's sponsorship and support to various violent groups in terms of sanctuaries, supplies and training. When pressurised in these interviews to be specific about a solution which he may have in mind, he said that an acceptable solution to holding a referendum or a plebiscite envisaged in the UN Resolutions of 1947 and 1948. But he wanted these resolutions to be applied only selectively without implementing the provisions in these resolutions for vacation of the territory of Jammu and Kashmir by Pakistani raiders and regular Pakistani armed forces. In an interview to *Gulf News*, just 48 hours before his arrival in Delhi. Pervez Musharraf stated that neither the Shimla Agreement nor the Lahore Declaration and accompanying documents, have any relevance to the summit at Agra. These were the agreements which have not served any purpose, according to him. His Foreign Minister, and he himself of course, claimed that he was quoted out of context by the Indian media. That he was willing to take cognisance of the Shimla and Lahore agreements as bench marks for the future of Indo-Pakistan relations.

Addressing a women's delegation in Islamabad in the first week of July, he said that he desires a new status for the entire state of Jammu and Kashmir unlinked from India. When the ladies delegation asked him what he thought of Kashmir valley being given to Pakistan and Jammu and Ladakh remaining with India, his reported response was that there must not be any ill-informed suggestions on these lines. He told these ladies delegates that there are Muslims in Ladakh and Kargil and in Jammu. They cannot be abandoned. So the whole state of Jammu and Kashmir has to be perhaps be de-linked from India to move towards a solution.

Responding to speculation whether the Line of Control in Jammu and Kashmir could be a basis for a solution, he said a week before arriving in Delhi that the Line of Control is the problem. How it can be a solution, implying that he does not accept the relevance or sensitivity of the Line of Control. He also kept hairpins on the point that he was the first Head of Government and State of Pakistan who has persuaded India to invite him to come and discuss only the Kashmir question. Under instructions from him his Finance Minister Aziz and his Commerce Minister Daud made public pronouncements in the second week of July that Indo-Pakistan cooperation can be structured only after the Kashmir problem is solved. Musharraf did not show any response to suggestions regarding Nuclear Risk Reduction, in the context of nuclear weaponisation of India and Pakistan. In fact, he re-affirmed the legitimacy of Pakistani nuclear weapons and missiles as a deterrence against India and linked it to the Kashmir issue. He also remained adamant about tripartite talks with Pakistan, Hurriyat and India being participants, to find a solution to the Kashmir issue. Though he agreed at individual suggestions that the contacts with the Hurriyat should be separately undertaken by India and Pakistan, but he insisted that Hurriyat should be acknowledged by India as the sole representative of Jammu and Kashmir which is politically and factually unjustified. He then announced just three days before the summit that he is not bringing his finance minister and Commerce Minister but only his Foreign Minister Abdus Sattar for the talks with the Foreign Secretary in the delegation consisting of his personal staff and foreign office officials.

These signals should have been sufficient for us to realise that he was coming for the summit with a narrow Agenda and the single aim. That is either to proclaim to the world after the summit that India had accepted the Jammu and Kashmir issue as not just very important item of discussion but the only and the most important item of discussion. And if he did not succeed, to proclaim to the world that despite special effort that he made to come to India, India remained obstinate and unreasonable.

Leaving aside the cosmetic type which surrounded his engagements in Delhi and Agra, he pushed through the one-sided Agenda without inhibitions and without any concern about its consequences. After giving initial indications that his meeting with the Hurriyat will depend on Government of India's views, not only was the Hurriyat invited to Pakistan High Commissioner Asharaf Jehangir Gazi's tea party but they had a 25 - minute meeting with Musharraf in which he repeated the contents of the letter which he wrote to them just before the summit, extending them full support and acknowledging them as the sole represent actives of the State of Jammu and Kashmir. In his banquet speech at the Presidential banquet on the evening of 14 July he adopted a admonitory and hortatory tone urging India to solve the Kashmir problem. It should be mentioned in this context that he not only wanted Kashmir to be the sole item on the Agenda but he also wanted a solution to the Kashmir problem within a definite time-frame (Almost like an ultimatum).

Then came the calculated theatrics aimed at aborting the summit meeting. He addressed a breakfast meeting of senior Indian and foreign editors on the morning of Monday the 16th July, without telling them in advance that his address to them in the discussions would be filmed and broadcast by the Pakistan T.V. It was a highly aggressive performance in which he emphasised that Pakistan cannot give up the primacy of Kashmir in discussion Agenda with India. He stated that he considered confidence building measures irrelevant unless the fundamental confidence building measure of a solution of Kashmir problem is not implemented, a solution which should be acceptable to Pakistan. He went on to say that if India did not trust him, why did India invite him. He justified his aggression in Kargil as a response to India supporting the Liberation struggle of Bangladesh and India occupying Siachen in 1984 (He ignored the fact that Indian action in Siachen was a pre-emptive step against impending Pakistani moves in the area). No head of Government or a senior Government delegate holds an abrasive press conference justifying his negotiating stance in the middle of negotiations while they are still going on. Even if one agrees that Sushma Swaraj's Press briefing on the 15th of July was somewhat one-sided, there was no need for Musharraf to address the Press after the Pakistani delegation had responded to Swaraj's interview. Parallel to this exercise, tactical moves were made to prepare the ground work for a Pakistani publicity and diplomatic offensive against India. Foreign Minister Sattar told the media that there is likelihood of a joint press statement while it was clear by Sunday night that there was going to be a deadlock. Simultaneously, Pervez Musharraf undertook a lengthy one to one discussion with Vajpayee to give the impression that he was struggling to forge a compromise which in fact was not the case according to information, which one has, Musharraf's response to Vajpayee's invitation was predicated on wrong assumptions. He thought that India was vulnerable to external pressure; (b) that the Government and the security forces of India had reached levels of exhaustion where they would not be firm about responding to Pak-sponsored separatism and terrorism in India; (c) he thought that the coalition led by Vajpayee is faction-ridden and that Vajpayee faces pressure from the opposition because of which he would not be able to take firm stand against Pakistani advocacies.

He felt that in this context, he would wrest a compromise from India within the framework of the Pakistani Agenda on Kashmir. He also felt that Vajpayee could not afford to see a failure of the summit organised at his initiative. Discussions on the 15th and 16th of July have proved that he was completely wrong in these assumptions. His alternative game plan that if the summit failed, he would tell the world about his reasonableness and India's obstinacy has partially succeeded. This also suits the vested interests of his survival in power with the support of the armed forces and the Islam-pasand parties who do not wish peace or a realistic compromise on Kashmir.

Though one is disappointed at the failure of the summit, in overall terms it might be good for India. We have given a clear message about our firmness in protecting our interests in face of tentative and uncertain prospects of peace with Pakistan. There is no need for India to be down-cast or desperate.

Discernible Political and Strategic Concerns of India Post-September 11, 2001-A Retrospective Analysis

The fall out of the terrorist attacks in New York and Washington is mostly analysed in operational terms of the campaign against international terrorism being conducted by the United States. What is more important are new trends of power equations, even possible hegemony which may evolve out of the emerging policies of the major powers, particularly, the United States. India's historical experience of foreign invasions and colonialism should make India concentrate not only on countering internal trends of divisiveness by political, socio-economic and constitutional means, but India should also be alert about negative projections about India by other powers.

India is, and should remain unperturbed by the deliberately motivated and pernicious strategic image as a self-opinionated hegemony,being projected by certain foreign think-tanks and academic circles. Compared to the US, and China and Russia (even after the break up of the Soviet Union); India does not have any ambitions or capacities to create an area of influence in South Asia. The USA's involvement with creating a new world order, China's general approach towards South East Asia and Russia's continuing anxities to exert intrusive influence in Eastern Europe and Central Asia merit apprehension regarding hegemony more than Indian policies. India must interpret such inclinations and accusations as motivated by a desire to keep it under pressure and ensure its not achieving a status in the international community commensurate with its size, resources, capacities and commitment to democracy.

Out of the three powers mentioned, it is possible to accept the fact that the capacity of the Russian Federation for exercising intrusive influence stands limited because of its own domestic, political and economic problems. But in the long run Russia's innate capacities will motivate it towards Great Power status again.

Having enumerated and assessed the fundamental and more abiding security concerns of India, one moves on to the more specific theme of Indian perspective about global political and military strategies which have emerged after September 11, 2001.

The main characteristics of the new political and military orientations in the policies of the major powers of the world have certain common or parallel strands which could be summed up as follows.

First, that the western democracies led by the United States have a special, even exclusive responsibility of structuring a new world order. Secondly, that this new world order should consist of nation-states which conform to their terms of reference of good governance, democracy and respect for human rights. International arrangements for economic management should be structured on the principles and practices of free market economy and competition (which need not necessarily be fair). The competition will be subject to the innate competitive capacity of nation-states.

The new world order should ensure free access to energy and natural resources. Terrorism and religious extremism should be resisted and eliminated, particularly terrorism and religious extremism which threatens the security and stability of western democracies. This political and military campaign against terrorism of necessity has to be carried out by a coalition of nation States which have the resources—military and technological capacities and consensus in political will to carry out the campaign. Therefore, such a coalition has to be primarily a coalition of western democracies led by the United States.

Given this requirement, the United Nations can play only a secondary and supportive role in this campaign against terrorism and religious extremism. A different exercise in politico-strategic engineering ensuring security and stability in conflict-prone areas of the world is underway.

Compared to the military alliances which the US forged in the 50s and 60s to contain Soviet Union and China, the approach now is that of not having formal military alliances. The alternative chosen is to have a pattern of strategic and security consultative arrangements and regional security, consultative mechanisms providing the basis for cooperation to ensure political stability.

Setting up pre-emptive action arrangements to ensure security and to avoid conflicts. These arrangements are now being underpinned by organising direct US military presences in various parts of the world. Since September 11, US forces stand located in Azerbaijan, Uzbekistan, Pakistan, Afghanistan and the Philippines. This is apart from the presence of the US Navy in the Indian Ocean, in Diego Garcia and in the Straits of Hormuz and off the western coast of Pakistan at Gwadar and Pasni. US military presence has the additional potentiality of preventing, to a great extent, horizontal nuclear proliferation and nuclear confrontation inherent in this US military presence is also the potential capacity of the US to destroy the nuclear assets of countries like India, Pakistan (not to speak of Iraq and Iran).

Countries of Central Asia like Uzbekistan, Kazakhstan, and Turkmenistan are already involved in the extended security arrangements of the NATO under the "Partnership for Peace" mechanism. Important Asian powers, the Russian Federation, China and India have either acquiesced or reconciled themselves to these developments, particularly because these arrangements meet certain categories of the respective national interests of these countries, and partially because no country in the region has the ability to resist these developments.

It is obvious that the increased American politico-military presence qualitatively enhance its political clout in the region, its access to the natural resources of Central Asia and the vast markets, stretching from Turkey to ASEAN and from the Russian Gulf to China. In the longer term perspective, political and strategic developments since September, 2001, have seeds of future competitions, even conflict situations between the United States on the one hand, and Russia and China on the other. It also has seeds of resentment which may grow in India over a period of time despite the current positive orientations in Indo-US relations.

These are the perceptions which constitute the perspective in which India visualises political and strategic developments in the Asian region over the coming two decades. These perceptions also constitute the evolving operational challenges which India's foreign policy has to cope with.

India shall complete 54 years as a modern independent country on the 15th August, 2002. It has been subject to external threats, wars, internal turbulence and disharmony. It has had to adjust to momentous changes in the international situation in the power equations and in the regional as well as the global security environment. Compared to the track record of most of the countries which emerged as independent entities after the Second World War, India's achievements would pass muster by any criteria. It is the new challenges which India faces post-September 11, 2001 which will determine India's position in the emerging global order.

The Sub-continental Crisis—Europe's Ambiguous Attitudes

India's specific focus has been on attitudes of the United States on the current Indo-Pakistan stand off. What one tends to overlook is that apart from the bilateral diplomatic exchanges with the US and other western democracies individually, European Community is getting collectively interested in international crisis situations in the context of their recent decisions to evolve a common foreign and security policy for Europe. The European Union as a collectivity has been incrementally interested and concerned about the Indo-Pak stand off since December last. What is important to note is that despite the existing direct access to the sub-continental developments, Europeans still look to England to interpret the Indian sub-continent to them.

Four senior British officials have visited India since the beginning of the year. The British Foreign Secretary Jack Straw, the British defence Secretary, Geoffrey Hoon, Mr. Chris Patten, a Commissioner of the E.U. (who is a Britisher) and then Sir David Manning, special envoy of the British Prime Minister Tony Blair. There is a perception that Britain's experience and knowledge about India endows them with some special capacity to influence India. Therefore, the British representatives in the various fora of the European Community are an influential voice about India and Pakistan. It is the British Members of the European Parliament who recently convened a special meeting of the Foreign Affairs Committee of the European Parliament to hold a hearing on the current Indo-Pakistan confrontation and the Kashmir issue on the 20th of June in Brussels.

I participated in this meeting on behalf of India. The perceptions and attitudes of Europe towards our predicaments should be an important factor in fashioning our international diplomatic moves on the ongoing crisis with Pakistan.

There were presentations by four main speakers, lasting for about one hour followed by a two-hour exchange of views with members of the European Parliament. I participated in this hearing as the keynote speaker. The other speakers were Pakistan's Ambassador in Brussels Shaukat Umar and two professors Vernon Hewitt from England and Dr. Jean-Luc Racine from France.

The Pakistani presentation as expected was basically a historical justification of Pakistan's claims on Jammu and Kashmir and the manner in which India had obstinately rejected and resisted these claims. Professors Hewitt and Racine while deliberately providing a detached and impartial analysis, nevertheless emphasised that the current troubles between India and Pakistan originated in Pakistan being the base from which terrorist subversion is launched against India. Both these speakers also emphasised that India has to overcome the alienation of a segment of the people in Indian Jammu and Kashmir by providing them a political solution responsive to their aspirations. Both these professors also implied that the Indo-Pak dimension of the solution to this aspect of the problem is based on the ground realities and the line of control between India and Pakistan in Jammu and Kashmir. What was more interesting and relevant was the reactions of the Members of the European Parliament and the nuances in their attitudes on the Kashmir issue.

My perceptions about reactions of these European interlocutors are the following :

There is a general appreciation for the political and military restraint with which India has reacted to Pakistan-sponsored terrorism during the last 7 months.

It is accepted that it is primarily Indian restraint which prevented a war in the sub-continent and a nuclear confrontation.

There is also the view that war has been avoided partially due to Musharraf declaring his intention to stop supporting cross-border terrorism.

It was felt that Indian restraint and Musharraf's speeches on January 12 and May 27 were a result of international political and diplomatic pressure generated particularly by the United States and western democracies in Europe.

The advocacy was that India should continue to remain restrained in the larger interest of stability and peace not only in Asia but in global terms.

These reactions were as expected but the comments and questions on the presentation reflected certain nuances which we in India should take note of.

While there was acceptance that terrorism originated in Pakistan and terrorists under the control of Pakistan, there is still a great amount of hesitation to acknowledging direct links between General Musharraf, the Pakistani government on the one hand and across the border in India on the other. The theory is that Musharraf is trying to do his best but he cannot completely control extremist Islamic terrorism because he has to counter terrorism on three fronts : in Afghanistan, against India and in his own country.

Secondly, the view was expressed that India should give President Musharraf some elbow room and some time to implement the promises which he has made in his policy pronouncements since January.

More than this, India should strengthen his (Musharraf's) capacity to act more firmly against terrorist organisations functioning in Pakistan and Pakistan occupied Kashmir by making more substantial concessions in terms of moving back our security forces and agreeing to a dialogue at the political level as early as possible.

While there was agreement that cross-border terrorism should be stopped and that the sanctity of the Line of control should be respected, there was a consensus that Pakistan has a legitimate locus standi on the Kashmir issue regardless of the legality or otherwise of the Accession of the Princely State of Jammu and Kashmir to India.

India meaningfully seeking a practical compromise on the issue with Pakistan has become even more important and critical due to the nuclear weaponisation of both the countries.

While India's policy stance that the issue should be resolved through bilateral negotiations is respected, there seems to be an incremental feeling that India should not remain negative about some kind of external mediation or facilitation by friendly governments in finding a solution with Pakistan.

Members of the European Parliament had no reticences about proposing some kind of a referendum, joint Indo-Pakistan sovereignty over Kashmir or creation of an independent state of Jammu and Kashmir. When I firmly pointed out the impracticability of all these suggestions, the response was that India should not be hesitant to explore all possibilities of this type. And when I emphasised that Kashmir is more than a territorial dispute, that it affects the very plural democratic terms of reference of the Indian Republic, the response I got was that Indian democracy is strong and stable enough not to be disrupted or de-stabilised by territorial and political concessions on Jammu and Kashmir. Ultimately, I had to categorically emphasise that the question of territorial alienation of Jammu and from the Indian Republic just does not arise whatever its cost, my audience was not pleased with this affirmation but I think there was some realisation that half-baked suggestions without any comprehension of the sub-continental realities would not be accepted by India.

All my European interlocutors accepted the high priority and importance that the Indian Government attaches to the holding of legislative assembly elections in Jammu and Kashmir in September without any disruption from Pakistan or by Pakistan-sponsored terrorist groups. More knowledgeable among them suggested that India should give a political package response to the people's aspirations to the maximum extent possible. Officials of the Council of Europe and European Commission were more inclined to accept the practicality of fashioning a solution to the Jammu and Kashmir issue on the basis of the Line of Control but with some adjustments.

I told them that while the Government of India cannot examine this proposal, given Pakistan's continuing subversive activities, I personally felt that a solution could be sought with some adjustment in the delineation of the Line of Control combined with a political package for the people of Jammu and Kashmir responsive to their concerns and aspirations.

European officials stated that after the current tension is completely defused and after some progress being made for a political dialogue such suggestions can be put on the table by India and that they would be supportive of India if there is such a modification in India's negotiating stance on Jammu and Kashmir. They agreed that reaching this stage in any negotiations would take some time, but neither India nor Pakistan should have a static and absolutist approach to resolving the Kashmir dispute.

It was interesting to note that there was not much enthusiasm or inclination to refer back to the UN resolutions on this issue. Nor was there any great enthusiasm for the UN to play any role. There was concern about the spread of Islamic extremist terrorism and Islamic orthodoxy in the Central and South Asian region. There was special concern about the status of women, the role of Madrasas and prospects of violation of human rights if Islamic orthodoxy finds a place in the power structure of Asian countries.

There is also an assessment that Musharraf is the only safeguard between moderation and the resurgence of highly assertive and violent Islamic forces in Pakistan, which then would affect the ongoing processes of stabilisation of Afghanistan. There was also a feeling that the revival of violent Islamic forces in Pakistan can have a ripple effect in Central Asia and in the Gulf, de-stabilising the whole region.

India must be clear in its perceptions that western democracies are not interested in the internal dynamics or the deeper political and ethnic and religious complexities affecting the Kashmir issue or Indo-Pakistan relations. Their concerns in order of priority are : First, that the Kashmir dispute should not lead to a nuclear war between India and Pakistan. Second, that Indo-Pak confrontation should not disrupt their campaign against these facets of international terrorism which affects them and their regional security interests. Third, there is a concern about human rights and good governance in general terms but not in terms of any passionate commitment. It is clear that it would be unrealistic to expect any substantive support from Europe or western democracies on our concerns about Jammu and Kashmir or Pakistan's subversive policies against us. India has to deal with this struggle on its own.

Pakistani Jamat Leader Fazlur Rehman in India

Maulana Fazlur Rehman, Secretary General of Muttahida Majlis-e-Amal has been in Delhi in the third week of July. He had a remarkable extensive discussions with different leaders of our civil society, including with the Prime Minister of India. Remarkable because given general perceptions about him in India as a religious extremist, a person who reportedly had links with the Taliban, a supporter of anti-India Jihad, and a patron of organisations like the Harkat-ul-Ansar, it was difficult to imagine cross-section of Indians willing to have dialogue with him and the group of Parliamentarians who he led into India.

The openness with which he was received is in conformity with the democratic ethos of our country. But one need not feel excessively virtuous about this. There was undoubtably a streak of curiosity about this man. Who whatever our perceptions, is a prominent charismatic leader in Pakistan politics.

I had the privilege of meeting both Maulana Fazlur Rehman and Kazi Hussain Ahmed when I was Indian High Commissioner in Pakistan from 1989 to the end of 1991. The relevance of my mentioning this point is that the meetings were not accidental on social and public occasions. Both of them specifically came to see me to have a general exchange of views on India-Pakistan relations as the internal situation in Jammu and Kashmir was becoming critical. Their message to me was that India should accept that there is a dispute in Kashmir, and that it should be resolved not on the basis of flat unilateral assertions by India and Pakistan but through a compromise based on the principles on which the Partition took place. This was to be expected from them. I gave them a hearing at that time and conveyed that no country can voluntarily destroy its unity and territorial integrity.

More than 12 years have passed since this exchange of views. The situation in the sub-continent has undergone profound transformation through critical events in Indo-Pakistan relations. Similar momentous changes have been characterised in international politics.

So the question is whether Maulana Fazlur Rehman has come to India with a change of mind and inclination to adopt and advocate a new policy on the issue of Kashmir and on Indo-Pakistan relations. The answer to all these questions necessarily involves some kind of an assessment of the personality of the Maulana in the general context in which he has visited India. He has been on the cards of Jamiat-ul-Ulema Islam for long years. He is one of its foremost leaders. He is an orthodox Muslim. He has links with Deoband in UP and belongs to a faction which supported the partition of India when the majority of Deobandis were opposed to the Partition. He believes in two-nation theory and therefore supportive of the secessionist movement in Jammu and Kashmir. There have been media reports about his links with the leadership of the Taliban but there is no categorical confirmation now and how close this relationship was. He was close to former President Zia ul Haq and has been in favour of Islamisation of Pakistani political institutions and the Pakistan army. He has transformed himself from being the leader of a very well organised religious party which was on the margins of Pakistani politics in the mid-90s to being a member of a party, the Muttahida Majlis-e-Amal which now rules the strategically important Provinces of North West Frontier Province and Baluchistan, in Pakistan. He is a contender for the role of Leader of the Opposition. It is only the strength of the People's Party of Pakistan in the legislature which has prevented him from virtually assuming this role. He and his party are not at all happy with Musharraf's joining the Americans in their anti-terrorist campaign in Afghanistan or Musharraf's endorsing the American military operations in Iraq.

The domestic political context in Pakistan in which he came to India is equally interesting. Musharraf remains entrenched in power. His acceptance and legitimacy in the eyes of the Western democracies has increased. He has brought in necessary economic inputs to ensure minimum levels of stability in Pakistan. He has brought in a defence assistance package which keeps the Pakistani army satisfied though all its expectations are not fulfilled.

The downside however is that Pakistani public opinion feels that Musharraf has reduced the status and credibility of the country as an independent player in regional and international politics. Majority of governments in Islamic countries feel that he has gone beyond the requirements of practicality in joining the United States. Public opinion in Muslim countries certainly find him and his government insensitive to the emotional and psychological feelings of the Muslims of the world. He is also seen as not being able to follow a purposive policy in relation to India.

This is the right ground for all the political parties in Pakistan, particularly, the Jamaat to lay the ground work for increasing their national role and ultimately capture power, if possible. Maulana Fazlur Rehman's visit is partially an exercise underpinned by this lait motif.

Prior to analysing or assessing the substance of his discussions, it would be pertinent to take note of general tenor of his pronouncements. He implied that the Partition of India was an existentialist reality, a debate on which would be an unnecessary exercise. He emphasised his connections with Deoband and pointed out that though India and Pakistan are two separate states, Muslims in the sub-continent share much in common. He talked about centres of Islam, religious and cultural interests, being revered by Muslim world, places like Deoband, Bareilly and the Dargahs of Moinuddin Chishti of Ajmer and Nizamuddin in Delhi. He said it is the message of these saints which should guide the lives of the people of India and Pakistan. He asserted that Kashmir is not an insurmountable problem. He referred to media reports about General Musharraf saying that he has 10 or 12 options to possibly solving the Kashmir issue and speculated that at least one of these options should serve the purpose of solving the problem. He stressed that Indo-Pakistan dialogue and solution of pending issues should be within the framework of the Shimla Agreement and the Lahore Declaration and to the extent possible under what was discussed during the Agra summit. He categorically opposed any mediation or Facilitation by third parties, like the US. He said it would be unwise to respond to a camel's request to share your tent as you will end up being outside the tent.

This is the gist of what he said in different fora. But what he did not say is equally significant. He did not at all talk about Jehad or its legitimacy. He did not make any reference to the right of self -determination. He did not talk about the resolutions of the United Nations or a plebiscite. He welcomed Prime Minister Vajpayee's peace initiative and General Musharraf's positive response to it. He outlined his general approach in his public pronouncements that a solution can and should be found through peaceful dialogue with people in the sub-continent and a solution should be found which should be acceptable to India, Pakistan and people of Jammu and Kashmir.

All that he said in India as summarised above, seems rational. But the question is of ideology and of convictions. Maulana Fazlur Rehman remains a votary of the two-nation theory and therefore he believes that Jammu and Kashmir should belong to Pakistan or become an independent Muslim entity. He does not want any third party mediation or facilitation because it will impose restrictions on militants and violent activities of Pakistan-based separatist organisations. His not mentioning self determination and to UN Resolutions to Indian audiences is astute political tactic, and in any case being a seasoned politician he knows that his options are no longer available. Equally importantly, his visiting India and projecting his support for the Vajpayee's peace initiative and Indo-Pakistan dialogue is a message to the international community, especially the major western governments that he and his party, are a responsible party participating in political processes in Pakistan and that they are not Islamic extremists. He is also positioning himself in domestic politics as a leader who believes in asserting a sense of self and independent identity of Pakistan instead of just playing second fiddle to the USA. A projection which would appeal not only to the Pakistani public opinion, but even to sections of Pakistani armed forces, the bureaucracy and intellectuals. One acknowledges that there is important gap in this analysis. It should be interesting to know what Maulana Fazlur Rehman told Prime Minister Vajpayee and what Mr. Vajpayee's assessment about what was conveyed to him.

India and Pakistan—A Further Slide Down

In the ongoing adversarial *Tamasha* between India and Pakistan, another contretemps occurred in the second week of February. The acting High Commissioner of Pakistan Jalil Abbas Jilani was declared *persona non grata* and expelled from India for having allegedly given some money to a couple of Hurriyat workers in support of their subversive activities against India. As expected, Government of Pakistan reacted by expelling India's Acting High Commissioner Sudhir Vyas along with four other officials of the Indian High Commission in Islamabad. The declared details about the incident are in the public knowledge. What is more important is to examine whether the decision taken by the Government of India was a measured one based on incontrovertible evidence or did the Government's decision have other orientations/ motivations. Even more important is to assess the implications of this latest bout of diplomatic confrontation.

Information put out by the Government of India about the decision to expell Jilani so far indicates that the evidence about Jilani's giving money to the Hurriyat workers is mostly circumstantial. First question needing an answer is, how is it that a senior diplomat of the experience of Jilani personally decided to get involved in such a transaction when Indo-Pakistan relations are highly tense and even more relevantly when the Pakistan High Commission is under general and constant surveillance by Indian authorities. Secondly, Hurriyat cadres who went into the High Commission must be aware of this surveillance. In spite of it what made them indiscreet or non-challant enough to go in and carry the money out. The lady from the Hurriyat instead of being taken into custody soon after getting out of the High Commission was only arrested a kilometre or two away. If she was to be caught red-handed, why not near the Pakistan High Commission. Our police authorities say she mentioned money being given to her by Jilani. But according to newspapers she did not mention Jilani by name in her statement, when she was produced in court. The case gets curiouser when one takes note of the fact that a senior Delhi Police official stated in a press conference that the Lady Anjum Jamrood was to take the money and deliver it to some contact in Bangkok. If the money was to be used from Bangkok, could not the Pakistan embassy in Bangkok disburse the money instead of this being done by the Pakistan High Commission in New Delhi.

Then again senior diplomats and heads of mission normally do not get directly involved in such intelligence operations. It is highly unusual for a head of mission himself to get personally involved in such transactions. Unless there is physical, electronic or photographic information about Jilani actually giving the money to Ms. Anjum Jamrood. The evidence remains circumstantial unless our authorities have some incontrovertible proof. The point being made is that these questions need to be answered by the Indian Government —both to our Parliament and to our public to confirm the logic of the decision. The same questions would have to be answered because they would be posed by Foreign governments who would be concerned and interested at heightened Indo-Pakistan tensions resulting from this decision. If the evidence we have is incontrovertible then the action taken against Jilani and four of his colleagues, expelling them, one accepts, was both inevitable and unavoidable. It must be kept in mind that Pakistan has given no specific reasons for expelling our Acting High Commissioner and four of his colleagues. Pakistan would however not have to face the type of questions which I have mentioned above about our decision. They would just have the simple answer that they have made a retaliatory diplomatic move.

Another worrisome aspect of our decision in this matter is that of the entire exercise being orchestrated and controlled by the Home Ministry, and police authorities. There was no, or very little consultation with the Ministry of External Affairs or perhaps even the PMO before the decision was finalised. One has been told by reliable sources that the Ministry of External Affairs came to know of the incident and follow up action first on the television. The first statements about the incident and follow up action being considered were made by a Joint Commissioner of Police, and so on. One cannot escape the conclusion that the Ministry of External Affairs stood marginalised instead of the spokesman of the Ministry of External Affairs being the principal articulator of the details of the incident and the action which followed. So the question arises whether the Home Ministry is becoming the principal determiner of India's foreign policy Agenda.

The implications of this recent development in our bilateral relations are :

- India has given the signal that it has now reached a decision to take decisive and drastic action against Pakistani diplomatic links with separatist elements in Jammu and Kashmir and other parts of India, regardless of the status and rank of the Pakistani officials involved.
- An equally clear message has gone to Hurriyat and other such groups that they would now be subject to more drastic remedial action by the Government of India about their net-working with Pakistani authorities.
- India-Pakistan relations have deteriorated further which will make the resumption of bilateral dialogue more difficult.
- Major powers of the world, particularly the United States of America, would react to this development critically and would interpret it as

India's unwillingness to make some move to restore some normalcy in Indo-Pak relations.

- Musharraf will utilise the incident to increase hostile and subversive activities in India and to launch a diplomatic offensive against India on the basis of this incident.

- It will increase his ability to assuage the Islampasand parties of Pakistan who are critical of his siding with the USA in its anti-terrorist campaign.

- While Pakistan is isolated to some extent as a state harbouring terrorists, Pakistan's credibility as an ally of the USA remains undiminished. Given this fact, the United States will generate pressure on Musharraf's behalf on India to resume the dialogue with Pakistan without pre-conditions.

- As always the large Muslim citizenry of India will again get concerned about heightened levels of Indo-Pakistan hostility.

- With the United States planning military operations against Iraq, high levels of Indo-Pakistan confrontation will be considered by the US and its allies as a factor disturbing USA's anti-terrorist and anti-Saddam campaign. This would be so in the context of Government of India having reservations about USA's impending military plans against Iraq.

- Sustaining levels of positive equations with the USA will be an important task for India's foreign policy in the coming weeks. As far as Pakistan is concerned some serious thought should be given to additional options in the linear logic of expulsion of Acting High Commissioner Jilani. Government of India should examine freezing bank accounts and other financial assets of the Hurriyat and other separatist groups operating in India, particularly those with links with the ISI.

India should consider declaring Pakistan a terrorist state taking the legal implications into account, a step we have not taken so far. We have limited ourselves to advocating to other countries, that Pakistan be declared a terrorist state. Consideration could be given to closing down diplomatic missions of Pakistan in India and India in Pakistan, for a brief period. Interest sections of both countries could continue to function in friendly embassies in each other's capital to maintain minimum levels of contact.

India's Pakistan policies should have two macro-level ingredients. First to respond decisively in terms of retaliatory action against any further major terrorist violence organised by Pakistan in India. Secondly, we must think about commencing a dialogue at some appropriate official level with Pakistan in some third country by the autumn or winter of this year.

Pakistan has reacted in a very base manner to the Indian decision on the expulsions. Pakistan has simply said it is part of ongoing attempt by India to malign Pakistan. What is more interesting is that Pakistan has refused to respond to Indian suggestion that a new Pakistani charge d' Affaires could be posted to New Delhi. The likelihood is of Pakistan not sending such an officer.

The Indian response has been simplistic at the political level. The Government has taken a smug self-righteous line without bothering to respond to the doubts which could arise about the decision mentioned earlier. The Congress Party considering this a national issue transcending party politics, has given general support to the Government. All the major Indian political parties should keep in mind that they have to explain or endorse the decision in a convincing manner both at home and abroad. A complete break down of communications and relations with Pakistan is not a practical predicament either for India or Pakistan. Political strategies and strategems apart, we must remember that neither India nor Pakistan can wish away the geographical reality of being neighbours.

There is one more serious, and to some extent introspective question which both our Parliament and our public opinion should consider. Are Government of India's present orientations in its Pakistan policies only a foreign policy move, or are the most recent decisions motivated by considerations of domestic politics and the general elections which are just an year away. There is speculation about this in Indian public opinion.

Pakistan-USA Relations—The US Congress Moves on Pak-based Terrorists

The US House of Representatives has proposed a Bill which is likely to be passed which could generate more pressure on Pakistan, to move back from its involvement in terrorist activities across the border against India.

The bill introduced in the US House of Representatives on July 11, is a follow up of the agreement reached between President Bush and President Pervez Musharraf during the latter's visit to the US at the end of June.

President Bush had announced a $ 3 billion package of economic and defence assistance to Pakistan during his discussions with Musharraf at Camp David. The amount is to be disbursed to Pakistan in annual instalments of between 600 and 700 million dollars per annum. An interesting caveat on this agreement for assistance to Pakistan was that the release of the funds to Pakistan would be subject to Congressional Approval every year.

The Bill introduced on July 11 in the House of Representatives stipulates that US aid to Pakistan from the fiscal year 2005 would be subject to three pre-conditions.

The Bill requires that the US President must certify that the Government of Pakistan has closed all known terrorist camps operating in Pakistan and in Pakistan-held Kashmir.

Secondly, that Pakistan had established tangible, serious and identifiable measures to prohibit and prevent the infiltration of Islamic extremists across the Line of Control into India. And third, condition is that US President should certify that Pakistan has stopped the transfer of weapons of mass destruction, including any associated technologies to any third country or terrorist organisation.

Indian media has not given much attention to this bill. Whatever attention has been given is in the tradition of our media getting over-optimistic and over-enthusiastic about this Congressional Move as a major shift in US policies putting Pakistan in the dock and supporting India's concerns about across-border terrorism. Our media in its preliminary analyses went on to imply that this is some kind of autonomous initiative by the US Congress separate from and differing from the attitude of the Executive branch of the US Government on these issues in relation to Pakistan. In fact, this is not an accurate analysis.

Official reports on Bush's discussions with President Musharraf indicate that there is congruity between what President Bush told President Musharraf and provisions of the Bill introduced in the House of Representatives which is likely to become law in some weeks. Bush had insisted on three conditionalities with Musharraf about US assistance to Pakistan, namely, Musharraf should remain committed to fight terrorism to which Bush added a caveat that terrorism is unacceptable in any form and in any part of the world. Bush secondly emphasised that Musharraf should move towards democracy in Pakistan and thirdly, Bush emphasised that Musharraf should stop sales of nuclear and missile technologies and related material to "Rogue nations", as defined by the US.

So the bill in the US House of Representatives is a re-statement of these conditionalities with greater elaboration. The bill should also be viewed in the context of the separate discussions which US Deputy Secretary of State Richard Armitage had with General Musharraf. In these discussions Armitage gave details of Pakistan-sponsored terrorism in Jammu and Kashmir. Armitage showed Musharraf maps and locations of terrorist camps in Pakistan operating against India. Armitage emphasised that the anti-terrorist campaign of the US is not limited only to Al Qaeda, and that the campaign also targets Pakistan-based terrorist organisations like Lashkar-e-Toiba and Jaish-e-Mohammed. Armitage rounded off his presentation with formal request to Musharraf that purposeful and comprehensive efforts should be undertaken by Pakistan to stop terrorist activities against India. Armitage mentioned in this context that Members and leaders of these groups operating against India are still at liberty in Pakistani territory and not under any effective restrictions.

The US House of Representatives, therefore has only followed up on the general policy orientations of the US Government articulated by President Bush with President Musharraf. One must of course take note of the significant additional dimension of this legislative move that the US Congress has decided to define and articulate definite terms of reference about the release of economic and defence assistance to Pakistan, even before any specific proposal on the subject was submitted to the Congress.

Leaving aside specific proposals, even the general presentation of budget for the next year or two, by the President to the US Congress is still weeks away.

Additional facts of contextual relevance to be noted are that this is not the first time that the US Congress has tried to impose restrictions on the flow of assistance to Pakistan. The Glen and Symington Amendment of more than a decade ago had sought to impose similar restrictions on Pakistan in view of its ongoing nuclear weaponisation programme. The restrictions are to be imposed by US Congress itself, but then the Amendment proposed by Senator Pressler known as Pressler Amendment delegated the authority to the US Administration and Senior President Bush gave clean chits to Pakistan during his tenure except towards the end of his period in office. While the US Congress has stipulated specific conditionalities, it must be remembered for the remaining part of President George Bush's tenure, the US Congress will have a Republican majority. And this majority is not likely to go against policy decisions of President Bush regarding Pakistan when the chips are really down.

We must take note of the fact that while giving background briefings on President Bush's discussions with Musharraf mentioned earlier in this column, US officials stated that the conditionalities or suggestions made by President Bush are not absolute conditionalities and bench marks which have been arrived at on the basis of agreement between President Musharraf and President Bush.

What then is one to make out of this move by the US House of Representatives :

- First, it is clear that levels of anxiety against religious extremist terrorism have increased in the US Government and US public opinion due to the following factors :
- Anti-US terrorist activities continue in Afghanistan and Iraq, despite large-scale US military presence in these countries.
- Islamic terrorist continue their activities successfully in countries considered by them to be friendly with the United States.
- Large-scale terrorist violence has occurred in the Philippines, in Indonesia and in Jordan, even inside Pakistan, and in Israel.
- The Al Qaeda network and relationship with other like-minded groups remains operational despite massive intelligence and military operations undertaken against them over the last 18 months.
- Public resentment amongst Muslim countries against the US is palpably on the increase.
- New findings by the CIA and FBI have confirmed more substantial evidence about the linkage of these terrorist groups with segments of the power structure in Pakistan and Saudi Arabia.
- Discussions between senior officials of the US Government and leaders of not only government but other political parties in India over the last six to eight months have made US aware of the larger regional negative security implications of Pakistan being allowed to carry on terrorist activities against India.

The three conditions stipulated in the bill introduced in the House of Representatives imply a more objective and factual understanding of the ground realities of terrorist activities against India originating in Pakistan. The conditionalities imply :

The US Government formally acknowledging the existence of terrorist camps in Pakistan operating against India and Pakistan with the connivance, if not support of the Pakistani Government. This perception also includes the realisation that even if Musharraf is serious about acting against these terrorists, Islampasand Muslim political parties and cadres, with their present political and legislative strength can limit Musharraf's ability to control the situation.

Secondly, the US acknowledges that terrorists from Pakistan-based camps are perpetrating violence in Jammu and Kashmir in India and that Government of Pakistan take concrete steps to stop this intrusive and subversive activities against India.

Thirdly, US authorities confirm and acknowledge Pakistan being source of proliferation of nuclear weapons and related technologies to other countries like North Korea, and perhaps even to some other Muslim countries.

The purpose seems to be to convey a clear message to Pakistan to fall in line with the international community's mainstream campaign against terrorism and perhaps also convey a message to the US Government that despite President Bush's equations with President Musharraf and Musharraf's cooperating with the USA, Pakistan should be subjected to more insistent advise to desist from terrorism.

Reactions from the Pakistani Government have been measured and subdued with Pakistani media responding with agitation and disappointment on this bill. The most important question to be answered is whether there is a justification for India to be over-optimistic about the Bill's reducing the nature and content of US-Pak relations.

My assessment is that there is reason to have some satisfaction that the US Government and Legislators are accepting the realities of terrorism in our sub-continent. But this does not mean that the bill will tilt the balance against Pakistan. Pakistan remains a reliable and active ally of the United States, in the assessment of the US power structure.

While India-US relations have gained in substance, USA's South Asia policy will continue to treat the South Asian sub-continent as a collective geo-strategic factor and not as an exercise in favourites of one country or the other.

2
Indo-US Cooperation

Indo-US Defence Cooperation—New Beginnings

General Padmanabhan, Chief of the Army Staff and Chairman of the Chiefs of Staff Committee of Indian Armed Forces has proceeded on a week-long visit to the United States on the 21st of April at the invitation of his US counterpart. The visit takes place in the context of expanding defence cooperation arrangements with the US, beginnings of which could be traced back to the proposals in Indo-US Defence Cooperation made by General Krik Leiter of the Central Command of the USA in 1990. When we commenced our policy of closer relationship with the US in anticipation of the end of the Cold War and the disintegration of the Soviet Union. Though our Defence Minister Sharad Power visited the US in the early 90s following a visit by the US Defence Secretary during the Administration of the Senior President Bush, operational consultations and substantive defence collaboration had not occurred. The earlier proposals remained a matter of discussion and prospects of cooperation remained a phenomenon of general political discussions. Issues related to defence cooperation remained in a drift during the Gujral and V.P. Singh Administrations.

Given the BJP's traditional pro-US orientations in foreign policy, some beginnings were made immediately after Mr. Vajpayee came to power. But they went off into a negative spin in consequence of India's nuclear weapon tests in May 1998. Political relations became brittle, proposals for defence cooperation went on hold with imposition of US economic and technological sanctions against India. This, however, did no result in intractable confrontation. Prolonged discussions between External Affairs Minister Jaswant Singh and Deputy Secretary of State Strobe Talbot between late 1998 and the beginnings of the year 2000, reduced distances and removed misunderstandings to a great extent. President Clinton's support to the Indian standpoint on the Line of Control during the Kargil conflict and his advising Nawaz Sharif government to pull back from the Line of Control perhaps can be considered a possible watershed in Indo-US relations. Clinton's visit to India in March 2000, generated impulses of Indo-US relations which have not only continued but have expanded their impact on India's relations with the US.

Prime Minister Vajpayee's discussions with President Clinton in September 2000, and the discussions between Foreign Minister Jaswant Singh and National Security Advisor Brajesh Mishra on the one hand and their counterparts in Bush Administration between November 2000 and March 2001 revived the various proposals for military and Defence cooperation and laid the foundations of the current phase of Indo-US defence cooperation. The military coup in Pakistan, incremental threats of international terrorism and most importantly the terrorist bombing inside the United States on September 11, 2001, are factors which have contributed to qualitative and quantitative expansion of Indo-US cooperation in the sensitive spheres of regional security, defence and the present anti-terrorist campaign. The rationale of this phenomenon is the broad convergence of interests and consensus on these issues between India and the United States. The present Republican Administration under President Bush is less didactic and intrusive on non-proliferation issues compared to the Clinton Administration. This has also helped reduce mutual tensions on the issue though differences of opinion on the substantive issues related to non-proliferation still remain between India and the US.

It would be pertinent to mention the details of multi-faceted defence cooperation that is evolving between India and the USA, before analysing the strategic and security environment in which this new dimension in Indo-US relations is taking place. Defence Secretaries Parry and Cheney of previous administrations had interacted with their Indian counterparts during the decades of 80s and 90s of the last century. Visits and exchange of views between senior military commanders of India and the US had commenced by 1992, joint consultative mechanisms on defence policy, on security issues were established since 1992, barring the ambiguities and drifts between 1995 and end of 1998, these mechanisms have not only stabilised themselves institutionally but have increased and expanded their scope of consultations. A joint Experts Group on countering terrorism has been in existence since the end of 1999, its terms of reference and responsibilities have gained in substance and expanded since the US launched its campaign against cross-border terrorism and the Al-Qaeda.

The Indo-US Defence Policy Group is now revived and fully functional to discuss proposals of cooperation and implementing them at the policy level. The US side being led by Mr. Douglas Feitch, Under Secretary for Defence Policy in the Department of Defence and the Indian side being led by Defence Secretary Mr. Yogendra Narain. Its first meeting took place after US removed sanctions against India on the 22nd of September, 2001. General Padmanabhan's visit to Washington precedes the next meeting of the Defence Policy Group which is scheduled to be held in Washington on 21st and 22nd of May. Arrangements for cooperation between the armed forces of the two countries have also been institutionalised. Joint executive steering groups between the army, navy and air forces of the two countries have been created (a separate steering group for each Branch of the Armed Forces). These steering committees have met over the last four months. The chairman of the Joint Chiefs of Staff of the US General Myers visited India earlier this year, the first ever visit by US Chairman Joint Chiefs of Staff, to India. (since the establishment of US-JCS in 1986). The Chief of the US Army General Shelten and Commander in Chief, Pacific, Admiral Blair have visited India during the last six months. US Defence Secretary Donald Rumsfeld visited India in November 2001, soon after the US launched its anti-terrorist campaign in Afghanistan. Our Defence Minister George Fernandes was in Washington in mid-January this year to continue the high level interaction on defence and security matters. The US Navy participated in the International seminar titled: "Bridges of Friendship" organised by the Indian Navy in Mumbai in February 2001, the first time the US Navy participated in a Fleet Review organised by the Indian Navy. There is now an Indo-US agreement on cooperation between Navies of the two countries to secure maritime trade routes between the Suez and Straits of Malacca. The Joint Training exercises were held by the two Navies as recently as in the month of March. An increasing number of officers from the Indian Armed Forces are proceeding for training in military institutions in the US as is the case with officers of the US armed forces to come to National Defence College, New Delhi and the Defence Services Staff College at Wellington in South India. Cooperation in military training projects is expected to double under the IMET programme of the US in the coming year.

This pattern of cooperation between India and the strongest military and technological power in the world, adds an important strategic dimension to India's Foreign and Defence policies. That Indo-US defence cooperation is increasing on a long-term basis despite continuous positive involvement of the US with the Musharraf government in Pakistan is significant. It is clear that while US-Pak cooperation is predicated on the objectives of containing Islamic extremist violence and countering international terrorist organisations in Afghanistan and in West and Central Asia, with the additional objective of Pakistan being the southern anchor or protecting US strategic interests in the Gulf, USA's incremental defence involvement with India has broader political and strategic objectives in dealing with power equations in the Asian region and the Indian Ocean. Future structuring of India's defence cooperation policies with the US also has to take place in the contact the expanded physical military presence of the US from Turkey, Georgia, and Azerbaijan in the north, to the Philippines in South East Asia. This includes US military presence in Afghanistan, Uzbekistan, Pakistan and the offer of military facilities to the US by countries like India and Bangladesh.

Our defence relationship with the USA has also to be nuanced in terms of our substantive defence cooperation relationship with the Russian Federation and our general political relations with China. While there is no basic conflict of security interest between the US and India, one cannot wish away some differences of approach in the details of US and Indian views regarding the fashioning of the Asian regional security environment, about operational objectives regarding the elimination of terrorism and about regional objectives of India's foreign policy. For instance, the importance of India's relations with Iran or on the issues of arms control and disarmament.

General Padmanabhan as Chairman of India's Chiefs of Staff committee will be therefore dealing with not only an important but complex agenda of Indo-US cooperation during his current visit to Washington. The most significant political dimension of this aspect of Indo-US relations is that the differences of opinion are not wished away nor are they lead to an adversarial atmosphere. The approach on both sides is of reasoning together and expanding mutual relations, more importantly relations between US are becoming an important factor in India's defence policy—a logical development in the context of the current realities of regional and international power equations.

Indo -US Relations—The Technological Dimensions

An important Indo-US bilateral discussion took place in the second week of November to review and revive bilateral technological cooperation between India and the United States after a gap of nearly two-and-a-half to three years. The discussions were crucial since this was the first exercise to comprehensively review this vital aspect of bilateral relations and to revive bilateral technological relations which have been in general hiatus since India's nuclear weapons tests of May 1998. Before one comes to an assessment of this most recent development of initiatives and prospects, it is relevant to examine technological interaction between India and the United States over the years. The cooperation in this sphere, however does not and cannot occur in a vacuum. It necessarily is dependent on the guiding political and strategic considerations in the foreign policies of both countries.

The over-arching influence on Indo-US relations till late 1980s was the chemistry of the Cold War and the Central point in American foreign policy was the question whether the democratic west led by the United States could more effectively meet the objective of successfully responding to the rising expectations in developing countries, particularly in a large developing country like India, which also claimed the additional virtue of being a democracy. The end of the Cold War between 1989 and 1991 has in a manner reduced the centrality of the question mentioned above, as US diplomat and scholar Dennis Kux asserted in the mid-1990 "now that the Cold War is part of history, India has slid down the ladder of US priorities although it's continuing effort to develop as a democracy does remain significant." Kux goes on to add the significant conclusion "one can hardly make support for democracy as a guiding principle of American foreign policy. Yet ignore what happens in a democracy in a country where 860 million people live, one out of every six being on earth" Kux wrote this in 1994. But at the most fundamental level this remains the basic consideration in the dilemmas in USA's South Asian policies. The way out was articulated in the draft US Defence Planning Guide which was leaked to the *New York Times* early in 1992. The portion related to India partially read as follows:

"We (USA) will seek to prevent the further development of nuclear arms race on the Indian sub-continent. In this regard we should work to have both countries, India and Pakistan, adhere to Non-Proliferation Treaty and to place their nuclear energy facilities under International Atomic Energy Agency's safeguards. We should discourage Indian hegemonic aspirations over the other States in South Asia and on the Indian Ocean. With regard to Pakistan, a constructive US-Pakistan military relationship will be an important element in our strategy to promote stable security conditions in South West Asia and Central Asia. We should, therefore endeavour to re-build our military relationship with Pakistan given acceptable resolution of our nuclear concerns."

Though this approach might have been modified in articulation in the final official document, the basic considerations influencing US policies as mentioned above have not altered. This is the basic orientation underpinning USA's sub-continental policies particularly so in respect of technological cooperation.

The history of Indo-US technological cooperation has been a chequered one. While on the one hand, it is the inputs from the US which initiated our space and nuclear programmes, cooperation in these spheres was always subject to US concerns about horizontal proliferation and military imbalance between India and Pakistan and in the sub-continent. There was a certain reluctance on the part of the US to assist India developing its infrastructural industries, particularly in the steel sector which only changed after the Russians gave this assistance and the resulting competition brought in the British and the Germans. The 1974 underground nuclear tests by India resulted in re-imposition of technological and economic sanctions against India, slowing down bilateral cooperation. An attempt was made to remedy matters half way during President Reagan's tenure when a Memorandum of Understanding for technological cooperation was signed between the USA and India in 1984 which included arrangements for close cooperation in the spheres of computer technology and certain aspects of space technology for peaceful purposes. These arrangements did not take off the ground because of Iraq-Kuwait crisis and the anxieties about horizontal proliferation in countries like North Korea, Iraq, Iran, Pakistan and India.

Regimes like the missile control technology regime, the NSC Agreement by the Nuclear Suppliers Group, the nuclear non-proliferation Act of the US came into operation. Similarly doctrines of dual use technology, the need to prevent such technologies falling into the hands of "Rogue" or "irresponsible" states created a general restrictive atmosphere on prospects of Indo-US cooperation in the spheres of sophisticated technology.

1998 nuclear weapons tests by India compounded the situation as far as Indo-US cooperation was concerned. The United States imposed across the board economic and technological sanctions putting into operation its "enhanced proliferation control initiative". Two hundred Indian organisations or entities were put on the prohibited list under what was called a catch all connotation. No US company or entity trade or interact with these two hundred Indian entities. Any trading arrangement was subject to Export Licences predicated on a priori negative decision. Even contracts between individuals in these agencies and their US counterparts stood suspended. The more recent developments in this sphere of India-US relations commenced with the Jaswant Singh-Talbot talks in 1999 resulting in about 50 or 60 Indian entities being removed from the above mentioned prohibited list. Now 150 entities still remain on the list.

It was only in September 2001 that the Bush Administration removed all sanctions against India and Pakistan though certain restrictions have remained in place under the US Non-proliferation Act and related Congressional stipulations. Now only 24 entities remain on the Restrictive list. These entities are India's nuclear facilities which are not under IAEA safeguards, the Defence and Research Development Organisation, Bharat Electronics, Indian Rare Earth Organisation. India's importing sophisticated technologies now is not subject to the comprehensive negativism of the Enhanced Proliferation Control Initiative. US Export Licences are still necessary but the applications are predicated on positive response. The Bush Administration which came into power in January 2001, not only continued but expanded the qualitative positive orientation towards India initiated by Bill Clinton in the last year of his tenure. While Bush Administration remained committed to its global non-proliferation and Arms control objectives, there was a certain adjustability in their approach on these issues rooted in USA's strategic and security interests. There was more political realism. India, therefore, decided to engage the United States in a discussion to reduce restrictions on technological cooperation, particularly in the spheres of Space, Nuclear Technology and Dual Use goods and technologies given the label of TRINITY.

External Affairs Ministers Yashwant Sinha broached this subject when he was in Washington on the 9th of September 2002. The item also formed part of the Agenda of Prime Minister Vajpayee's discussions with President George Bush. The response was positive. Dr. Rangarajan and Dr. Kakodkar, Chiefs of our Space and Atomic Energy Departments followed up on this political dialogue when their US counterpart Dr. Meserze came to India. US Under Secretary of Commerce Ken Juster also visited India give more substance to Indo-US exchanges on this subject. There is a joint Indo-US High Technology consultative Group tasked with working out plans of bilateral technological Cooperation across the board. This, however, does not mean that their would be no differences of opinion between India and the United States on this issue. The cooperation has to be structured subject to the general obligations of the US Government to its legislative Non-Proliferation obligations. However, the political and strategic considerations affecting US policies towards India seem to be changing. The President of the United States has to present a National Security Assessment to the Congress once during every tenure. Bush made this presentation in September 2002. It is significant that he referred to India in this presentation under the chapter of emerging centres of global power, underlining the strengthening of relations with India as an important item on USA's foreign policy Agenda. The Indo-US trade in technology, particularly the non-atomic energy factor forms a major segment of Indo-US bilateral trade and it is growing at the rate of 35 to 40 per cent per annum. The US seems to reluctantly acknowledge India's nuclear weapons status and more importantly, India's capacities to function as a responsible nuclear weapons power (even though the US does not recognise India as a nuclear power legally). Further meetings of the High Technology Consultative Group are scheduled for next year and it is reasonable to presume that cooperation in the technological sector would be a cementing factor in Indo-US relations. This prospect, is of course subject to overall strategic stipulation that India's policies do not radically contradict or challenge the global and regional order envisaged by the US policy planners. The extent to which India can conform to USA's world views in the context of Indian interests constitutes a challenge for India's foreign policy planners.

3
India Beyond Borders

India-China Relations—Post-September 11, 2001

The United States of America and Pakistan have been the operational focus of India's foreign policy since the terrorist attacks on the US in September, 2001. The focus on Pakistan increased after the Jaish-e-Mohammed's terrorist attack on the Indian Parliament on December 13 2001. The major powers whose attitudes and policies on Pakistan's links with cross-border terrorism against India which are of importance to India, are those of the United States and China. There has been a greater clarity in US policies in this regard in Indian perceptions due to two reasons. Links between the Al Qaeda movement, the Taliban and Pakistan-based terrorist organisations active against India, secondly, the continuous high level interaction between the Governments of India and the United States since September 2001.

In contrast, there have been ambiguities about China's attitudes and policies in Indian perceptions. Chinese Prime Minister Zhu Rongji's visit to India early in January has to some extent clarified these ambiguities. India has been host to two senior Chinese leaders since the second half of the year 2001. Former Prime Minister and Number two in Chines ecommunist Party's hierarchy Li Peng was in India with a large Chinese delegation earlier and Mr. Zhu Rongji was in India early in January 2002. Both Li Peng and Zhu Rongji came to India amidst the changing strategic and security environment in the world and particularly in sub-continental Asia in the context of the US-led campaign against international terrorism. The discussions with these leaders and Indian leaders signified, first that the controversies which afflicted Sino-Indian relations in the aftermath of the India's nuclear weapon tests in 1998 have been set aside and that both countries are trying to get bilateral relations back on track. Secondly, the discussions emphasised the revival of continuity in Sino-Indian relations which began with President Narayanan's visit to China. The visit of Prime Minister Zhu Rongji has been interpreted in positive terms by sections of the media and political analysts. His visiting India at a point of time when India's relations with Pakistan were in a state of high tension has been interpreted as reflecting China's desire to have an even-handed and impartial relationship with India and Pakistan in contrast to the close political and strategic involvement of China with Pakistan.

One must examine whether this assessment is entirely accurate. Recalling the immediate background of Premier Zhu's visit would be pertinent. General Musharraf visited Beijing twice towards the end of last year. The second visit took place in response to Indian diplomatic and military pressure on Pakistan in reaction to the terrorist attack on the Indian Parliament. Though media reports asserted that General Musharraf got a "frosty reception" in Beijing and that unlike in 1965 and 1971, the Chinese did not generate any overt political and military pressure on India, the fact is that China has given both financial assistance and defence supplies to Pakistan in recent months since September 2001. This has been done on the rationale that China apart from continuing its traditional defence relationship with Pakistan is strengthening Pakistan as a partner and ally in the global struggle against international terrorism. It is interesting to note that the US Government and media have interpreted this recent assistance as a proof of China's support to the US-led coalition against terrorism.

Whatever the interpretation, the net result is that Pakistan's military capacities are sustained and enhanced by this assistance which cannot be ignored by India. We must realise that while sustaining its close substantive strategic relationship with Pakistan, China is engaged in an exercise of structuring a political balance in power equations in the sub-continent by simultaneously engaging the Indian Government in high levels of interactions. Zhu Rongji came at a point of time when USA's strategic presence is increasing in South and Central Asia. The Gulf War in 1990-91 initiated this process. While forces of the Pacific and Central Command of the USA converge in their jurisdictional role across the Pacific and Atlantic, in the Indian Ocean and the Gulf, the US Central Command's physical presence is now there in Uzbekistan, Kyrgyztan, Afghanistan and Pakistan. The Chief of the US Central Command Lt. General Tommy Hanks stated during his visit to Pakistan that the United States will continue its military presence in our region for some time to come. President Bush's State of the Union message on 30th January 2002 underpins this indication. He stated that the campaign against terrorism is just beginning and will last a long time. He indicated that North Korea, Iraq and Iran, could be the subsequent targets of the US campaign.

There is US presence now at Peshawar, Abbotabad and at the ports of Pasni, Gwadar and Karachi. The US military presence at Gwadar has complicated China's naval presence at the Pakistani port. It is logical, therefore, for China to structure its South Asian policies in the context of the challenge which the US poses to Chinese influence in the area by its planned long-term strategic presence. This in a manner could encourage China to have practical and stable relationship with India, while sustaining to the maximum extent possible its equations with Pakistan. This is the logic of Zhu Rongji's recent visit to India, more than China's desire to be impartial between Pakistan and India.

We would do well to remember that in relative terms relations with the USA and Pakistan remain a matter of higher priority in Chinese foreign policy, due to the economic and political reasons.

This is the context in which one has to assess the current state of short-term prospects of India's relations with China. Six significant bilateral agreements were signed with China during Prime Minister Zhu's visit. These were a resumption of direct civil aviation contacts between Beijing and New Delhi, on cooperation in the fields of tourism, space, science and technology and to cooperate in countering terrorism through the institution of Sino-Indian joint working group on the subject. Both Li Peng and Zhu Rongji emphasised China's interest in expanding cooperation in economic and technological spheres, especially in the area of information technology. These are positive trends as far as they go, with one rider as far as bilateral economic relations, particularly trade relations go. The prospects are of more competition than complementarity in Sino-Indian relations in this respect. One area of cooperation underpinned by some complementarity is the Track II discussions between India and China to establish and expand cooperation between Southern China (Yunan), North eastern states of India known as the 'Kunming Initiative' which is supported by the Chinese Government. This exercise must be subject to the caution of China's politico- strategic orientations where there is no dilution of its claims on the state of Arunachal Pradesh in India. It is regarding political issues of substance that India and China have still long way to go. The Sino-Indian Joint Working Group on the Boundary question has not yet completed the task of removing discrepancies in the delineation of the Line of Actual Control between the two countries.

Though an increasing number of confidence building measures have been agreed upon they have not become fully operational, though they have progressed. There has been no move by either side to discuss a solution to the boundary question, setting aside the burdens of past negotiations. Though India recognises Tibet as an autonomous region of People's Republic of China, Tibet's progressive political and cultural and ethnic integration with China, disregarding the assurances of autonomy for Tibet remains a matter of concern to India, as Tibet's remaining a buffer zone between India and China is a matter of interest to India. The location of Chinese missiles and air bases in Tibet remain a matter of security concern to India.

Whatever justification China gives to us about its defence relationship with Pakistan, it remains an arrangement impinging on India's security, given the present state of Indo-Pak relations. Long-term stabilising of Sino-Indian relations depends on these issues being addressed by both sides with foresight. Given the convergence of views, between India and China on issues like, opposition to hegemonies, the need for non-discriminatory and comprehesive disarmament, agreement on working towards a just and fair economic order and the potential for bilateral technological cooperation, there is a basis for structuring a durable and practical relationship between India and China despite the undercurrents of competition and the legacy of mutual suspicions.

Zhu Rongji's coming to India at a time of sub-continental crisis and his statements here indicate that possibilities of such Sino-Indian cooperation exist.

Visit to Brussels to Participate in the Hearing of Foreign Affairs Committee of European Parliament

Dear Jaswant Singh ji,

I write to briefly report to you on my recent visit to Brussels to participate in the hearing of the Foreign Affairs Committee of the European Parliament on Jammu and Kashmir and Indo-Pakistan relations.

I was technically invited as an independent non-governmental participant in this meeting. But I understand that you took the decision to depute me for this meeting and directed the Ministry of External Affairs to provide me with all the logistical support for this visit.

First of all, therefore, please accept my thanks for providing me with this opportunity for high level exchange with Members of the European Parliament on a matter of vital interest to us in India. The report on my presentation to European Parliament and the summary of the discussions which followed my presentation have already been sent to the Ministry, to the concerned officers and Divisions by our Ambassador in Brussels, Mr. P.K. Singh.

The purpose of this letter is two-fold. First to inform you of my impressions of reactions of the Members of the European Parliament and the Council of Europe to the critical developments in the Sub-continent. And secondly, to convey some suggestions for expanded interaction with the European Community for your consideration.

The main hearings were held at the premises of the European Parliament on the 20th of June. The hearings were held for two and half to three hours. There were four main speakers in this meeting. Ambassador Shaukat Umar, Pakistan Ambassador in Brussels, Prof Vernon Hewitt of the Universities of Sussex and Bristol, Dr. Jean -Luc Racine of the Foundation for Humanities and Social Sciences of Paris, France and myself.

The Pakistani presentation as expected was basically historical justification of Pakistan's claims on Jammu and Kashmir and the manner in which India had obstinately rejected and resisted these claims. Professors Hewitt and Racine while deliberately providing a detached and impartial analysis, nevertheless emphasised that the current troubles between India and Pakistan originated in Pakistan being the base from which terrorist subversion is launched against India. Both these speakers also emphasised that India has to overcome the alienation of a segment of the people in Indian Jammu and Kashmir by providing them a political solution responsive to their aspirations. Both these professors also implied that the Indo-Pak dimension of the problem can be resolved in a practical manner only if a solution to this aspect of the problem is based on the ground realities and the line of control between India and Pakistan in Jammu and Kashmir. The hearings of the Foreign Affairs Committee of the European Parliament were chaired by Baroness Emma Nicholson, Vice Chairman of the Committee though in the initial stages Mr. Brok Chairman of the Committee was in the chair. Baroness Nicholson is a Member of the European Parliament from the UK belonging as far as I recall to the Liberal Democratic Party of the United Kingdom.

Apart from this meeting I had discussions with the Director General for Political and Military Affairs of the Council of Europe, Mr. David Cooper on deputation from the British Foreign Office. He is a senior advisor to Mr. Jeavier Solana. In addition I had meetings with Mr. Richard Arndell, Director General for External Relations of the European Commission

Mr. Jon Greenwald, Vice President (Programme), of the International Crisis Group of Europe (of which Shri I.K. Gujaral is a member) and Ms. Vicky Bowman, Special Assistant to Mr. Chris Patten. I also addressed a meeting of the European Institute for Asian Studies.

My perceptions about reaction of these European Interlocutors is the following :

1. There is general appreciation for the political and military restraint with which India has reacted to Pakistan-sponsored terrorism during the last 7 months.

2. It is accepted that it is primarily Indian restraint which prevented a war in the sub-continent and a nuclear confrontation.

3. There is also the view that war has been avoided partially due to Musharraf declaring his intention to stop supporting cross-border terrorism.

4. It was felt that Indian restraint and Musharraf's speeches on January 12 and May 27 were a result of international political and diplomatic pressure generated particularly by the United States and Western democracies in Europe.

5. The advocacy was that India should continue to remain restrained in the larger interest of stability and peace not only in Asia but in global terms. (The latter consideration is based on the assessment that such restraint will avoid polarisation between Islamic countries and other governments).

6. These reactions were as expected but the comments and questions on the presentations reflected certain nuances which we in India should take note of.

(a) While there was acceptance that terrorism originated in Pakistan and territories under the control of Pakistan, there is still a great amount of hesitation in acknowledging direct links between General Musharraf, the Pakistan Government, on the one hand and across the border in Indian on the other. The theory is that Musharraf is trying to do his best but he cannot completely control extremist Islamic terrorism because he has to counter terrorism in Afghanistan, and in his own country.

(b) Secondly, the view was expressed that India should give President Musharraf some elbow room and some time to implement the promises which he has made in his policy pronouncements since January.

(c) More than this India should strengthen its capacity to act more firmly against terrorist orgainsations functioning in Pakistan and Pakistan occupied Kashmir by making more substantial concessions in terms of moving back our security forces and agreeing to a dialogue at the political level as early as possible.

(d) While there was agreement that cross-border terrorism should be stopped and that the sanctity of the Line of Control should be respected, there was consensus that Pakistan has legitimate locus standi on the Kashmir issue regardless of the legality or otherwise of the Accession of the Princely State of Jammu and Kashmir to India.

(e) India meanigfully seeking a practical compromise on the issue with Pakistan has become even more important and critical due to the nuclear weaponisation of both the countries.

(f) While India's policy stance that the issue should be resolved through bilateral negotiations is respected, there seems to be an incremental feeling that India should not be negative about some kind of external mediation or facilitation by friendly governments in finding a solution with Pakistan.

(g) Members of the European Parliament (as distinct from the Representatives of the Commission and the Council), had no reticences about proposing some kind of a referendum, joint Indo-Pakistan sovereignty over Kashmir or creation of an independent State of Jammu and Kashmir. When I firmly pointed out the impracticability of all these suggestions, the response was that India should no be hesitant to explore all possibilities of this type. When I emphasised that Kashmir is more than a territorial dispute, that it affects the very plural democratic terms of reference of the Indian Republic, the response I got was that Indian democracy is strong and stable enough not to be disrupted or de-stabilised by territorial and political concessions on Jammu and Kashmir. Ultimately, I had to categorically emphasise that the question of territorial alienation of Jammu and Kashmir from the Indian Republic just does not arise whatever its cost, my audience was not pleased with this affirmation but I think there was some realisation that half-baked suggestions without any comprehension of the sub-continental realities would not be accepted by India.

(h) All my European interlocutors accepted the high priority and importance that the Government of India attaches to the holding of legislative assembly elections in Jammu and Kashmir in September without any disruptions from Pakistan or by Pakistan-sponsored terrorist groups.

(i) More knowledgeable among them suggested that India should give a political package to the maximum possible extent to the people of Jammu and Kashmir.

(j) Officials of the Council of Europe and European Commission were more inclined to accept the practicality of fashioning a solution to the Jammu and Kashmir issue on the basis of the Line of Control but with some adjustments. I told them that while the Government of India cannot examine this proposal given Pakistan's continuing subversive activities, I personally felt that a solution could be sought with some adjustments in the Line of Control combined with a political package for the people of Jammu and Kashmir responsive to their concerns and aspirations.

(k) European officials stated that after the current tension is completely defused and after some progress being made for political dialogue such suggestions can be put on the table by India and that they (Europeans) would be supportive of India if there is such modification in India's negotiating stance on Jammu and Kashmir. They agreed that reaching this stage in any negotiations would take some time, that neither India nor Pakistan should have a static and absolutist approach in resolving the Kashmir dispute.

(l) It was interesting to note that there was not much enthusiasm or inclination to refer back to the UN resolutions on this issue. Nor was there any great enthusiasm for the UN to play any role. There was concern about the spread of Islamic extremist terrorism and Islamic orthodoxy in the Central and South Asian region. There was special concern about the status of women, the role of Madrasas and prospects of violation of Human Rights in Islamic orthodoxy finding a place in the power structures of Asian countries.

(m) My assertion that the question of mediation in any form does not arise and that the maximum that India acknowledges is possibilities of indirect facilitating role in persuading Pakistan to give up terrorism and subversion against India and to come to the negotiating table with a practical approach was tentatively accepted. I was told however that if some forward movement is not there, direct international involvement could become inevitable given the prospect of nuclear war between India and Pakistan.

(n) There is also an assessment (a wrong one in my opinion) that Musharraf is the only safeguard between moderation and the resurgence of highly assertive and violent Islamic forces in Pakistan. Which then would affect the ongoing processes of stabilisation of Afghanistan.

(o) There was also a feeling that the revival of violent Islamic forces in Pakistan can have ripple effect in Central Asia and in the Gulf, destabilising the whole region.

The conclusion I reached was that the officials of the European Commission and the European Council were perhaps more knowledgeable about and more practical in dealing with Indo-Pakistan issues. Members of the Foreign Affairs Committee of the European Parliament tended to have a kind of moralistic approach without much understanding of the complexities of the issues involved.

In overall terms, the Members of the Foreign Affairs Committee were not deeply interested because only about 15 or 20 out of the 65 to 70 members of the Foreign Affairs Committee attended the hearings. Some specific suggestions I have for your kind consideration are :

1. We must send eminent and impartial non-government Indians to Brussels and Strausburg to explain our policies. Persons like Mr. George Verghese, Mr. Raja Mohan, Professor Amitabh Mattoo, could be sent.

2. We must examine the possibilities of sending the articulate women from Jammu and Kashmir from both communities to state our concerns and our case.

3. We must receive proposals from members from the Institutions of European Union and give them an opportunity of exchanging views with our leaders and think-tanks as well as with leaders of Jammu and Kashmir.

4. It might be worthwhile inviting Solana and Baroness Emma Nicholson to visit India in the coming months to give them first hand knowledge about our policies and our predicaments. I think the resources both human and financial of our embassy in Brussels and the major European capitals should be enhanced with the stipulation that these additional resources should be utilised primarily to inviting leaders of Europe involved in Europe's collective political and diplomatic activities directed at our region.

I have imposed a longish letter on you. I do hope that you would have the time to read through it given your many important pre-occupations. But I thought that it is relevant to keep you directly informed of my assessments resulting from this visit.

Yashwant Sinha's South Asian Diplomatic Initiative—Context and Prospects

Yashwant Sinha has certainly signalled a pertinent diversification of India's foreign policy focus since assuming charge as the Minister for External Affairs. Jaswant Singh's tenure in the foreign office from end-1998 till 2002, was characterised by our concentration on relations with the USA and other important power centres of the world particularly those which were allied to the US. This was to some extent necessary because India had to deal with the fall out of its nuclear weaponisation due to its heightened adversarial relationship with Pakistan, and due to the terrorist attacks on the US on September 11, 2001. The Indian Parliament and Jammu and Kashmir Legislative Assembly being targeted by international terrorist groups was an additional impulse for a closer interaction with the major powers.

Sinha took over charge when a certain statistic was achieved in criticalities affecting India's external relations. It was time to attend to India's relations with its immediate neighbours as well as with the Arab countries, relations with whom suffered a certain amount of neglect. Sinha completed a round of visits to practically all the countries of the SAARC region early in August. He has visited Afghanistan, Maldives, Sri Lanka, Bhutan, Nepal and Bangladesh. The only country left out of this tour itinerary was Pakistan for obvious reasons. The post -September 11 global context in which Sinha's South Asian tour took place must be noted. All the countries in the SAARC region are part of the US campaign against international terrorism in one form or the other. Senior political and official figures from the US have visited South Asian countries except Maldives and Bhutan. Pakistan and Bangladesh have stationing-of- forces agreements now with the United States. The consequence, though not openly acknowledged, is a greater de facto involvement of the United States in the SAARC region. While all the countries in the SAARC region, including India welcomed this US involvement as a positive development in the campaign against international terrorism and as a phenomenon which might increase US economic cooperation with all the countries of the area, India's other neighbours welcomed this involvement due to additional reasons, viz. that the USA's activist posture in South Asia would balance off the political apprehensions and economic/ military threats they perceive from India (whether these are factually accurate or not). The US presence is also considered by these neighbours as a tempering factor controlling the implications of the nuclear weaponisation of India and Pakistan.

Leaving aside the macro-level global context. The ingredients of the regional context are of specific relevance to the diplomatic initiative taken by Yashwant Sinha. There are reticences and resentments against India shared by practically all her neighbours which can be summed up as follows : Because of its territorial size, demographic, technological, military and economic strengths, compared to her neighbours, India has an over-weaning and assertive stance against all her neighours. India has a series of disputes territorial, economic and political, with all her neighbours. India is not willing to grant concessions or come to compromises on these disputes. India has a factorable balance of trade with all her neighbours but is not willing to take any steps in terms of granting tariff and non-tariff concessions to remedy this imbalance in favour of the small neighbours. Despite being a regional economic power, India seems to have the additional ambition of being a completely domineering economic power. India takes its neighbours for granted and does not take any special measures to nurture relations with her neighbours in a manner responsive to their needs and sensitivities. India is obsessive in its apprehensions about the smaller neighbours developing extra-regional equations which in India's opinion may affect India's security.

The escalating stand off between India and Pakistan poses a serious threat to regional stability and security. These conceptual threat perceptions of India's neighbours find expression on specifics in India's bilateral relations with them. Dispute on Jammu and Kashmir with Pakistan falls in a category by itself. Even otherwise, India has territorial disputes with Nepal (Kalapani issue), with Bhutan by implication. India wants Bhutan to settle its border with China in tandem with Sino-Indian boundary settlement. With Bangladesh (border enclaves still have to be exchanged and finally settled between the two countries, settlement of the rival claims on New Moor islands still hangs fire). With Sri Lanka (about free access for Indian fishermen at Kachchativu Island). India has not settled its maritime boundary with Bangladesh and Pakistan. Then there are political and economic issues. Bhutan and Nepal desire India to take active interest in resolving their bilateral disputes about Nepalese expelled from Bhutan and about terrorist activities inside their territories originating from Indian dissident groups, Bangladesh being a base for anti-Indian terrorist activities, the issue of illegal migration of Bangladeshis, the treatment of

Hindu minority in Bangladesh remain issues on which there are differences of opinion between India and Bangladesh. Sri Lankan Government continues to seek India's endorsement of the ongoing peace initiative with the LTTE but more importantly Sri Lanka wishes India to curb support for the LTTE's separatist activities from Tamil Nadu.

In the economic sphere, India's neighbours wish India to give more trade concessions to their exports to redress the imbalance in trade which they have with India. But at the same time theirs seems to be a one-sided approach in that they wish India to give concessions but they are not willing to take initiative on their own which will help solve the problem. A case in point is Bangladesh's reluctance to export natural gas to India, purely on political grounds despite the proposition being logical and feasible from the economic and technical points of view. Then there are comprehensions on the part of India about her neighbours having too close relationship with Pakistan or China in the context of the undercurrents of India's relations with China and Pakistan. The relationships of her neighbours with Pakistan are a matter of particular concern because Pakistan's motives are not just to improve relations with these countries but to utilise these relations to generate negative pressures on India. President Musharraf's visits to Nepal, Bangladesh and Sri Lanka which preceded Yashwant Sinha's visit are assessed by India through the prism of this perception.

Given this critical background, Yashwant Sinha's visits to neighbouring countries in July and August were timely initiative to mend fences, to remove misunderstandings and apprehensions, and to bring back India's bilateral relations with these countries back on track, to the extent feasible. Sinha assured the Nepalese authorities about India's continuing help to overcome the violence and de-stabilisation generated by Maoist dissidents in that country. He indicated that India would be willing to discuss all other issues on which there is a difference of opinion with an open mind and with a practical problem-solving approach. Sinha also sought the assistance of Nepal in controlling Pakistan-sponsored terrorism originating in Nepalese territory and permeating the Indo-Nepalese border.

In Bangladesh, while giving similar assurances he made it clear that India has no wish to impose on Bangladesh about export of natural gas from that country. He gave the categorical assurance that it is for Bangladesh to decide on the issue. While India would welcome the supply of natural gas from Bangladesh, if Bangladesh has reservations the India would resort to other options respecting Bangladesh's sensitivities. Sinha also promised further relaxation of import duties on Bangladesh exports to India. Most significantly he did not press the demands which are of interest to India regarding transit facilities or on the issue of illegal migration and so forth. His extending an invitation to the Prime Minister of Bangladesh to visit India, to some extent cleared the impression that India has reservations about the Government of Begum Khaleda Zia. Here again he expressed India's willingness to have substantive discussions on pending issues with Bangladesh. The visits to Sri Lanka, Bhutan and Maldives did not involve dealing with any major controversial issues. Here Sinha's line with these countries was that India would be supportive in meeting the political and economic concerns of these countries to the maximum extent, trying to transcend previous technical and narrower perceptions of the Indian Government.

With his background of economic diplomacy during his civil service days, and his political experience as the Finance Minister, Mr. Yashwant Sinha seems to be animated by a certain approach towards regional relations. This appears to be that in his view trained human resources, the competitive labour force, the availability of raw materials, natural resources and the large market of South Asian region should attract other countries of the world to this region. An environment of political stability and a proven capacity for coordinated economic performance within the region are prerequisites to achieve this. The emergence of democratic political systems, the restructuring of national economies in conformity with global trends, and the shared attitude of the people of South Asia to move beyond conflict and mutual antagonisms provide the necessary basis for a concerted effort by South Asian countries to meet the above objective. The positive ramifications of interaction with the EEC, the APEC and ASEAN or NAFTA need no emphasis.

India has a more complex and difficult role to play in this process, compared to the other countries in the region. It has to reassure its neighbours, while being firm about, and safeguarding its substantial political, security and economic interests. India's predicament is difficult because some of its neighbours judge its bona fides towards them on the sole criterion of whether it accepts their suggestions in toto for resolving problems and inherited attitudes and the compulsion of realpolitik combine to create a volatile atmosphere in which all nations are seeking to fashion reasonable institutional mechanisms for meeting their more fundamental aspirations. India being the largest polity in the region necessarily has to take a lead in forging stable regional equation.

It is not unreasonable to speculate that Yashwant Sinha has initiated a process of reviving both multi-lateral and bilateral cooperation in the South Asian region.

A Significant Hiccup in Sino-Indian Relations

The satisfaction and the acclaim about Prime Minister Atal Behari Vajpayee's visit to China in the last week of June stands diminished in public perception by the confrontation between the Chinese Border Security Personnel and an Indian Border Patrol Party consisting of personnel from the Intelligence Bureau on the 26th of June. Vajpayee was still in Shanghai when the incident took place at Asaphi La sector of the Line of Actual Control. This sector on the Line of Actual Control along with seven other sectors are areas where there is difference of opinion between India and China on the location of the Line of Actual Control.

The incident was more or less accidental and not a consequence of any pre-planned mutually intrusive patrolling exercise by either side. What is a matter of concern is, however, the manner in which the Chinese side handled the situation. According to reports in the media, the Chinese were aggressive in their discussions. They detained the Indian personnel, disarmed them, interrogated them and then sent them back to the Indian side of the LAC according to Chinese perception after which their arms were returned.

The controversy was further exacerbated at a press briefing given by a spokesperson of the Chinese Foreign Office early in July. Press Trust of India's correspondent in Beijing, apparently referring to the border incident asked a question as to why China had intruded into the Indian side of Arunachal Pradesh. The Chinese spokesperson's response as anticipated was that China does not recognise Arunachal Pradesh as a part of India. This is not a new stance. China has been sticking to this claim on Arunachal Pradesh since the mid-50, when the Sino-Indian boundary and the validity and legitimacy of the MacMahon Line became an issue between India and China. One is prepared to take note of the textual relevance of the fact that the Chinese did not ratify the Tripartite Anglo-Tibetan-Chinese Convention defining the border between Tibet and India. It was negotiated by Sir Henry MacMahon the then Foreign Secretary of India. But it is equally relevant to note that India did not consider the China's non-ratification a hurdle to exercising sovereign territorial jurisdiction in the area now known as Arunachal Pradesh, and formerly known as NEFA, North Eastern Frontier Agency.

That the Chinese side was not disinclined towards a practical compromise with India on Arunachal Pradesh, if India agreed to cede territory in the Western Sector of the Boundary with China (Aksai Chin), in exchange. This was inherent in the suggestions sent by the then Chinese Prime Minister, Zhou en-Lai and Jawaharlal Nehru. It is reasonable to deduce that Deng Xiaoping in his discussions with Rajiv Gandhi in December 1988 was indirectly re-affirming this approach when he talked about resolving the Sino-Indian boundary on the basis of equality, mutual accommodation and mutual understanding.

Whatever the circumstances of the provocation, the behaviour of the Chinese border guards at Asaphi La and the strident tone of the Chinese Foreign Office spokesperson on Arunachal Pradesh, shows not only consistency in China's basic approach to the issues related to the Line of Actual Control and the boundary and also an approach where there is no inclination towards moderation and creating an atmosphere of reasonableness on these issues. The Sino-Indian Joint Working Group on the Boundary is to continue with discussions on the delineation of the Line of Actual Control and move forward operationally on further confidence building measures. The two special Political Representatives designated to discuss the substantive question of the Boundary by the two Prime Ministers during Vajpayee's visit are to commence their discussions on this basic issue. The Indian side will do well to take note of China's policy articulations on the Asaphi La incident and on Arunachal Pradesh in their future negotiations.

It is clear that the media, the Parliament and Indian public opinion should assess the critical developments following Vajpayee's visit to Beijing not in terms of a partisan manner, of electoral politics, or unreasonable nationalistic jingoism. While it is true that Indian official response to these as it has come out in the media smacks of an anxiety not to offend the Chinese or diminish positive publicity on the result of Prime Minister Vajpayee's visit to China. The official spokesperson of the MEA made the following points which are factually valid to the extent that they go :

- The incident involving the Indian patrol and Chinese border guards in Arunachal Pradesh was not pre-meditated by the Chinese. The confrontation was accidental.

- Chinese and Indian patrols happen to run into each other often all along the 2500-mile long Line of Actual Control.
- The Chinese Patrol's action against the Indian patrolling party did constitute a breach of the November 29 agreement on Confidence building measures in the military field.
- The matter has been taken up through diplomatic channels with the Chinese both at Delhi and in Beijing.
- The incident will not come in the way of moving forward on various bilateral initiatives for improving relations as agreed upon during Vajpayee's visit to Beijing.
- China's assertive statement on Arunachal Pradesh was provoked by a question by an Indian journalist.

Arunachal Pradesh is part of India.

Minister for External Affairs Yashwant Sinha repeated more or less the same points in his statement in the Lok Sabha on these issues.

All the relevant points of a response have been made but what is a matter of concern is the excessive and unnecessary conciliatory tone of our response. The Chinese side has been exonerated by agreeing that the incident was accidental. But the point is the way the Chinese patrol party behaved was in complete contradiction not only of the operational details of the CBMs of the 1996 agreement but of the policy between Governments of China and India on maintaining peace and tranquility on the Line of Actual Control signed on 7th September, 1993 in Beijing. Article1 of this treaty clearly said that neither side would use or threaten to use force against the other by any means.... In case the personnel of one side cross the Line of Actual Control, upon being cautioned by the other side, they shall immediately pull back to their own side. When necessary the two sides shall jointly check and determine the segments of the Line of Actual Control where they have different views as to its alignment.

Article 4 of the 1993 Treaty clearly states : "In case of contingencies or other problems arising in the areas along the Line of Actual Control, the two sides will deal with them through meetings and friendly consultations between border personnel of the two countries".

The Chinese patrol challenging the Indian patrol, disarming them, detaining them, interrogating them, is in clear violation of these two articles, leaving aside the general spirit and content of the Sino-Indian agreements on the LAC and Confidence Building Measures, of 1993 and 1996 respectively.

As far as Chinese Foreign Ministry spokesman categorically asserting China's claims on Arunachal Pradesh is concerned, it is not sufficient to say that the statement was provoked because of an Indian journalist's question and that the Chinese have not said anything new. And that it in the end stated in passing that Arunachal Pradesh is part of India. This is what one gathers from media reports on the official response of the Government of India. A point of importance agreed upon by India and China in 1993 Agreement was that all discussions related to the Boundary question will be within the guiding principle of mutual equal security (Article 2 of the 1993 agreement).

Being measured and reasonable should not diminish clarity and firmness in the articulation of our positions and policies. Formal statement categorically stating that Chinese border patrols's behaviour was in violation of 1993 and 1996 agreements and that Arunachal Pradesh is an inalienable part of the territory of the Indian Republic should have been made with adequate publicity. The same points should be conveyed formally to the Chinese government underlining that in the interest of continuing the initiatives for peace and normalcy, China should be more reasonable and tempered in its responses so that misunderstandings due to intemperate communications which spoiled Sino-Indian relations between 1956 and 1961 is not repeated.

One would do well to remember Winston Churchill's advice on the phenomenon of Appeasement in inter-state relations : "Appeasement in itself may be good or bad according to circumstances. Appeasement out of fear or just to avoid unpleasantness can be disastrous. Appeasement from a position of clear policies and strength might be surest, and perhaps the only road to peace."

Some Thoughts on National Security

The provocation for this article is the comparatively more attention given to issues related to National Security at the brain-storming session of the Congress Party at Shimla between the 7th and 9th of July. The President of the Indian National Congress, Mrs. Sonia Gandhi, made the following points in her inaugural address at this meeting.

She stated that the present government has polarised the Indian society on communal lines using terrorism as an excuse instead of combating terrorism decisively and strongly.

She stated that Government has weakened India's National Defence not only by mismanaging the crisis which it has faced over the last five years from the military point of view by not spending funds allocated to modernise and re-organise the Armed Forces of India.

She has asserted that ambiguities, delays and inefficiencies in managing economic reforms has jeopardised country's economic security.

Following this, referring to foreign policy and national security issues, the final declaration (Sankalp) of the Shimla meeting emphasised that the Congress is firm to build a framework of foreign policy which has in-built flexibility to respond to the dynamics of the changing world, keeping national interests paramount.

The meeting defined non-alignment in its true conceptual context as envisaged in its origin, that it essentially means a capacity to exercise independence in taking foreign policy decisions according to national interests.

The Congress Party also showed realism about India's newly acquired nuclear weapons status. While emphasising the need for universal nuclear disarmament, the Congress Declaration talks about the need for a dialogue with other nuclear weapons powers, particularly, our nuclear neighbours for confidence building measures and for managing the implications of India's nuclear weaponisation.

Neither time nor space allows a detailed description of the lively exchanges which took place on the issue of national security and foreign policy, but the aspects which attracted attention and about which there was general consciousness merits attention and discussion by a wider audience and larger public.

The security challenges for India in the medium and long-term can be listed as follows:

- The requirement of India to structure new equations with important power centres of the world after the end of the Cold War and the disintegration of the Soviet Union, because of the disappearance of leverages which India had in fashioning its foreign and security policies for the last 50 years, since the end of the Second World War.
- An important dimension of this concern is the creation of a stable and calibrated relationship by India with the USA without losing India's independence of options in taking decisions in foreign and security policies.

- Managing the prospects of Fax-Americana to be undertaken by India.
- South Asia constituting nearly 1/5th of the world's population, also happens to be one of the poorest areas of the world, barring perhaps Africa, South of Sahara. Meeting socio-economic developmental requirements through appropriate domestic and external policies is another challenge.

Within the ambit of the above concerns, particular attention has to be given by all South Asian countries for ensuring energy security, particularly in terms of hydro-carbons and hydel power. A rational and practical management of energy resources of both these categories moving away from the narrow political considerations is imperative.

Then there are some fundamental security concerns affecting South Asia. These are consolidating identities of different countries on the basis of pluralism and religious and ethnic diversities. The challenge is made more complex because there are several nation states in the region. The religious, ethnic and linguistic characteristics of civil societies of these nation states overlap with each other. This overlapping results in apprehensions about respective national identities. The challenge is to resolve the contradictions between the nature of the civil societies and anxieties about consolidating individual national identities, promoting civic nationalism that is integrative rather than ethno-religious nationalism which is separative.

The complexes and apprehensions generated by the asymmetry between India on the one hand, and the South Asian countries on the other, in terms of size, population, levels of development, technology and military power has resulted in tensions in inter-state relations in the region. A purposeful effort is required to overcome these tensions. India has a special responsibility in this regard, while the other countries need to make an effort to overcome the burdens of history of the last half a century or so.

Migration of people due to socio-economic pressures borne of the land to people ratio, is going to be a major problem. While politically South Asia is characterised by different nation states, South Asian land mass is, normatively speaking, one economic region. Structuring cooperative and contentful regionalism is the only solution.

Establishment of SAARC was an attempt at such regionalism. It has been stalled primarily due to political tensions. The solution is, therefore to deal with the political problems in a pragmatic manner to move on to the more desirable and logical objectives of regional cooperation.

Adjusting to the ongoing process of globalisation remains an important challenge in terms of security for all South Asian countries. The challenge is made more complex due to the undercurrents of restrictive and acquisitive economic and technology regimes forming part of the policies of the major powers of the world.

Last but not the least, the internal centrifugal forces affecting the unity of the nation states of the region has to be coped with. This requires not only strengthening of democracy in each of the nation states making them safe for diversities, but also the establishment of harmonious relations between South Asian States.

Some of the issues in which a broad structure of our foreign and security policies have to be laid down are :

Non-alignment

It is necessary to make a distinction between Non-alignment and Non-aligned Movement. The Non-aligned Movement in its traditional form has faded away. The terms of reference of the Movement which were relevant to the Cold War era, are no longer relevant to current trends in international relations.

Non-alignment as a governing principle in foreign policy, however, remains absolutely relevant as originally envisaged by Pandit Jawaharlal Nehru. It simply means India retaining its freedom of choice of options in foreign and security policies decisions without being subjected to external influences and foreign persuasions to the maximum extent possible.

To sum up, India adhering to sustain its capacity to formulate and implement an independent foreign policy, responsive to India's national interests at a given point of time.

In contrast, the Non-aligned Movement now lacks unity, different regional, sub-regional groups have different priorities and their own independent contacts with power centres of the world. The capacity of the movement in its traditional identity to work in unison is not there today. The need, therefore, is for Members of the Non-aligned Group of countries to create new terms of reference to function together based on conscious and thoughtful exercise of finding areas of own interest beyond which they can work together. India could and should play a leading role in this exercise, if other like-minded countries are responsive to this requirement.

Non-Proliferation

India's nuclear weaponisation in 1998, requires a change in India's approach to issues related to non-proliferation. There is a shift in international non-proliferation policies. The mainstream Agenda of the international community is not so much comprehensive disarmament but elimination of nuclear weapons as graduated area control aimed at preventing further horrizontal proliferation of unclear weapons.

The question of India giving up its nuclear weapons and missiles capacities does not arise. Maintaining and nurturing this military, technological strategy is necessary.

Accordingly, our approach to problems of non-proliferation and disarmament has to change, including the last effort made by Shri Rajiv Gandhi at the UN Special Session on Disarmament in 1988. India's approach could be :

(a) Complete elimination of weapons of mass destruction by all countries in a gradual and practical manner, should be our overall objective.

(b) In the long term an attempt should be made to replace the Nuclear Non-Proliferation Treaty by a new Convention on non-proliferation of nuclear weapons should be suggested, both in bilateral discussions and in multilateral fora. The stipulation in this convention should be applicable equally to all countries, regardless of whether they are nuclear weapons powers or not.

(c) The legally recognised nuclear weapons powers should in the meanwhile accept the reality of India having become a nuclear weapons power, and to treat it accordingly.

(d) India on its part should clearly emphasise its determination to keep its nuclear and missile assets sealed and updated where necessary. In doing this, the Indian endeavour should be to formulate policies and project an approach where India assures the major powers of the world that it is a responsible country and that its nuclear weapons capacities in no way threaten the strategic and security interests of the major powers of the world.

(e) While adopting this approach, India should indicate its willingness to participate in negotiations for a new nuclear weapons non-proliferation convention and related sub-agreements. These later agreements should not have discriminatory clauses as the CTBT, FMCT, etc.

(f) India should also urge that other regulatory regimes related to non-proliferation like the NSC-Nuclear Suppliers Club, WASSENAR, agreements should become non-discriminatory.

(g) Arguing for our clear proposals for nuclear and comprehensive disarmament would lack credibility, given our own acquisition of nuclear weapons.

(h) These efforts at the multi-lateral level should be backed up by bilateral agreements with important nuclear and missile powers.

Vajpayee's Visit to China—Prospects of Equations in a Changing World

Prime Minister Vajpayee will be in China from the 22nd of June on an official visit. This is the first visit by an Indian Prime Minister to Beijing after a gap of nearly ten years, the last such visit took place in September 1993 when Prime Minister Narasimha Rao had an exchange of views with Prime Minister Li Peng and President Jiang Zemin in Beijing.

Sino-Indian relations have seen ups and downs during the last decade. Vajpayee's mentioning China as a major security factor compelling India to conduct nuclear weapons tests, Defence Minister George Fernandes describing China as an adversary between 1998 and 1999, were the low points in Sino Indian relations. However, the general orientations in India's China policy set by Rajiv Gandhi's visit to Beijing in December 1988 has been more or less sustained through diplomatic channels and high level exchanges. Chinese Prime Minister Zhou Rongji and President Jiang Zemin have visited India between 1996 and 2000. Defence Minister George Fernandes has visited Beijing. The tension characterising Sino-Indian relations in 1998-2000 has faded. Vajpayee's journey to Beijing takes place at an important juncture in international relations and regional politics. The visit takes place after the changes brought about in the priorities in the international agenda, foreign policies and security matters in the aftermath of the terrorist attacks in the United States of America and in other parts of the world. The visit also takes place after the assertive confirmation of the uninhibited assertion of a unipolar position of influence by the United States in world and regional affairs as manifested in the war in Iraq and removal of Saddam Hussain regime. The non-proliferation agenda has shifted away from a macro-level objective of reduction and alienation of nuclear weapons and nuclear missiles to arms control and selective disarmament primarily concentrating on horizontal non-proliferation.

While China endorsed the mainstream of this Agenda, India with its newly acquired nuclear weapons capacities remains opposed to discriminatory arrangements and selective non-proliferation. While both India and China attach importance to their relationship with the USA, at the fundamental level, both are opposed to a unipolar hegemony in world affairs. China now has a new leadership which is the first of its kind with no personal and political linkages with the generation of leaders who were part of the Communist Movement and the Long March. The present state of bilateral relations is steady. The arrangement for maintaining peace and tranquility on the Line of Actual Control stipulated in the Sino-Indian Agreement of 1993 and agreement on confidence building measures signed in 1996, are holding. No major controversy has occurred on the Line of Actual Control in recent years. As the preparations for this visit have been on the anvil for nearly an year, political significant ingredient in the process have been a meeting between Vajpayee and President of China Hu Jintao in St Petersburg late in May, and External Affairs Minister Yashwant Sinha's meeting with his Chinese counterpart Li Zhaoxing in Phnom Penh in the week preceding Vajpayee's arrival in Beijing.

Vajpayee and his Chinese counterpart Wen Jiabao will have wide ranging discussions on global, regional and bilateral issues normal for such high level exchanges. Some specifics, however, which form the substance of the discussions and will constitute the framework of relations between China and India at least for coming five to ten years would be :

- Management of the emerging new world order subject to the unipolar power of the USA. A trend the imbalances of which has to be redressed.
- Dealing with the shortcomings and aberrations of international economic and technological arrangements under the W.T.O.
- Exploring possibilities of mutual cooperation and playing an effective role in world security arrangements work and the ASEAN Security Forum, the ASF.
- Examining possibilities of working together on reviving the role of the United Nations in world affairs, including its reforms.

More importantly, substantive issues affecting bilateral relations would form part of the exchange of views which would include a review of the progress made by the Sino-Indian Joint Working Group on the boundary question in relation to the agreed delineation of the Line of Actual Control.

- Initiating steps to deal with the substantive issue of resolving the Boundary issue.
- A candid discussion on the implications of Chinese defence cooperation and defence supplies arrangement with Pakistan on Indian security specifically and regional security in general.
- Coming to mutually acceptable and transparent equations on issues related to Tibet and status of Sikkim, issues about which there are ambiguities rooted in differences of opinion.
- Charting out a substantive scheme for expanding bilateral trade, technological and economic relations.

Official pronouncements from China from the second week of June onwards indicate that China is willing to expand and encourage positive trends in Sino-Indian relations. Chinese official spokespersons have pronouced the Vajpayee visit as an important landmark in bilateral relations. Chinese spokespersons however underlined that recent policy orientations of both India and China on the security dimension of their equations indicate that Vajpayee and his counterpart Wen Jiabao have redefined strategic and security terms of reference of bilateral relations between the two countries.

The logical expectation should be that China and India would affirm intention in their policies towards each other not to threaten each other's security. Chinese spokespersons have also indicated the willingness of Chinese Government to move on to discuss the substantive aspects of the boundary issue while the residual problems related to Line of Actual Control are getting sorted out. This is apart from these spokespersons indicating a positive attitude about expanding bilateral relations across the spectrum in various dimensions mentioned above.

While all the right noises and all the right gestures are being made about Vajpayee's visit to Beijing, the outcome and the prospects need an assessment in terms of realities and practical possibilities. The boundary question is a vexed one. The most recent pronouncement of the Chinese that they would like to resolve the issue on the basis of equality, mutual understanding, mutual accommodation and mutual adjustment.

As far as the status of Sikkim and Tibet go, India should stand by its policy decision of Chinese jurisdiction over Tibet. China should parallely recognise Sikkim as an integral part of India. While we should express our concern regarding Chinese military cooperation with Pakistan, and Defence cooperation arrangements with Myanmar, there is no point in complaining to the Chinese about it. The solution is to tell the Chinese that we view their defence relationships with these two countries with concern, that they should not object to India adopting defence doctrines about increasing its defence capacities to meet the challenges resulting from their cooperation with these two countries.

Forging a cooperative relationship with China while keeping in mind possible aberrations which may affect this exercise, is the practical approach. Vajpayee's visit to Beijing provides the opportunity to forge such relationship. If such relationship becomes a reality, it will have a farreaching and positive impact on regional and global security and stability.

4

Efforts Continue

Vajpayee's ASEAN Visit - Looking East—Mostly Looking

Prime Minister Atal Behari Vajpayee has just concluded his visit to Cambodia and Laos in connection with the first Indo-ASEAN summit. A number of bilateral agreements were signed with Laos and Cambodia also during the visit. Media as usual have reported positively on the visit in terms of the events attendant on the visit. The prognosis on India's relations with ASEAN countries has to be based on the more recent interactions between ASEAN and India in term of substantive relations. It is equally important to compare Indo-ASEAN interactions with the evolving relations between the ASEAN, on the one hand and major regional powers like China and Japan on the other.

A little bit of historical recall would also be relevant in this process. ASEAN countries had invited India to join their regional grouping in the mid-60s as a full member but India refused in the context of the Cold War and the situation in Vietnam at that time. It is between 1987 and 1989 during the second half of Rajiv Gandhi a tenure that India conveyed its interest in being associated with the ASEAN. The initial response of ASEAN governments was reticent because of socialist-oriented economics arrangements in India and a certain concern about Indo-Pakistan tensions being injected into the deliberations and activities of the ASEAN, if India were to be admitted. By 1990 however, both global and regional politics had undergone qualitative changes. The Soviet Union was in the process of disintegrations, and Cold War had ended. India under the Narasimha Rao Government had embarked on a substantive and wide-ranging programme of economic reforms, restructuring and liberalization, thereby bringing the Indian economy in line with the economies of the ASEAN countries. The existent complementarities between the economies of the ASEAN countries and India became crystallized. The market for commerce and investment could serve a combined population of nearly 1.3 billion people of India and the ASEAN countries. ASEAN Governments responded to Indian overtures in 1992 and between 1992 and 1996 India first became a spectoral dialogue partner of the ASEAN and in 1996 became a full dialogue partner. India also joined the security entity of the ASEAN, the ASEAN Regional Forum, in 1996. India's initial suggestion to join the Security Forum were rejected by the ASEAN. The reason being, ASEAN's reluctance to have the complex politico-military tensions of the subcontinent becoming part of the discussions. This reasoning had validity because once India became a dialogue partner of the ASEAN, Pakistan Government actively lobbied to become part of ASEAN on similar lines. Pakistan's additional reasoning was its Islamic Identity particularly with Malaysia and Indonesia. The point to note is that it took nearly nine years from 1987 to 1996 for India to become a stable participant in the ASEAN process which finally eliminated in the first ASEAN-India summit held in Phnom Penh between the 4th and 6th of November. The omnibus statement summarizing the conclusions of India-ASEAN summit declared that the strategic vision of the new linkage (established in the summit) at the highest level would be translated into reality with concrete programmes of cooperation. The Statement also asserted that this cooperation will comprehensively combat non-traditional security threats, including that of terrorism within the framework of the existing ASEAN Regional Forum (The regional security entity of the ASEAN). The statement also confirmed that the India-ASEAN summit now onwards will be held once every year. The collective leadership of the ASEAN and Prime Minister Vajpayee agreed that the existing programmes and projects of economic and technological cooperation should be expanded. More significant was Prime Minister Vajpayee's suggestion that the programmes of economic cooperation be expanded to explore possibilities of the creation of an ASEAN-India Free Trade Area by the year 2012.

India also took some specific initiatives to strengthen economic cooperation with Laos and Cambodia in the bilateral segment of the visit. In discussions with Cambodian Prime Minister Hun Sen and Laotian Prime Minister Bounnhang Vorachit, Vajpayee, offered Dollar 10 million credit line to each of the countries.

Bilateral agreements were also signed with Laos and Cambodia to combat illegal trafficking of drugs, defence cooperation and expansion of trade and investment relations. In terms of formal, agreements and decisions, the India-ASEAN Summit has led to the most substantive results after a gap of nearly a decade. The last occasion marking such decisions was former Prime Minister Narasimha Rao's visit to the ASEAN countries in the summer of 1993. The framework for result-oriented directions have been finalized but future prospects have to be assessed on the basis of two criteria. First a comparison between the content of cooperation between ASEAN's relations with China, Japan and Korea, and secondly, the record of cooperation between India and the ASEAN over the last decade. India's participation in the Regional Security dialogue under the ARF too had hiccups because of India's nuclear weapons tests of 1998 and the Kargil conflict and high levels of Indo-Pakistan tension. This should not be a matter of too much concern because the decision taken regarding these events were in India's interests.

It is however on the economic side that one should be thoughtful. China and the ASEAN have also signed an agreement on the creation of a Free Trade Zone which will have a market of nearly 1.7 billion people and this free trade area is likely to become operational within three to five years. Compare this to the decision only to "explore possibilities" of creating such a zone between India and the ASEAN over a period of ten years. Given the pace and substance of our economic performance such caution is realistic, though disappointing. One suspects that caution is more on the part of ASEAN than India.

The record of Indo-ASEAN economic cooperation is also not encouraging. The projects envisaged for cooperation in the civil aviation sector (the Singapore Airlines Project), in the sector of building of highways with a Malaysian Consortium, the lack of satisfactory progress about establishment of Information Technology Parks in States of Karnataka and Tamil Nadu, have not increased India's credibility in the ASEAN countries, though leaders friendly to India, like Prime Minister of Singapore Goh Tok Chung and Prime Minister of Malaysia Mahathir Mohammed continuing to bat on in favour of India. It is also relevant to note that while ASEAN has agreed to a collective, summit dialogue with China, Japan and South Korea they have not included India in this collective summit exercise, obviously not because India is not in the league of these countries in its economic performance and policies. Secretary in the Ministry of External Affairs, R. Abhayankar correctly assessed India's performance in relation to ASEAN when he said during Vajpayee's visit to Cambodia that "India unfortunately has ignored ASEAN and its strategic and economic potential in the past. India is now trying to redress this balance. With increasing engagement, India hopes that ASEAN will gain a better understanding of India's, economic and security concerns. The importance of ASEAN for India cannot be over-stated. It is a mutually re-enforcing relationship." A valid "mission statement". One hopes it, will be translated into operational realities. Otherwise I would have to recall a remark made by a senior official of the ASEAN Secretariat to me two years after my retirement in 1996. He said: "We keep hearing your policy makers talk about 'India's Look East' policy, but you just keep looking not doing much about it."

One hopes that the Cambodian visit will preclude, expressions of such views from friends in ASEAN in future.

Future of the SAARC in the Context of Indo-Pakistan Confrontation

The next SAARC summit scheduled to be held in Islamabad between January 11 and 13, now stands postponed because of Prime Minister Vajpayee's decision not to go to Islamabad because Pakistan's subversive terrorist activities against India. There have been accusations from the official spokesman of the Pakistan Foreign Office Kamran Mirza that India is deliberately sabotaging the prospects of South Asian cooperation by its obdurate approach of putting irrelevant pre-conditions, for participation in the summit. There is obviously a different Indian view on this point, but what is important is to examine the relevance of SAARC in its present form as an instrumentality of regional cooperation in the context of the record of its performance over the last 17 years since 1985.

The SAARC came into formal existence in December, 1985 in Dhaka on the basis of a proposal initiated by the late President Zia-ur-Rehman of Bangladesh in January 1981. India was initially reluctant to join this regional forum because Mrs. Indira Gandhi correctly anticipated that given Pakistan's India policies and Bangladesh's emerging distances from India, the grouping would be more an arrangement to exert various kinds of pressures on India rather than as an instrumentality to forge regional cooperation. She, nevertheless, decided that India should join the organisation as South Asian Cooperation would be a geo-political and economic myth if India kept out of this regional arrangement.

It is that SAARC has had a chequered career over the last two decades. India is not the only country which has decided to absent itself from SAARC summits, over the years. Sri Lanka, Bhutan, and even Pakistan have been instrumental in postponement of summits. The reasons at given points of time were different. In Sri Lanka's case, it was the resentment against India during the ethnic crisis in Sri Lanka in the mid-80s. The fall of the Babri Mosque delayed the summit in the early 90s, critical developments in Indo-Nepalese relations, Kargil conflict all resulted in non-participation of Heads of Government of one country or the other, leading to the postponement of the summit.

This break in the continuity of meetings is in fact a symptom of a fundamental shortcoming in the conviction of the Members of the organisation about regional cooperation. The lack of conviction is a result of Numbers of the SAARC not adhering to the terms of reference of the SAARC Charter on the basis of which South Asian Cooperation was sought to be forged. The basic term of reference was that member states of the SAARC realising the existence of a number of issues in bilateral dispute between them, agreed that that should be dealt with separately while they will collectively focus on economic, developmental, cultural and technological aspects to serve the larger and more pertinent objective of the well-being of the peoples of the SAARC countries. What has happened in fact is that Members of SAARC, particularly Pakistan have deviated from this term of reference, formulating their policies on proposals on regional cooperation on the basis primarily of narrower political considerations rooted in the disputes mentioned above.

Governmental and non-governmental discourse on the working of the SAARC manifest two thought processes. In terms of normative aims, based on considerations of regional stability, security and development, there is a consensus that the SAARC should be strengthened, made effectively functional providing a foundation and impulse for regional cooperation. But when it comes to operational details, specific projects and programmes of cooperation, controversies and contradictions of bilateral relations between Members of the SAARC, not only delay decisions but even prevent the very initiations of such projects. It is and it should be a matter of critical concern that the predicament and deliberations at the SAARC are in direct contrast to trends in regional cooperation in other regions of the world. The general context in which the disabilities and ineffectiveness of the SAARC should be viewed is worth recalling.

The older arrangements of multilateral cooperation which characterised international politics till the decades of the 80s of the last century are fading away. The trans-continental bonding of developing countries for political and development purposes have become a phenomenon of the past. The Non-aligned Movement, the Group of 77, the Group of 15, are now institutional shells which do not contribute in substance to processes of cooperation or evolution of joint policies. Even organisations like UNCTAD which are part of the United Nations system exist in form. The substance of work in the spheres of developmental and economic cooperation has been taken over by organisations like the WTO and multi-lateral financial institutions. The phenomenon of globalisation has accentuated this trend. The other equally important development over the last two decades has been the emergence of new regional groupings, more focussed on specific pattern of interests and geared to creating new equations between Governments of States to meet these interests. Entities like the European Union, APEC, the NAFTA, the ASEAN and similar regional cooperation arrangements in Africa, South America and Central Asia, have replaced the older multilateral arrangements, and are becoming incrementally influential and effective.

The SAARC is proving to be an unfortunate exception to these broad trends in regional and inter-regional cooperation. The reasons for SAARC not taking off even after two decades of existence, should be taken note of without inhibitions and courteous obfuscation. First and foremost is, India being disproportionately large and strong geo-political and economic presence in the region when compared to other members of the SAARC. The apprehensions generated by this asymmetry are accentuated because the cultural, linguistic, religious and ethnic identities of the civil societies of all the other member-states of the SAARC overlap with such identities which constitute Indian civil society. Thirdly, India's relations with Pakistan are characterised by a number of disputes, the most important being the Kashmir issue which resulted in Pakistan deliberately cultivating adversary attitude towards India which in turn translates into subversive and intrusive policies of Pakistan, threatening the unity and integrity of India. There are disputes though characterised by lesser intensities in terms of threat perceptions with Bangladesh, Nepal and Sri Lanka. All these result in twin negative ramifications. India's smaller neighbours entertain a general apprehension about India's potentiality of becoming a regional hegemon if there is too much of an integrated effort at regional cooperation. Secondly, Pakistan particularly, and other neighbours of India generally tend to structure their policies on regional cooperation relating them to the disputes they have with India. It is also true that India responds in a similar manner at times on this second ramification. The most important project of cooperation discussed in the SAARC over the last decade has been the creation of a South Asia Preferential Trade Arrangement which was supposed to evolve into South Asia Free Trade Area. On all accounts, it has been a still born experiment, particularly because Pakistan refuses to cooperate and links such cooperation to the solution of the Kashmir issue on Pakistan's terms. Technological, cultural and other aspects of cooperation have been a sporadic and somewhat disjointed phenomenon. The reasons for this abiding hiatus are, first, there is not genuine and broad-based mutual trust between the Members which is necessary basis for fruitful cooperation. Secondly, all the countries of the SAARC region are subject to patterns of political instability and tension, due to one reason or the other. Governments of the region are so enmeshed in dealing with the fall out of these instabilities that they cannot move on to bold and substantive initiatives for regional cooperation, howsoever desirable it is.

A realistic assessment of the prospects of Indo-Pakistan relations on the basis of the most recent policy orientations of the Musharraf Government makes it clear that holding of summits and attendant meetings at various levels is not going to result in any substantive cooperation under SAARC arrangements. It is time for India to examine whether SAARC in its present form constitutes a relevant framework for South Asian cooperation. There is no point in participating in an arrangement which is hamstrung by Pakistan's complexes and patently negative motivations towards India. It would be more practical for India to commence structuring new equations for cooperation with each of her neighbours individually which can then evolve into various forms of sub-regional cooperation in due course.

Given India's political, economic and technological capacities, it would be relevant for India to look beyond the narrowly defined SAARC region to structure cooperation arrangements more substantially again on bilateral basis with countries of South East Asia, Central Asia and West Asia.

Putin in India—A Reality Check

President Putin of the Russian Federation paid a second visit to India between the third and fifth of December. It was logical for the Government as well as the Media to attach high importance to the visit. Given the more or unchallengeable supremacy of United States in world politics structuring equations with other important powers to balance off this unipolar influence is logical for India. This balancing off does not mean getting into a confrontationist mode with the US or of having any unrealistic aspirations that equations between other important powers of the world can challenge undoubted influence of the US particularly, in the context of the significance of relations between other important countries and the USA which constitutes a more potent factor in global equations today.

Putin's visit was marked by an Indo-Russian Joint Declaration, by a Memorandum of Understanding and of the signing of eight agreements related to establishing strategic consultation mechanisms, the creation of a Joint Working Group on counter-terrorism and putting in place arrangements for cooperation in the spheres of economy, trade, science, technology and tele-communications. The economic and technological cooperation agreements were the result of negotiations between the Russian Deputy Prime Minister Klebanov, and his Indian Counterparts in the Ministries of Defence, Communications, Atomic Energy, and so on. A clear convergence of views emerged on some significant political and security issues during these discussions. But more about it a little later.

It would be relevant to go beyond the factual aspects of the visit and assess the context in which it took place and the prospects of Indo-Russian relations rooted in this context. Putin's last visit to Delhi was in the year 2001; Prime Minister Vajpayee paid a return visit in 2001, setting in motion the process of annual summits which were agreed upon during Putin's first visit. The most important nuance in Russia's foreign policy brought about by Putin after assuming power was to diversify the entirely Euro-centric orientations of Russia's foreign policy under Boris Yeltsin and his Foreign Minister Kozirev. While maintaining a continuity in ensuring a substantive and incremental pattern of relations with the United States and West Europe, Putin acknowledged the need for Russia to revive equations with other power centres, particularly in Asia. (Japan, China and India), to introduce trends of multi-polarity in Russia's foreign policy to the extent feasible. Given the present state of political, and defence cooperation, and economic relations of Russia with important Asian powers,, it is clear that President Putin is succeeding in this exercise.

Some important events have occurred since Putin's last visit to New Delhi which have profoundly influenced international politics as well as Russian attitudes and policies. Putin's present visit to New Delhi took place after September 11 terrorist attacks on the US and the consequent anti-terrorist campaign launched by the US in the Asian region. He came after dealing with a traumatic terrorist attack in a theatre in Moscow against which he took successful retaliatory action. He came to Delhi after attacks on the legislative building in Jammu and Kashmir and on the Indian Parliament by Pakistan-sponsored terrorists. The other events were the US decision to heighten its campaign against President Saddam Hussain of Iraq the confirmation of the Al-Qaeda group remaining active in countries stretching from Algeria to Indonesia, and the heightened ethno-religious tension against the Russian Government in Chechnya and Dagistan. The visit also took place after the withdrawal of the US from the anti-Ballistic Missile Treaty and the decision to deploy theatre missile defence and national missile defence to which the Russians have reluctantly agreed. The visit took place in the context of the most recent expansion of NATO, including the East European countries, formerly under the area of influence of the then Soviet Union (the membership increasing from 19 to 26).

The visit also follows the extension of USA's political and military presence in the Gulf and in South and Central Asia. The point being made in recalling this context is that President Putin is faced with the task of resolving the contradictions between his desire to make Russia resume a pre-eminent position in world affairs and the compulsions born of his anxiety to reconcile to the expanding political strategic and technological influence of the US and its allies. His visit to China and India are clearly an attempt at resolving this contradiction through creating a pattern of relations with major Asian powers which would temper the assertive dynamics of USA's dominance of world politics.

Assessed in this background, the concrete results of Putin's latest visit indicate that there is a parallelism, even convergence of interests between the Russian Federation and India. Putin has been more direct in acknowledging President Musharraff's linkages with cross-border terrorism against India. He shares Vajpayee's view about punitive action being planned against Iraq, having to be under the umbrella of the United Nations. He has agreed to expand defence supplies relationship between India and Russia, both in content and range, and has agreed to cooperation in sophisticated spheres of technology about which the US and other Western countries have some reticences. This includes technology related to peaceful uses of space and atomic energy, as well as to supply and construction of 2000 megawatt nuclear power stations in India, the project reports on which have now been completed (Kudankulam Nuclear Power Plant). Under most recent agreements Russia is to supply what they called the 5th generation advance fighter aircraft and a whole range of military equipment including rockets, armour, Radar Communications equipment, etc. There are also 12 working groups to plan projects of cooperation covering the spheres of trade, non-conventional sources of energy, hydrocarbons, metallurgy, science and technology, civil aviation, and so on.

The latest declarations made and agreement signed, strengthen the institutional framework for Indo-Russian relations but these relations still have to acquire sufficient substance, Indo-Russian trade stood at 1.26

billion dollars in 1998-99. It went up to 1.57 billion dollars in 1999-2000. During the period 2000 to 2002, there has been a decline in the volume of bilateral trade which now stands at 1.33 billion dollars. This volume of trade is way below the potentialities and mutual complementarities between India and Russia. President Putin made an interesting suggestion that the monies owed by India to Russia rooted in the credit arrangements at the time of the Soviet Union could be released to set up Indo-Russian joint ventures in India which could meet both the domestic needs as well as exports. In an overall sense, Indo-Russian economic relations in volume and content are much less than what India has with western democracies if one leaves the defence supplies arrangements outside this calculation.

We must acknowledge that while there may be an element of strategic considerations in Russia giving India defence supplies, the basic impulse is Russia's need for foreign exchange and resources. It is to be noted that prospects of Indo-Russian defence and political cooperation should be assessed in the light of Russia's defence supplies and cooperation arrangements with China (much larger in value and volume), and Russia's continuing commitment to sustain close relationship with the US and its allies. This is the realistic framework within which Indo-Russian relations should be assessed and a prognosis speculated upon.

At the macro-level, India-Russia relations are of relevance and significance to both countries. As far as India is concerned we must recognise that despite the loss of super-power status, Russia remains a strong nation-state and has potentialities of re-emerging as important power in world politics because of its economic, technological and military strength.

While Russia wants to consolidate its relations with the US and western Europe, it has concerns about a unipolar world dominated by the United States. Therefore, Russia would like to sustain a strong relationship with countries like India and would like to retain its influence to the extent feasible in Central Asia and West Asia. Russia at present is equally interested in having a good equation with China and more importantly to some extent with Pakistan. We must note that Russia has offered to cooperate with Pakistan in the energy sector. There is a convergence of interests between Russia and India on cross-border terrorism and threats to pluralistic nation-states. Russia remains an important existing and potential source of defence supplies to India and of hydrocarbons, energy resources and technologies. These factors have manifested themselves in one form or the other during President Putin's discussions with Vajpayee.

Russia, therefore, should remain an important factor in our foreign and security policy calculations.

India and the US—New Beginnings with Bush Jr.

The New Ambassador of the United States, Mr. Robert Blackwill, arrived in New Delhi on Friday, the 27th of July. He brings to his assignment multifaceted experience as career foreign service officer, a political campaign strategist for the Republican Party for more than a decade and a distinguished academician specialising in security and strategic affairs. That President Bush has chosen a person of high professional experience instead of nominating a politician as his Ambassador to India indicates the seriousness with which he wishes to attend to Indo-US relations. (Not that US politicians have done badly in India as Ambassadors, the academicians and carrier officers seem to be better).

Ambassador Blackwill's appointment would be welcomed by those who have more than a general interest in Indo-US relations. The Bush Administration has now been in place for eight months, a sufficient period to assess the initial indications about how the new dispensation in Washington plans to structure its relations with India. There were two speculative and anticipatory schools of thought in India about President Bush's likely India policies. The first that Republican administrations tend to have a cautious and distant approach towards India. Second, that Bush and his advisors will find it difficult to the performance of Clinton during the last two years of his Presidency in intensifying Indo-US relations. Both these assumptions seem to be less than accurate. Comparisons are invidious, but the Clinton Administration took notice of India only during the second half of his second tenure. To quote his first Assistant Secretary of State for South Asia Ms. Robin Raphael : "India was not much of a blip on the foreign policy radar screen of the United States". There is no doubt that Clinton and his Advisors compensated their neglect of India handsomely in 1999 and 2000. This attention to India by Clinton was impelled by three factors. India's nuclear weapons tests of 1998, a certain convergence of interests in countering international terrorism and potentialities of mutual benefit for India and the United States in the Information Technology capacities of India. Bush Administration's orientations towards India were in contrast positive, ab initio, even before he assumed the Presidency. In his main foreign policy speech in the Presidential campaign, there was a specific reference to the importance of nurturing close relations with India. The speech was made in California. External Affairs Minister Jaswant Singh and National Security Advisor

Brajesh Mishra were in contact with the advisors of Bush from September 2000 onwards.

A senior foreign policy figure in the Bush Administration made an interesting point in a conversation with me; that despite the general impression about Bush Jr.'s inexperience in foreign affairs, he focussed on India during the campaign. During foreign policy discussions he referred to India's importance not only in terms of its strategic, economic and technological importance but he reportedly spoke with conviction and wondered about a billion people of Indian State with so many diversities, remaining a democracy. It appears that Bush's interest in India is rooted in the profound factor of a political value system which he considered important. There was no doubt that the more active role played by the Indian diaspore in the US, influenced his views on India to some extent.

Prime Minister Vajpayee was supposed to meet him in September 2000, an appointment which he could not keep due to various reasons which are in the public knowledge. But Bush and Vajpayee spoke on the telephone to each other on prospects of Indo-US relations four months before Bush assumed his Presidency.

President Bush's interest in India was not general, but focussed is proved by the fact that high level inter-governmental contacts between India and the US have been the most frequent, perhaps in last four or five days. Jaswant Singh has had a meeting with Secretary of State Colin Powell, National Security Advisor Condoleeza Rice and with President Bush. Bush set aside protocol and transcended conventions when he invited Jaswant Singh for an unscheduled and long discussion in the Oval Office. Brajesh Mishra and Foreign Secretary Chokila Iyer have also been to Washington during this summer. Deputy Secretary of State Armitage visited India to give our foreign office briefing on US plans for the NMD. The visit was followed by Chairman Joint Chiefs of Staff General Henry Hugh Shelton who visited India in July, the first ever visit by the Chairman of the US Joint Chiefs of Staff. This was followed by the visit of the US Assistant Secretary of State for South Asian Affairs, Christina Rocca to New Delhi in the third week of July. US Trade Represenative Zeleck is to visit India in the coming month. This is apart from detailed discussions which took place between Jaswant Singh and Brajesh Mishra, on the one hand and Vice President Dick Cheney and Secretary of Defence Donald Rumsfeld, on the other. Equally significant was Vice President Cheney receiving the Indian leader of the opposition, Mrs. Sonia Gandhi during her visit to the US in June. These top level interactions apart from signifying a more intense pattern of interactions also imply the desire and intention of both the governments to engage each other to lend substance to Indo-US relations.

All this, however, does not mean that there is an across the board agreement on all issues affecting Indo-US relations. It would be pertinent to assess the attitudes of the Bush administration on issues impinging on India's relations with the USA. Basic differences remain on non-proliferation issues between US. But there is a qualitative difference in the Bush Administration's on the issue towards India. The new US administration is moving back from the admonitory and punitive posture against India on the nuclear issue. While remaining committed to the traditional non-proliferation Agenda, the US would persuade India to cap its nuclear weapons capacities and missile capacities at present levels, and to see that India remains committed to the policy decisions announced after India's nuclear weapon tests. That of not conducting further tests, no first use, and so on. The US would also advocate that India refrains from enhancing its missile capacities to ICBM levels. The macro-level US policy stance would be to bring India within the ambit of its general non-proliferation agenda. The US will not question India's sovereign discretion to endow itself with weapons systems which it considers necessary for ensuring India's security. But the US will firmly convey the negative implications of India enhancing its nuclear and missile capacities from the US point of view. The US approach would be practical and realistic, not confrontationist. There are also indications that some of the sanctions imposed against India would be gradually removed, not because US considers the sanctions inappropriate, but because the sanctions have not made any tangible impact on India. They have only limited potentialities of expanded cooperation between the two countries.

The US welcomes the general endorsement given by India to the NMD but the US realises that India has not supported the weaponisation of outer space. India's response has been meticulously crafted. India has only supported those segments of the rationale of the NMD which aim at elimination of nuclear weapons and missiles. This is a nuance which is not taken note of in public perceptions. But the Bush administration understands the logic of India's response on the subject. While the USA acknowledges the potentialities of expanded economic and commercial cooperation, the US has reservations about the manner in which some of the important US projects in India have run into difficulties ; the foremost among them being Enron Project. Zeleck's visit hopefully will serve the purpose of clarifying each other's stand. There should, however, be no illusion about USA diluting views on WTO issues specially in the context of current down-turn in US economy.

US reactions to the Indo-Pak summit at Agra have been significantly nuanced. The Bush administration has refrained from any value judgement or critical evaluation of the manner in which the summit ended. Official US spokesmen welcomed the initiative of Prime Minister Vajpayee and stated that despite the apparent failure of the Agra summit, they endorsed the decision of India and Pakistan to continue bilateral talks at the political and official levels. The US has also been meticulously and politically correct in underlining that while the US would encourage the process, US has no desire for any mediatory role. Two issues on which there is convergence of views between India and the US are the expansion of bilateral economic cooperation and institutional consolidation of bilateral arrangements to counter terrorism. One should expect initiatives from both sides, governmental and non-governmental, to make cooperation in these two spheres contentful. One should also note that out of the many invitations that President Bush has received from foreign countries, he has accepted an invitation to visit India.

All this leads one to the conclusion that Indo-US relations have at last reached a stage where one can expect a stable and realistic structuring of Indo-US relations on practical lines.

There are still segments in the Indian public opinion and establishment which perceive USA in the mould of the Cold War image of the country. A Republican administration fashioning a constructive interaction with India as it is trying to do, would be particularly effective in transcending such perceptions.

Richard Armitage's Visit—Emergence of Realism in Indo-US Relations

US Deputy Secretary of State Richard Armitage was in Delhi, for the fourth time since terrorist attacks on the US in September last, during the 4th week of August. One has to go beyond the published reports on the discussions held between Armitage and his Indian counterparts to comprehend the undercurrents in Indo-US relations which are of quite an importance for India as well as for the larger issues affecting South Asian Region's stability and security.

The operational impulses behind Armitage's visit to New Delhi and Islamabad was the continuing state of tension between India and Pakistan. The objective of Armitage's shuttle diplomacy is based on two assessments of the Government of the United States which is shared by all its important allies. First, that though the prospects of an imminent military conflict between India and Pakistan have partially receded, Indo-Pakistan tensions remain a matter of high priority concern; second, that to keep the lid on this tension, diplomatic and political pressure should continue to be generated on Pakistan and India particularly India because India's restraint is reaching the limits of its tolerance threshold.

The more recent context of Richard Armitage's visit which is relevant to the present state of Indo-US relations has not attracted sufficiently detailed assessments. It is pertinent to undertake this exercise. Handling the situation in Afghanistan which involved a fair amount of cooperation and consultations between India and the USA, is descending into a pattern of uncertainty isolated and the contradictory cross-currents of Afghan politics and the ethnic and regional patterns of confrontation which is characterising that country. The intensity of the anti-terrorist campaign in Afghanistan is abating. Even the anti-Taliban and anti-Al-Qaeda in the North-western areas of Pakistan is tapering off. The focus of US attention has shifted to the preparation for launching of campaign against Saddam Hussain. President George Bush's decision in this regard is subjected to controversies both within the US Government and between the US Government and a majority of important powers of the world.

Despite the importance that India attaches to functioning in cooperation with the US in countering terrorism, India is opposed to a military campaign against Iraq particularly a unilateral military campaign led by the United States. India conveyed this view to Arab Ambassadors posted in Delhi and to the Syrian Foreign Minister just a week before Armitage's arrival in New Delhi.

Caliberating relations with India and Pakistan has become somewhat problematic by the US, because of Musharraf's policy stances and India's responses during the last three weeks. The levels of intrusions from the Pakistani side of the Line of Control remain at dangerous levels. Separatist terrorist groups attacked Hindu pilgrims going to Amar Nath. They continue to target our security forces in Jammu and Kashmir and even more critical is the systematic campaign of assassinations being carried out against political figures in Jammu and Kashmir, who have indicated a willingness to participate in the legislative assembly elections of the State in September. General Musharraf did not help matters by announcing his value judgement that the elections in Jammu and Kashmir being organised by the State Government and Government of India are a farce, in his address to the Nation on Pakistan Independence Day on 14th August- nor has he responded to the tentative steps towards normalisation which India announced, in a speech of May the 27th. Instead he has made demands which he knows would be patiently unacceptable to India namely that India should not hold elections in Jammu and Kashmir without consulting Pakistan, that India should pull back its troops from the Line of Control and the International Border and that India should enter into unconditional dialogue with Pakistan early.

While India continues to be responsive to suggestions from the United States about remaining restrained against terrorist violence originating from Pakistan, India remains firm on not resuming dialogue unless there is clear evidence of Pakistan withdrawing support from terrorist activities and Pakistan refrains from disrupting the proposed scheduled elections in Jammu and Kashmir. The immediate challenge to USA's sub-continental policies is to cope with the intransigences of India and Pakistan towards each other.

US Secretary of State General Colin Powell indicated the lines on which the US plans to deal with the dilemmas of sustaining USA's close relationships with Pakistan given Pakistan's role in USA's anti-terrorist campaign and of consolidating the emerging positive trends in Indo-US relations. In public pronouncements during his last visit to the sub-continent he announced the ingredients of US policies as follows: The Government of Pakistan has taken steps to curb terrorist infiltrations into India but Pakistan could do more (He did not acknowledge any direct linkage between Government of Pakistan and anti-Indian terrorist activities in Pakistani territory); Kashmir is on the international Agenda as a matter of concern which USA will be actively interested in resolving; USA welcomed the scheduled elections in Jammu and Kashmir which is the first step towards finding a long-term solution to the problem of Jammu and Kashmir and lastly, US desires India and Pakistan to resume direct dialogue as early as possible. Apart from this context of direct impact on Indo-US relations there are other issues on which a certain divergence of opinion has emerged. Though India supported President Bush's decision regarding the National Missile Defence Project, India is not entirely happy about USA's withdrawal from the Anti-Ballistic Missile Treaty. India has reservations about USA pulling back from the Kyoto Convention on

Environment Management. President Bush not participating in the Johannesburg summit on Environment and Sustainable Development, and India's differences of opinion with the US policy orientations on environmental issues over the last decade since the previous such summit at Rio de Janeiro in 1992 underline difference of views on this important issue of international concern.

There is no need to over-emphasise reservations of India regarding USA's not fully implementing the WTO arrangements finalised in 1996, resulting in apprehensions of limitations of access of Indian exports to the US markets. While these divergences of opinion on specific issues were not unexpected and while they are being dealt with through normal diplomatic means, it is at the deeper levels of public perceptions in India and the USA that Indo-US relations are entering a somewhat critical phase. There is a general feeling of disappointment and rising criticism about the US not being sensitive and supportive about Indian concerns regarding Pakistan and terrorism sponsored by the Musharraf Government, despite the wholehearted support that India has given to the US since September last. There is added angst despite India's continuing endeavour to establish close rapport with the US since early 90s, the responses from the US have not been as reciprocal as India hoped for. It is a different matter that India unilaterally defined its expectations, realistically assessing how the US would calibrate its policies towards India.

India's new Foreign Secretary Sibal's speech at the Federation of Indian Industries in July articulated this disappointment which was critically noted by Deputy Secretary of State Armitage who enquired about its implications in a discussion with Ambassador Lalit Mansingh in Washington. Armitage's question was whether there is any shift in India's US policies. Singh's response was there was no shift but that Sibal's remarks were only a reflection of trends in India's public opinion. The sticking point as far as India is concerned, is US Government's insistence on not being critical of Pakistan's India policies. The approach remains evenhanded. State Department spokesman Richard Boucher in a statement on the 17th of July described Pakistan as the foremost and indispensable ally of the US in the war against terrorism. He went on to temporise: "We have condemned continuing violence. We believe that the situation cannot be resolved by this kind of conflict. It is vital to all sides in Kashmir to exercise restraint and take steps to reduce violence. The US continues diplomatic efforts to encourage India and Pakistan to move away from armed conflict". Boucher of course acknowledged that ensuring that infiltration across the Line of Control ends permanently, continues to be the highest priority for Pakistan. Then he gave a certificate to Musharraf. "As President Musharraf has pointed out Pakistan has also been the victim of terror and extremism and together we are fighting this scourge."

This approach while tailored to USA's interests, refuses to acknowledge the tense realities that India faces in relation to Pakistan.

Coming to the specifics of Armitages discussions in Delhi in August India appreciated the continuing interest and attention reflected in his visit to Delhi for high level discussions. His latest rounds of exchanges however were charaterised by his Indian interlocutors (particularly Brajesh Mishra) clearly conveying India's concerns and disappointments about USA not taking a sufficiently firm stance against Pakistan's intrusive and subversive approach against India in Jammu and Kashmir. He was also told that while India remains restrained, Indian restraint should not be taken for granted if Pakistan sponsored violence disrupts the political processes which India is trying to put in place in Jammu and Kashmir. Armitage had a two-point response. He stoutly maintained that Musharraf is committed to fulfilling his promises which he gave to the US about withdrawing support from terrorist activities in India. Secondly, that he will again urge Musharraf to speed up the fulfillment of his promises. India contrasts the assurances with the public pronouncements which he made in Islamabad after his discussions with General Musharraf-Armitage had to do tight rope walking in Pakistan and pulled back from any direct critical evaluation of Pakistan's India policies. Both Deputy Prime Minister L.K. Advani and National Security Adviser Brajesh Mishra have publicly stated that India while continuing to attach importance to Indo-US relations is also clear in its mind that India would have to deal with Pakistan on its own more or less without depending too much on support from the US and other powers.

Armitage's visit was also in preparation for Prime Minister Vajpayee's forthcoming meetings with President Bush in NewYork in September on the margins of the United Nations General Assembly session. Ambassador Robert Blackwill has proceeded to Washington on the 29th of August to finalise the framework of this mini-summit. The substances and atmospherics of Armitage's visit has served the purpose of both governments getting involved in a Reality Check on Indo-US relations. India should ensure that this emerging realism adds maturity and practicality in consolidating Indo-US relations. This process should not be disrupted due to disappointments and emotional and psychological levels of Indian Public opinion.

Restoring Dialogue with Pakistan—Vajpayee's Initiative ?

Prime Minister Atal Behari Vajpayee has been focussing on Indo-Pakistan relations in his public pronouncements since the second week of April. Following Yashwant Sinha's assertions about Indian's right to undertake pre-emptive strikes against Pakistan, Vajpayee said during his visit to Sikkim that India's basic approach is to resolve differences with its neighbours by negotiations, through peaceful means. Then over the weekend of 17th to 20th April during his visit to Jammu and Kashmir, he reiterated India's willingness to resume a dialogue with Pakistan to resolve all pending issues, including those related to Jammu and Kashmir provided the necessary atmosphere of, calm and stability is created by Pakistani ending cross-border terrorism. Vajpayee re-stated this approach in his statement in the Lok Sabha on the 23rd of April and in the Rajya Sabha on the 24th of April.

Other significant developments related to Vajpayee's pronouncements were his publicly endorsing Jammu and Kashmir Chief Minister Mufti Mohammed Sayeed's policies of reconciliation with all other opposition groups including militant groups in Jammu and Kashmir. Apart from the nomination of former senior civil servant N.N. Vohra as Central Government interlocutor with Kashmiri political parties to evolve a solution to the domestic dimensions of the Jammu and Kashmir issue, Vajpayee indicated that Vohra has an uninhibited brief to interact with all groups in Jammu and Kashmir. Vajpayee emphasised that India's approach is to resolve the Jammu and Kashmir issue on the basis of Democracy, Humanism and Kashmiri identity—Jamuriat, Insaniyat and Kashmiriat. Vajpayee added that augmented resources would be allotted for development in Jammu and Kashmir, responsive to the multi-dimensional needs and priorities of the people of the State. Vajpayee described his statement as India extending a hand of friendship to Pakistan, but that the exercise can be meaningful if Pakistan also extends its hand of friendship seriously and sincerely.

Before examining whether Vajpayee's statements signify a qualitative shift in India's Pakistan policies and the tentatively positive response President Musharraf gave to Vajpayee's statements, it is pertinent to discern the logic of the timing and content of Vajpayee's statements.

As military operations in Iraq are coming to an end, there have been messages to the Government of India from the US Government that USA will give more attention to preventing a sub-continental confrontation. Colin Powell's conversation with Yashwant Sinha following Yashwant Singh's advocacies regarding the legitimacy of pre-emptive strikes against

Pakistan, were of particular causation of the above message. Principal Secretary to the Prime Minister, Brajesh Mishra is proceeding to Washington towards end of April. US Deputy Secretary of State Richard Armitage and Assistant Secretary of State Christina Roeca are visiting Delhi during the second or third week of May. Indo-Pakistan relations and tensions related to Jammu and Kashmir would be the top item on the Agenda of the Americans in these discussions.

Prime Minister Vajpayee is also scheduled to visit France, Germany and the Russian Federation towards the end of this month, or in May. These important European powers are also of the view that India should resume dialogue with Pakistan at some suitable official level as soon as possible without stipulating the absolute condition of complete stoppage of cross-border terrorism from Pakistan.

Richard Armitage and Christina Roeca are to visit Pakistan also during their forthcoming Asian tour. Indications are that while they would exert more categorical pressure on Pervez Musharraf to stop cross-border violence, they will be equally firm in advising India to commence a dialogue with Pakistan, moving away from the absolute condition which India had stipulated. Parallely, Defence Minister George Fernandes was in Beijing from the 20th April when Vajpayee was making these statements. There are differences with China, particularly on the boundary issue, there is some parallelism between the Kashmir issue and the Sino-Indian boundary dispute in terms of the territorial dimensions of two disputes. Vajpayee's statement mentioned above was a message both to China and to Pakistan. Vajpayee's statements have this textual background. The rationale of his pronouncements was to convey to the major western powers, led by the United States that India is not obstinate and that India is willing to move forward to a dialogue with Pakistan. Inherent in the message was an unarticulated advocacy that western powers should exert direct and effective pressure on Pervez Musharraf government to stop cross-border terrorism, for bilateral diplomatic and political discussions. India would point out that with the onset of summer there can be further increase in Pakistan-sponsored violence in Jammu and Kashmir and therefore this is precisely the time that Pakistan should be asked to cease and desist.

Leaving aside the over-optimistic analyses and speculation in the Indian media about the positivism in Vajpayee's statements, the fact of the matter is that, though the rhetoric has become deliberately moderate there is no substantive change in India's stand on resuming dialogue with Pakistan. Musharraf's response has been as anticipated. He welcomed

Vajpayee's intention of resuming the dialogue with Pakistan. The Pakistan Foreign Office went into details saying that Pakistan is willing to nominate a senior person to commence discussions on the Agenda and modalities for resuming discussions, at any time and at any place of India's choice. Significantly, there is no response to India's suggestion that Pakistan takes meaningful steps to stop Pakistan-sponsored terrorist violence in India. Pakistan remains static in its stand that it has nothing to do with violence in Jammu and Kashmir.

It is in the internal dimensions of the Kashmir issue that Vajpayee signalled a change of attitude in the central Government. His endorsing Mufti Mohammed Sayeed's "healing touch policy", his announcing brief to Vohra that he can talk to all concerned, and his decision to expand economic and developmental activities in Jammu and Kashmir in support of Chief Minister Mufti's policies signal a positive shift in India's approach on internal issues of Kashmir to some extent. But here also Vajpayee missed an opportunity to state that the Central Government would be willing to take a fresh look at the political package required to meet the constitutional and political arrangements sought by the people of Jammu and Kashmir, particularly in the valley. May be he did not want to pronounce on this aspect till the discussions initiated by N.N. Vohra take definite shape. The Hurriyat and Shabir Shah Party refusing to talk to Vohra continue to pose a problem which has to be resolved. Vajpayee's visit to Jammu and Kashmir and his statements had two limited objectives. To project India's policies as conciliatory and reasonable and to give tentative assurance to the Government and people of Jammu and Kashmir that the Central Government is willing to be responsive to initiatives for normalcy being undertaken by Mufti Mohammed Sayeed. Whether even these limited objectives would be fully met is subject to uncertainties and deepseated inhibitions. Major powers would be convinced of our reasonableness only if we re-commence dialogue with Pakistan within a definite frame. The Government and the people of Jammu and Kashmir would assiduously monitor whether the policy pronouncements of Vajpayee acquire operational orientations in the weeks to come. There is no need or justification for over-optimistic interpretations or conclusions at this stage.

5

Indo-US Mind-Sets

The Vajpayee-Musharraf Pilgrimage to the US—An Assessment

Prime Minister Vajpayee and President Musharraf visited the US in the first half of September. The formal objective was to participate in the UN General Assembly session and to join the commemorative ceremony in New York marking the first anniversary of the terrorist attacks in the US last year. The substantive aim of both the leaders, however, was to utilise the opportunity for having a detailed discussion with President Bush so as to make USA's policies as responsive as possible towards the interests of Pakistan and India respectively.

Musharraf and Vajpayee went to New York in the background, of critical domestic developments both in India and in Pakistan. Vajpayee is coping with the inner contradictions of his coalition government and even within BJP itself. The elections in Gujarat and in Jammu and Kashmir have generated tense chemistry in the Indian politics. There has been no let up in subversive terrorism originating in Pakistani, in Jammu and Kashmir. The orientation towards modernisation and liberalisation of the economy in Indian policies is subject to short-term political and partisan ideological pressures, a predicament which will have a direct impact on Indo-US economic relations which are of particular importance to India.

Musharraf is facing widespread criticism from all political parties regarding the manner in which he has amended the Pakistani constitution and the procedural and legal requirement which he has put in place for the forthcoming general elections in Pakistan in October. The United States is less than satisfied not only about his performance in curbing terrorism but also because north-western areas of Pakistan have re-emerged as centres of activities by Taliban and Al-Qaeda cadres generating centrifugal forces in Afghanistan. Musharraf's specific objectives during his just-concluded visit to the USA could be itemised as follows :

He desires complete support from the United States for the political dispensation which, he is structuring for Pakistan atleast for the coming five years with himself as the Supreme Centre of the Pakistani power structure. He wants the restoration of multi-faceted defence supplies and weaponry to Pakistan by the USA. He desired an augmentation of financial commercial and technological inputs into Pakistan economy as a quid pro quo for the risks he has taken to support the USA's anti-terrorism campaign, He wanted to ensure US understanding of, if not support for his Kashmir policies vis-a-vis. India. He remains keen on direct US political and diplomatic intervention in the Kashmir issue with the objective of pressurising India into some kind of a compromise which would be acceptable to Pakistan. He must have made an effort to explain to President Bush the rationale of his "public stance" of opposing intended US military operations against Iraq.

Broadly speaking, except on the point regarding restoration of defence supplies, which he justified by accusing India of stockpiling arms and changing the balance of power in terms of conventional forces, Musharraf has received a generally positive response to his other advocacies. Vajpayee did not have too long a list of demands to present to the United States. His first priority was to convey India's concerns about Pakistan's continuing subversive challenge to India's unity and territorial integrity. Related to this issue was the aim of conveying to the United States that Musharraf has not adhered to his assurances given in his statements of June 12 and May 27th. Some agreements were reached for enhancing technological cooperation in the spheres of peaceful uses of space and nuclear energy. Limited information available on this point indicates that this cooperation will remain constrained to marginal technologies dealing with distance learning, water-sharing management, etc. It is reported that the National Security Advisor Brajesh Mishra did underline Indian disappointments about US responses on the question of Pakistan-sponsored terrorism. There was no signal that the United States was in a position to do more than what it has done so far, barring re-articulation of some general assurances.

What then could be the general assessment of impact of these exchanges between Vajpayee and Musharraf, on the one hand and Bush, on the other. Taking detailed note of the events in New York related to

President Musharraff's and Prime Minister Vajpayee's visit to the United States the visit of both these leaders and the discussions which they had with President Bush and other political leaders are of obvious significance for the critical situation in the sub-continent. Having objectively considered available information on what transpired in New York, one comes to the inescapable conclusion that general public expectations from these discussions between President Musharraf and Mr. Vajpayee and President Bush have been sadly unfulfilled.

President Musharraff's policy statement to the General Assembly at the United Nations and his public pronouncements in other fora clearly indicate that his intensely adversarial attitude and policy towards India remain unchanged. Two particular elements in his pronouncements should be taken note of. He remains mendacious by asserting that no cross border intrusions or terrorist activaties are taking place in the Indian side of Jammu and Kashmir from Pakistan side of the Line of Control. Secondly, he has affirmed without any inhibition that he will raise the Kashmir issue in every manner that he can on every occasion which is available to him. His objective of subverting the unity and territorial integrity of India remains unchanged. The government and the people of India should consider the responses to be given to his offers for dialogue, etc., in this critical context regardless of advice coming from other quarters to interact with him.

While Prime Minister Vajpayee reportedly had a useful exchange with President Bush on September 12, substantive results of the discussions and its impact on Indo-US relations remain uncertain and a matter of curiosity. One has not seen any new initiative of additional assurances coming from the US about holding President Musharraf and his government responsible for subversive terrorism engineered by Pakistan against India. Nor has there been any categorical affirmation from the US that it will question Pakistan's continuing attempts at disrupting elections in J & K. US continues to limit itself to an advisory role hesitating from generating direct pressure on Musharraf in the matter.

One is constrained to say that Prime Minister Vajpayee's UN statement in the UN General Assembly became a debating exercise rather than an assertive articulation of policy decisions and Indian intentions responding to Musharraff's clear indications that he will continue his anti-India policies in every respect. Countering the points made by Musharraf against India or questioning his views with satire is not enough. Unless the Government of India has decided otherwise, the General Assembly session was an occasion to convey a clear message to the international community that India's responses will now go beyond policy statements to neutralise Pakistani challenges to India's unity and territorial integrity.

According to reports, Bush told Vajpayee that he intends to exert more pressure on Pakistan to fall in line with the international anti-terrorist campaign particularly in relation to India. This has been conveyed to India by the US over the last six months. The question is whether Bush mentioned additional specifics about the pressure that he intends to generate on Musharraf.

There have been reports of President Bush and Prime Minister Vajpayee agreeing on expanding defence and technological cooperation. It is pertinent for the people of India to know whether this expanded cooperation is going to be substantive or just marginal and cosmetic. It is also necessary that the Indian people know what the connections and terms of reference of this expansion in Indo-US cooperation are.

Another issue of importance discussed by Prime Minister Vajpayee at the UN is the reported plan of the United States to launch military operations against Iraq. One hopes that the Government of India has conveyed firm and categorical opposition to any unilateral action being taken by the USA and its allies, in this matter. That the Government of India plans to be more active on this issue is indicated by the reported discussions between External Affairs Minister Yashwant Sinha, on the one hand and his Russian and Chinese counterparts Igor Ivanv and Tang Xiajuan, on the other.

Experience shows that military operations only increase sufferings of the common people of Iraq. Any action in Iraq should be based on a consensus in the United Nations Security Council and the General Assembly.

Indo-US Relations—Need to Change Mind-sets

President Bush's visit to Beijing in the first half of February should put to rest unrealistic speculations about a likely strategic consensus between China, the Russian Federation and India, to counter the dominant influence of the United States in world affairs. Bush and Jiang Zemin agreed that US and China have a shared responsibility to maintain world peace and stability, particularly in the Asian region. Expressing their views on Indo-Pakistan relations Jiang and Bush affirmed that they would encourage India and Pakistan to enter into a dialogue and resolve the Kashmir problem which they consider a factor of continuing tension in

South Asia. Though, theoretically all States are sovereign and equal Bush and Jiang affirmed the position of their countries as great power which have a higher responsibility to keep peace in this region. This Chinese assertion (with Bush), plus Chinese equations with Pakistan, should make Indian analysts desist from irrelevant and irrational exercises aimed at the much bandied about strategic equation theory. This assessment is also rooted in the inescapable reality that the Russian Federation needs to have good relations with the United States, given its economic predicaments and security concerns.

Putin's reactions to Bush's Strategic Defence Initiative, to US withdrawal from the ABM Treaty and the Putin's acquiescence of the dominant role of the western powers led by the United States in Afghanistan clearly indicate that, leaving aside political cosmetics Russia is not likely to have much of a stomach for a strategic equation with India to contain the US. It is obvious, therefore, that while sustaining a good and broad-based bilateral relationship with China and the Russian Federation, India has to continue focussing on its relations with the United States. The relationship with China and Russia can only be a balancing factor. It cannot be and should not be an exercise in countering the USA or containing it.

It is pertinent therefore to review the basic pattern of Indo-US relations during the last year, and to be clear about USA's priorities in relation to India. Significant characteristics of this pattern are the US seeking to intensify collaboration with India on the whole range of issues that currently confront the international community. The initiatives which India took since 1992 to establish closer relations with the United States 'particularly those which were taken after the terrorist attacks on New York and Washington last September, have resulted in President Bush being convinced of the relevance of a long-term positive relationship with India, as he said in his state of the union message in January 2002, "The US is working with India in ways which we have never before to achieve peace and prosperity. India and the United States are agreed on a long-term partnership to counter terrorism and religious extremism apart from structuring cooperative bilateral policies which have resulted in close collaboration between India and the US at the United Nations. Both countries contributed to the passing of the UN Security Council Resolution 1373 against terrorism and are now jointly working for the adoption of a comprehensive convention against international terrorism of which India is one of the original sponsors.

India and US working together to turn off the tap of financial resources of the terrorists as well as Indian advocacies leading to the US Government designating the Jaish-e-Mohammed and Lashkar-e-Toiba as international terrorist organisations exemplify that this cooperation is not declaratory but substantive. This does not mean that Indian concerns on terrorism are fully met. United States is being more patient and gradualistic than India, would wish in pressurising General Musharraf to pull back from supporting terrorist secessionism in Jammu and Kashmir, which is logical from the point of view of the US which considers partnership with Musharraf government important in its ongoing efforts at fighting terrorism in Afghanistan and stabilising of Afghan Government.

United State's Ambassador in New Delhi, Dr. Robert Blackwill indicated in a speech on the 26th of February that more than fifty American policy makers at the Assistant Secretary level and above have visited India since July 2001. There has been a matching number of visits by the Government of India to the US covering a wide-range of bilateral issues from trade and technology, to energy and environment. Leaving aside Pakistan's more active operational role in the anti-terrorist campaign in Afghanistan, the Governments of India and the United States have been jointly active in negotiations aimed at the stabilisation and development of Afghanistan. USA's and Indian special envoys Dobbins and S.K. Lambah, have been functioning in co-ordination at New York, at Bonn and Tokyo. The political significance is that India's role in stabilising the political flux in Central Asia and Afghanistan is acknowledged and established for the present.

The other spheres where bilateral relations have gained substance are those of intelligence and law enforcement, Defence cooperation, including discussions and joint exercises between the armed forces of the two countries, energy security, economic cooperation and significantly, civil, nuclear and space cooperation. Another important field in which relations have gained momentum is that of science and medical research. An elaboration regarding prospects of cooperation relating to energy security is relevant. While US multinational companies are engaged in oil and gas exploration in the South Asian region, there is a geo-strategic dimension in energy security where the interests of India and the USA converge. The US imports 50 per cent of its hydro carbons, from the Gulf. India imports 90 per cent of its crude oil. There is an emerging Indo-US agreement on ensuring the security of the Gulf and the international sea routes carrying these resources across the Arabian Sea and the Indian Ocean.

Though there is no dilution of opposition of the USA to nuclear and missile proliferation, it must be noted that Bush Administration has stopped giving hortatory tutorials to India on nuclear and missile weaponisation. A parallel practical and rational development is India and the United States reviving cooperation in the peaceful uses of nuclear energy and space.

Having recounted these positive features in India's relations with the United States, there are two issues on which there is a shortfall and concern. India is concerned about USA's relations with General Musharraf's government in Pakistan and the lack of meaningful progress in economic cooperation and US investments in India. Indian public opinion feels that the US should be more vigorous in bringing General Musharraf in line with India's concerns regarding his support to separatism in Kashmir. There is also a tendency in India to peg its value-judgements on Indo-US relations through negative prism of worries about US-Pak relations. This is an illogical approach. US structures its relations with Pakistan within the framework of its perceived interests. If this relationship affects India's interests negatively, the solution is not to demand that the USA scale down its relations with Pakistan. We should have the strategic political capacities and flexibility to counter this negative impact on our own initiative, without making Indo-US relations a hostage to this predicament.

As far as the slow progress in economic and investment cooperation goes, the ball is entirely in India's court. Cooperation in this sphere is not based on abstract political considerations or general goodwill. It depends on the content and efficiency of our economic policies. Unilateral demands cannot be a substitute for performance.

While Indo-US relations are on track, we must have a clear understanding of US priorities in this region. These are: eradication of terrorism and Islamic religious fanaticism in this region, stabilisation of Afghanistan is an important ingredient of this objective. Secondly, ensuring durable security to the countries of the Gulf and West Asia, where the US energy security interests are of paramount importance to them. Thirdly, it is within this context that the US gives high priority of normalisation of relations between India and Pakistan and a political solution to the Kashmir issue. US would be a willing facilitator for negotiations and would be inclined to directly intervene if the prospects are of an actual nuclear confrontation between the two countries. United States is interested in ensuring access to the energy resources and markets of Central Asia, an objective which would serve Indian interests also in the long-term. But the problem is the United States being reluctant to encourage moderate political processes in Iran and its militarily assertive posture against "the axis of evil" which is viewed with apprehension and criticism by the international community including some of USA's close western allies. The Macro-level US strategic objective is to sustain and encourage governments which would be supportive of USA's ideological orientations security and economic interests, and to establish a network of understandings with such governments.

India is an important factor in this scheme of things. The challenge to India foreign policy is three-fold: Sustaining and expanding Indo-US, relations while there are and there would be differences of opinion on significant security and economic issues. Secondly, to safeguard India's strategic and technological interests vital to Indian security and capacity for economic self-reliance, and third, and most important, while having close relations with the Unipolar power that the United States is, to maintain a balancing relationship with other centres of power in the world for the purpose of ensuring India's freedom of foreign policy and strategic options.

QUESTION-ANSWER SESSION WITH ME

You Joined the Congress because of Gujarat. Was that the only factor?

It wasn't. I have often heard the criticism that middle class fellows like me who have led a comfortable life sit around writing articles, giving lectures and value judgment on the margins. We don't want to get actively involved in doing something concrete to remedy the very situation which we criticise. I thought one should see what one can do. I joined the Congress because of its ideology and principles. My parents were Congress workers who worked with Mahatma Gandhi from 1921-1942. They went to jail and left politics on the day of independence. At some sub-conscious level, that too must have worked.

Many in the BJP have turned to you from time to time, yet you chose not to join them. What was it about the BJP that put you off ?

Basically, it is their misinterpretation of Hinduism which underpins their ideology. I am very proud of being a Hindu but their whole approach to the plural society of India is rather unidimensional. Their vision of Indian nationalism is authoritarian. It is not an inclusive and tolerant ethos which is the essence of Hinduism. To compound matters, you have its related organisations like the VHP and Bajrang Dal and, to a lesser extent, the RSS. Their approach fuels political problems, economic problems. It's not something one can agree with.

So you agree with what the Election Commission has done on Gujarat?

Absolutely, the Election Commission, has not delayed the polls with any political motive. Jimmy Lyngdoh is a friend of mine, very slightly younger than me in service. Look at the type of accusations made against him, that he is a Christian and some nonsense Modi said. Is this the way serious people in a state talk ?

And now the Central leadership is saying Modi is a good man. The Deputy Prime Minister is saying so. Some of his party workers are saying we must have a Narendra Modi in every state. We are a billion people, there are bound to be people with different political views. But it should not strike at the roots of the pluralistic image of India. And that is what these people are accidentally or deliberately eroding.

What should the Congress now do about Kashmir?

There are limited points on which I can express as a Congress partyman. The party president is the only one who went to Kashmir and campaigned. As far as I know, top leaders of no other national political party went there. Mrs Gandhi went in spite of advice not to go there. She went because she believed she should personally underline that Congress as a national party has a role in this important state at this critical juncture.

The aim of the Congress will be to be a part of a stable government. Being the oldest national party with the longest experience in dealing with Jammu and Kashmir and being part of the government will perhaps be helpful in negotiations with the Centre for the future political dispensation.

Is it time to resume talks with Pakistan ?

I am not speaking for the Congress but my personal view is that while we must not show a great amount of anxiety to resume dialogue with Pakistan we should certainly make preparations as early as feasible. Pakistan has also had elections. The likelihood is you will have to deal with a government led by Musharraf in the foreseeable future. We must make preparations to resume dialogue. But it should be step-by-step approach, not straightaway announcing we will have a political discussion.

But our Government says Pakistan is still exporting terror and there can be no talks till that ends?

That's where I think a two track policy is necessary. Response to major acts of terrorism should not only be decisive but my personal view is that we should now go into a pre-emptive mode. I am not saying pre-emptive mode across the border. When an incident happens, we must see if we can do something. While doing that on the one hand, we must give signals we are willing to resume the dialogue. It is not a realistic approach to say we will start the talks only when terrorism stops altogether. You cannot wish away Pakistan. The more you delay in resuming dialogue or showing your willingness to be flexible, the more external support for you will diminish.

Will border de-escaltation help? Do you think it's time?

I can understand the deployment along the LoC. But at the international frontier, you have massive deployment. You have done it for months, it's expensive, exhaustive. In my view, we must de-escalate from the international frontier. It is bad politics, it is bad defence policy to put troops on high alert for such a long time.

Could this form part of the agenda for the October 16 meeting of the National Security Advisory Boards?

I think most of it will be devoted to post-Kashmir election strategy. Of course, Pakistan will form part of the agenda but recent statements from the government suggest that there is no inclination to move away from a very static stand which they have taken.

Jaswant Singh justified pre-emptive strikes recently

I don't agree with Jaswant Singh's type of pre-emptive strike. You do not talk in advance about pre-emptive strikes, especially when you are in government. Advani says we will exercise the right of hot pursuit. You don't say in advance. You do it and then say this is why we did it. Under international law, it is recognised you have the right of hot pursuit. Do whatever is necessary with the decisiveness and appropriate element of surprise. When the other side starts whining, then you say this is the reason you went and did this.

What happens if President Bush strikes Iraq ? Where does that position India?

I don't think we should get actively involved in the US campaign against Iraq. Our question should be what have you done against our terror.

Our Government has been saying that about Pakistan...

We do not have to use the argument of an example of US action to do what is necessary for US. India should be not only self-reliant but its options should be exercised on the basis of independent objective judgement on what is good for her. There is no meaning in saying if you do it in Iraq, we can also do it in Pakistan.

Look at the European Union summit, it's a foreign policy disappointment. Our Prime Minister goes all the way to European Union and this Prime Minister of Denmark equates us with Pakistan, doesn't talk about terrorism and pontificates on India being restrained and talk to Pakistan. Their has been a shortcoming in the preparatory work for the summit.

Pravasi Bharatiya Divas—Fulfillment or a Farce

The much publicised Pravasi Bharatiya Divas was celebrated between the 9th and 12th of January 2003. It was the first conference of Indians settled abroad holding foreign citizenship and Non-Resident Indians living in foreign countries under various external legal facilities provided by foreign governments. The objective of the conference was to affirm that people and the Government of India now acknowledge that Indian diaspora abroad has become a significant factor in India's external relations, as well as in India's domestic politics. The diaspora is now being perceived as a possible source of influence and inputs, both abroad and in India, serving Indian interests.

A number of policy decisions were announced indicating Government's appreciation of the incremental role being played by Indians abroad., one of the most important policy decisions was granting of dual citizenship to certain categories of Indians living abroad who have acquired foreign citizenship. This apart from the facilities given to the Indian community about the issue of Identity Cards as Persons of Indian Origin (PIO cards).

The NDA Government of India for the last four years have extended them privileges and facilities about the grant of visibilities for technical and professional education for children of NRIs, and so on. The demand for dual citizenship was the most insistent and repeated demand which has now been granted.

I am opposed to this decision due to various reasons which rooted in some fundamental questions. The first question is how would the grant of Indian citizenship to people of Indian origin who have acquired foreign nationality serve India's substantive interests. What are the motivations of Indians abroad demanding dual citizenship and the Government of India granting it. The presumption or anticipation is that giving dual citizenship to Indians will give them a closer sense of identity with India. Secondly, the privileges about travel, acquisition of property, extension of educational facilities, etc, would result in their becoming more obligated and involved in the developmental and economic progress of India. Third that the grant of such citizenship will increase their commitment to India in the countries where they reside.

Indian residents abroad demand dual citizenship to get travel facilities rights to acquire property, at times to get safe tax havens and to gain social prestige in communities abroad where they are permanent residents.

My question is why this complementarity of motivations and objectives between the Government of India and the Indian community abroad should be based on the quid pro quo of the grant of dual citizenship. Is citizenship a phenomenon to be settled on the basis of a bargain? Secondly the objectives on the part of all concerned, which I have detailed above can be met without the grant of dual citizenship if the Government of India is sufficiently flexible in granting the facilities to people of Indian origin and if the Indian communities abroad are sufficiently emotionally committed to their linkages with India and India's causes.

The fact that Indian community abroad insists on dual citizenship implies that they predicate their involvement with India on India granting them privileges of citizenship despite their having acquired foreign citizenship voluntarily. This does not show much of a commitment or involvement with India.

The other reason why I consider the grant of dual citizenship an avoidable gesture is that of these privileges being granted on a selective basis. It is not being extended to all Indians who are foreign nationals living in all parts of the world. Out of 20 million Indians living in different parts of the world, dual citizenship is likely to be granted to four and a half to five million Indians living in West Europe, the USA, Canada and other prosperous countries like Japan and Australia. Foreign nationals of Indian origin living in other parts of the world will not be eligible for this facility. Then again the grant of dual citizenship is a conferment of facilities and privileges without obligations on the part of Indians who get this citizenship. They will not be part of political processes of India. There will be no obligation on their part to serve the Government of India if it becomes necessary; they can detach themselves from obligations towards India by claiming their basic national identity of a foreign country.

Leaving aside some marginal economic and social benefits, the grant of dual citizenship results in the phenomenon of ambiguous loyalty amongst those who get this dual citizenship, an ambiguity which leaves the option to decide on which citizenship to claim at given points of time to the foreign nationals of Indian origin; and particularly foreign nationals who are prosperous and living only in the advanced countries. The resentment and anger which the large numbers of persons of Indian origin in other parts of the world would feel about this selective granting of dual citizenship, can create tensions in Indian communities abroad as well as problems in foreign policy of India. This is apart from a fair segment of public opinion inside India which does not see any justification for the grant of dual citizenship. It is worthwhile mentioning that out of 184 countries which are members of the United Nations only about 40 countries have the practice of allowing dual citizenship to their communities living abroad. Apart from aberrations resulting from dual loyalties, the travel facilities, property facilities, etc, resulting from the grant of dual citizenship, it can create problems of security and socio-economic tensions within India. This is particularly so in a poor country like India where the proposal would give benefits to well to do Indians living abroad whose only merit is their having gone abroad and having become rich enough.

It must also be mentioned that this decision is rooted in many of the political parties in India, particularly the BJP depending on funds from foreign nationals of Indian origin living in the more prosperous countries of the world. India could have avoided this decision which is based essentially on narrow short-term motivations.

I have been abroad in the Gulf after this conference was over. A majority of Indian community in the Gulf is unhappy with the decision regarding selective grant of dual citizenship.

Two other decisions announced also smack of adhocism and lack of reason. The "Pravasi Bharatiya Samman" was accorded to a number of persons of Indian origin. No doubt all of them are eminent in their respective spheres of achievements, but an and award by the Government of India to a person of Indian origin living abroad should primarily be for activities by the individual concerned which have served India's cause or served Indian interests. Persons of Indian origin who might have established educational institutions in India, or contributed to social and developmental projects benefiting people of India getting this Samman Puraskar would have been in order. I certainly do not see the rationale behind giving this award to people like VS Naipaul who have lived abroad all their life and their only claim to the Samman was because they have got other forms of recognition like the Nobel Prize. I can understand the award going to a person like

Pandit Ravi Shankar who has enriched Indian music. But I cannot understand the award going to people whose work has not had any influence or impact on Indian affairs and Indian predicaments.

Then there is the decision to give facilities to children of persons of Indian origin to get admitted to Indian technical and scientific institutions. Is there any dearth of young Indians living in India to aspire for such academic facility and who have to go through a very hard process of competition to enter institutions of higher scientific and technological learning. How justified is it to extend this facility to children of Indian origin who are in any case well to do and who live in countries where such facilities are available. The only reason for giving this facility to children of Indians abroad is perhaps because these young people are not sure of making the grade to join foreign institutions through the competition there.

Another question requiring an answer is the quantity and extent to which the Indian diaspora has contributed to India's economic development in terms of investment, building up of infrastructure or augmenting India's economic growth through related economic activities. Barring a few individual cases of NRIs building educational institutions in some parts of India near their Alma Maters, one has not seen any significantly broad trend of NRIs, PIOs, etc, being involved in building up India. Had there been some emerging trend over the last decade, one would have accepted the hoopla between the 9th and 12th of January, as acceptable.

The last point which one should take note of is that vast sections of people of Indian origin even from North America and West Europe who were the major beneficiaries of this Pravasi Bharatiya exercises have kept away from this conference and have been critical of its proceedings as a purely partisan exercise by the BJP. It is a pity the Government of India forgot Jawaharlal Nehru's advice to the Indian communities abroad in the years following our independence where he said that these communities having decided to live abroad should integrate themselves fully with the peoples of the countries of their adoptions and that their first loyalty should be to foreign country of their choice. They should of course retain their sense of cultural identity and linkages with India but they should not be motivated by opportunistic considerations to revive legal and political links with India rooted in short term vested interests.

Pravasi Bharatiya Conference was in direct contradiction to this wise stipulation.

Same to You

Since 9/11, Pakistan has been on the backfoot trying to stave off accusations of it being a sponsor of international terrorism. Islamabad's close links with the Taliban regime in Afghanistan, its connections with Osama bin Laden, the Pakistani government harbouring Islamic militant organisations with links to Al-Qaeda, have been part of the substantive assessment of international terrorism not only in India but also in western democracies.

Pervez Musharraf's supporting the US campaign in Afghanistan and Iraq against terrorism and his pronouncements dissociating himself from terrorist activities originating in Pakistan have been some assistance to him in preserving his equations with the US and the West. But the activities of the Pakistan-based groups keep Musharraf and his government on the defensive.

The second accusation embarrassing Islamabad is its internationally confirmed role as a proliferator of nuclear weapons and missiles in collaboration with China and North Korea. These accusations involve Pakistan helping North Korea with its nuclear weapons programme and Chinese missile technology being made available to Pakistan through North Korea, and Pakistan being a transit facilitator of such technologies to Iran and Saudi Arabia.

All these accusations have riled the Pakistani authorities. Their reaction has been to mount a political and diplomatic offensive against India. The first salvo came in the form of Pakistan objecting to consular and diplomatic presence of India in Afghanistan and in southern Iran. Pakistan has also objected to Iranian authorities allowing an Indian consulate general to function at Zaidan. The basis of Pakistani objections is their publicly announced assessment that India is expanding its offensive intelligence activities against Ialamabad under the cover of these consular offices. Pakistani authorities have also implied that the objective of the Indian missions is to erode the Islamic identity of Afghanistan and Iran. That neither the Afghan nor the Iranian government has taken note of these allegations has been frustrating for Pakistan.

The second ingredient of the Pakistani political and diplomatic offensive is their accusations since end-June that India has been responsible for the violence in Karachi in Sindh and Quetta in Baluchistan provinces, including the destruction of natural gas pipelines in Baluchistan. Pakistan has also accused India of having 55 training camps for terrorists who have infiltrated into Pakistan for subversive activities. This has been followed up since end-July-early-August with categorical accusations about India proliferating nuclear and chemical weapons technologies to Iran. The accusation has been on the following lines:

That India and Iran have been expanding bilateral cooperation over the last decade to develop their nuclear and chemical weapons capacities.

Pakistani intelligence sources have reportedly asserted that Iran is improving its capacities to process nuclear fuel, to design nuclear warheads and to finetune its missile capacities. To lend authenticity to these accusations, the Pakistani government has asserted that Indian scientists are working with Iranian scientists at Talkhab and Chah-e-Lashkar, sites where Iranian nuclear research laboratories are supposed to be located.

Then there is the extraordinarily ridiculous accusation that India has deployed its Akash missile around these nuclear installations for their defence on the request of the Iranians. The accusations are ridiculous because of the well-known fact that Akash missile is still at its trial stage in India and that its deployment with the Indian armed forces themselves is uncertain. Pakistani authorities go on to accuse India of having an extensive military technological exchange programme with Iranian scientists, violating international stipulations of non-proliferation. Reports have been put out by Pakistan that a dozen to 20 Indian scientists are working in Iran's Zelzal missile plant near Esfahan. Indian scientists are also allegedly helping Iranian scientists in building a small nuclear reactor to process weapons grade nuclear fuel. Indian organisations like Bharat Dynamics, ISRO and DRDO are supposed to be functioning in close co-operation with Iranian agencies for developing Iran's nuclear missile and chemical weapons capacities.

The attempt obviously is to deflect the attention of the US and the major powers from Pakistan's long-standing programmes and arrangements with China and North Korea. The attempt is also to avoid the scrutiny of Pakistan's cooperation arrangements in these spheres with Iran, Saudi Arabia and Libya—apart from trying to prove that Pakistan is not a base for cross-border terrorism. What the Pakistani intelligence sources and establishment do not seem to take note are the factors which lend credibility to India as a responsible State in regard to issues related to non-proliferation and arms control. The question of India running training camps to send terrorists into Pakistan is ridiculous as there is no sizeable Hindu or non-Muslim minority in Pakistan which could provide logistic support to Indian subversives.

Though not a signatory to the NPT, India has adhered to the stipulations in that treaty aimed at preventing horizontal proliferation of nuclear weapons and related technologies. After conducting nuclear weapons tests in 1998, India has voluntarily declared a moratorium on further tests. It is true that India has cooperation arrangements with various countries on the peaceful uses of nuclear energy. But such projects are within the framework of the stipulation of the International Atomic Energy Agency. These projects are also subject to IAEA inspection. Then again, though not a signatory of the Missile Technology Control Regime (MTCR), India does not transfer military technology of this category to any country. If India had done anything of this kind, not only would countries like the US have taken remedial action, but they would have also publicised the fact to generate pressure on India. This has not happened.

As far as chemical weapons go, India is one of the founding signatories of the International Convention of Chemical Weapons and an active participant in the secretariat of the Organisation for the Prevention of Chemical Weapons at the Hague in Netherlands. In fact, India voluntarily cooperated with the US in the early Nineties, when some Indian companies tried to export chemicals to West Asia which could be used for weapons purposes.

India not only helped in retrieving objectionable cargo, but it took punitive action against the Indian companies and the shipping company involved in this case. While it is true that countries like Iran and Libya wished to acquire nuclear weapons and missiles, India's economic and technological cooperation with these countries has not drawn any critical or negative attention. Whereas direct and indirect Chinese and North Korean potentialities of cooperating with these countries through Pakistan as a catalyst remains a matter of concern for the US and western democracies.

Pakistan's offensive constitutes a significant dimension of the context in which the India-Pakistan peace initiative is evolving. Pakistan continues to aid and abet cross-border terrorism in J&K and in other parts of India. Militant Islamic organisations in India have confirmed and acknowledged contacts with terrorist organisations in Pakistan. Pakistan remains deeply interested in eroding India's international credibility and in disproving India's incontrovertible evidence regarding cross-border terrorism.

The recent people-to-people contact and exercises in Track II diplomacy revealed one fundamental orientation in Pakistani attitudes. There is no inclination to move towards a middle ground to resolve issues related to J&K on a realistic basis. This most recent political and diplomatic offensive only proves that the basic adversarial orientation of the Pakistani establishment against India has not changed.

The process of dialogue resulting from Atal Bihari Vajpayee's peace initiative retains its minimum momentum only because of international pressure on India and Pakistan; more so on Pakistan. The road to normalcy without doubt is going to be long and marked by hurdles. One should have no illusions in this respect.

6

International Dilemma

Can India become a Super Power?

One is glad that there in an inclination now in the community of political and strategic analysts to introspect about whether India can become a super power. This is a pleasant change, from the somewhat smug sub-conscious attitude in the collective Indian psyche that regardless of the realities of what India is, India is a super power and a major influence on international politics. This sentiment though not specifically articulated in this form underpined many of our attitudes and postures in foreign relationship, practically for the first two decades after Independence. The military defeat in the Sino-Indian conflict of 1962 and pressure which led to India giving concessions to Pakistan despite its military victories of 1965 and 1971 made us realize that we are afterall, subject to the pressures of Realpolitik and to our own limitations in terms of economic technological and military power, which clearly precludes our having any illusion about being a super power.

The question whether India can become a super power requires an answer to three criteria: First, what are the qualities and attributes which a State should have to become a super power. Secondly what are the assets and liabilities which characterise India within the framework of the criteria of the first category just mentioned. Thirdly, what are the potentialities and more importantly what are the possibilities of India becoming a super power.

The characteristics of super powers as one discerns them from contemporary historical experience are: first, the state or the nation concerned should have sizeable territory and demographic strength in terms of the size of the population. Secondly, such a state should have high levels of domestic cohesion, clear sense of national identity and stable administration based on strong legal and institutional arrangements. Thirdly, the concerned state should be economically well to do and should be endowed with food security and natural resources, particularly energy resources and infrastructural resources in terms of minerals and metals. Such a state should have a strong industrial base backed up by productive capacities and technological knowledge. Then the state concerned should have military capacities, particularly nuclear and missile weapons capacities, atleast comparable to, if not of higher levels than other countries which may have similar capacities.

The combination of all these ingredients and attributes of a particular state should be of far higher levels than those of the majority of states in the international community. Such endowments exceed the characteristics and capacities of other states aspiring to world power status. It is only then that a state can acquire the status of a super power and be acknowledged as such.

One, therefore, examines as to how far India meets the criteria described above. One would preface this section of the assessment by pointing out that India's quest for, or assertion of an influential status in world affairs in many ways had nothing to do with the substantive criteria described above. India's assertions regarding its influence were based on a perception that India was uniquely positioned to influence the world order because India's foreign policy was based on idealism and rooted in high moral principles. India's civilisational background and size were supposed to ensure for India an influential voice in international affairs. But this certainly was not a realistic claim.

Coming to the specific criteria, India has a large sized territory, equivalent to the whole of Europe excluding Russia. Its geo-strategic location at the southern end of Asia's land mass straddles its air space and trade routes between the Pacific and Indian Oceans. It has a population of over a billion people. It has trained human resources with technological capacities of a high order. India has the 4th largest army in the world and is now a nuclear and missile weapons power. It is among the seven or eight countries which have confirmed capacities in nuclear technology, space technology and other sophisticated spheres like laser, Robotics and Information Technologies. It is among the first fifteen economic powers of the world. These attributes should lead to the conclusion that India is well on the way to becoming a super power. Such a conclusion, however has to be conferred with practical, objectivity and caution. While India is a democracy with relevant institutional arrangements and experience stretching over half a century, the fact of the matter is that Indian democracy is still in its tenuous and experimental stage. The standards of governance in the Indian polity leaves much to be desired. There is no internal cohesion and unity in Indian civil society. This is not denying a general sense of national identity which Indians have. In reality, however India is subjected to centrifugal forces originating in castes, religions, ethnic, linguistic sub-regional contradictions. Nearly, one-third of India's population lives below the poverty line, generating socio-political tensions in Indian society. While we take satisfaction about the levels of our economic development and attendant technological capacities, the down side is in that Indian economy is weak in infrastructure and its protective capacities. India is dependent for energy for defence, supplies and for certain categories of high technology on foreign countries. India's internal social and economic problems are a limitation on its capacity to project its power abroad in a meaningfull manner. Over and above all, India does not seem to have the cohesion, the discipline and decisive political will to consolidate its strength and then to project this strength externally.

This is not a palatable conclusion but objectivity demands that this reality should be acknowledged.

Does all this mean that India cannot become a super power? The answer in terms of potentialities is that India has prospects of becoming one of the most important powers of the world. Territory, demography, economic potentialities and potential military capacities underpin India's prospects of becoming a great power. There are however certain prerequisites, a series of exercises in getting India's act together.

First and foremost a deliberate and conscious effort should be made by civil society and political classes in India to overcome the centrifugal impulses and trends which afflict our people.

An intellectual and emotional sense of a composite Indian national identity has to be consolidated. Secondly, policies have to be formulated and implemented to consolidate India's economic well-being in all its dimensions, of health, education, roads, and communications, productivity, food and energy security, and so on. India should be able to reach and sustain an annual rate of growth in the GNP of eight/nine per cent in the coming two decades.

India should focus on fashioning on stable pattern of relations particularly with its neighbours so that an atmosphere of peace and security which it could generate will enable India to focus on its political consolidation and economic development. India should sustain and up-date its military capacities in all dimensions especially in the fields of missile and nuclear weapons capacities.

Parallely, India should establish equations with the major power centres of the world, especially the United States, Western Europe, Russia and China which should ensure that these countries do not view India with apprehension. It is necessary that these important powers do not generate forces countering India's capacities and policies to emerge as a major influence in world politics. It is important that India develops its strength and capacities to match capacities of atleast China, France and the United Kingdom, to become a member of the super power club. Matching the economic and military capacities of the Russian Federation and the USA, is not a practical possibility in the foreseeable future. Hence the exercise to come on par with the lesser super powers of the world mentioned above.

All this is not going to be easy. The domestic dimensions of super power potentialities have to be met through democratic means which is clearly a difficult path, given the cross-currents of competing interests dissent which are endemic in a pluralistic nation-state like India. Similarly, the external dimensions of moving towards super power status would be subject to pressures which would be generated by countries in India's extended neighbourhood and even by the existing great powers. The solution here is to assiduously cultivate a harmonious relationship with India's neighbours and to strengthen relationship with countries like the US and Russia which assures then that India will function in cooperation with them to establish a stable international order. Most importantly, a clarity in objectives and persistent political will to work towards those objectives have to characterise our national attitudes and policies.

The possibility of India becoming a super power are there, but one remains uncertain of the extent to which we can acquire the political will to realize this potentiality.

Indo-Bangladesh Relations : Back to Negatives

Semi-confrontationist rhetoric has characterised the Governmental and media discourse between India and Bangladesh over the last three or four months. Smug, inaccurate, conventional wisdom of Indian analysts has been that, this was to be expected from the BNP Government led by Begum Khaleda Zia. That interaction between India and Bangladesh is acrimonious is a bit of an anti-climax because atleast the Government of India and some knowledgeable circles were not subject to the prejudice mentioned above. Prime Minister Vajpayee was among the first Asian leaders to send a message of congratulations to Begum Khaleda Zia when she came to power after the Bangladesh general elections of last year. The message was followed by a visit by Shri Brajesh Mishra, Principle Secretary and National Security Advisor to the Prime Minister, to Dhaka. The objective was to convey to Begum Khaleda Zia that the Government of India does not suffer from any a priori value judgement about her India policies. He also conveyed India's desire for positive and contentful relationship with Bangladesh, a relationship which would respect and serve mutual interests of India and Bangladesh.

Mishra made a special point during his visit that India will not pressurise or impose on Bangladesh on any aspect of Indo-Bangladesh relations as far as Bangladesh's policies do not affect Indian security and stability.

Foreign Minister Yashwant Sinha continued the process of high-level political interaction in line with his foreign policy assessment that India should give particular attention to its relations with its neighbours instead of marginalising them as was happening during the dispensation of his predecessor. Sinha had detailed discussions on substantive issues with his Bangladesh counterpart, including those related to migration, terrorism, economic cooperation, etc. The visit helped in reviving a good atmosphere for structuring bilateral relations. But since December 2002, relations have taken a negative turn.

The Government of India became critical of Bangladesh on two crucial issues, accusing the Government of Bangladesh about not cooperating on them. The first was about Bangladesh being a base for terrorist and subversive activities against India sponsored by the Inter-Services Intelligence (ISI) of Pakistan. The second issue being about Government of Bangladesh not taking any meaningful action to prevent illegal migration of Bangladeshis from Bangladesh to India. Deputy Prime Minister L.K. Advani and senior Home Ministry officials issued a number of statements over the last six weeks affirming this accusation. The situation was compounded by a fortnight-long confrontation between the BSF of India and Bangladesh Rifles in the northern sector of the Bangladesh-India border where a number of Bangladeshis tried to cross over to India and were stopped by BSF troops. This group of Bangladeshis remained stranded in the No-Man's land for more than ten days with an armed confrontation between the BDR and BSF barely avoided. This particular crisis was resolved after a telephone conversation between Foreign Minister Yashwant Sinha and Bangladesh Foreign Minister Morshed Khan, followed by latter's visit to Delhi between the 13th and 16th of February.

It is worthwhile examining the substance of the two issues of controversy in the current phase of Indo-Bangladesh relations. As far as Bangladesh being a sanctuary for separatist terrorist movements in the North East is concerned, it is a phenomenon stretching back to more than a decade. The Government of India had definite and fool-proof information about training camps for these movements run by the ISI in collaboration with some segments of Bangladesh Intelligence Agencies. India also had definite information about the sanctuaries and the banks in which separatist groups like the ULFA and the Bodos had their bank accounts in Bangladesh.

Between 1991 and 1994, the then Home Secretary N.N. Vohra and I as Foreign Secretary had visited Dhaka and given detailed information on this matter to our counterparts in the Government of Bangladesh. There was a two-point response from Bangladesh to our presentation. About sanctuaries and bank accounts, the response was that they will investigate the matter and take remedial action for closing them down. As far as the existence of training camps was concerned, Bangladesh categorically denied the existence of such training camps and the activities of the Pakistani Inter-Services Intelligence.

The Government of India has also referred to the critical issue of large-scale illegal migration from Bangladesh to India for nearly a decade and half. Bangladesh has repeatedly denied the occurence of any such migration.

Estimates are that between seven to nine million Bangladeshis have migrated to India and are illegal residents within Indian territory. The phenomenon of migration is a more complex one. The origins of such migration perhaps pre-dated the creation of Bangladesh. Our Governments in Assam in the 60s of the last century encouraged migration of Bangladeshis Muslims and smaller number of minorities into Assam allowing them to merge with the population of Assam and giving them voting rights. This was a deliberate and narrow extercise in electoral politics of Assam. Chickens came home to roost in anti-Bengali riots in Assam in the 60s.

The second wave of such migration was during Bangladesh War in 1971. The third wave was Chakma tribals from Bangladesh's Chittagong

Hills Tracts migrating into Tripura and Mizoram and to some extent into Manipur. Here also local political leaders had an inclination to absorb these migrants for electoral purposes. But fortunately things did not go out of control. There was also a separatist movement of these migrants receiving support from the Indian authorities for a brief period. Fortunately the issue was resolved by negotiations and many of them went back to Chittagoan Hill Tracts. The last wave of migration is a continuous phenomenon. In all objectivity one must acknowledge that the Government of Bangladesh is not actively sponsoring this migration. The land to people ratio of Bangladesh is becoming increasingly critical. Social and economic conditions in Bangladesh particularly in the rural areas, is bad and subjected to extreme poverty and unemployment. The consequence is large groups of Bangladeshis seeking opportunities across the border for employment and survival. This migratory movement has been going on for nearly two decades. While Bangladesh Government may not be sponsoring this illegal migration, they certainly are not inclined to take any purposive steps to stop it for the obvious reason of reducing their own socio-economic burdens.

The levels of migration must have reached a point where it is de-stabilising the demographic, social, ethnic and linguistic balance in the Indian States. Hence the Government of India's open articulation of the issue and more assertive stance on it. The solution does not lie in Indian accusations and Bangladesh denials. The two governments should sit together and negotiate a practical solution. If regional economic cooperation arrangements or sub-regional cooperation are to be in place, Bangladeshis could be given work permits for temporary residence arrangements. So that the migrants stand identified and do not become part of the political processes within India which has obvious pernicious and negative implications for Indian polity. Such a solution will take some time but some steps need to be initiated. The proposed arrangements should also include security considerations.

As far as Bangladesh being a base for anti-India terrorist activities goes, Bangladesh's denials are not going to cut any ice. The involvement of intelligence agencies of Bangladesh with the ISI is rooted in the Khalida Zia government being in a coalition with Jamat-e-Islami. The Jamat of Bangladesh has links with Jamat and other Islampasand parties in Pakistan. Added to this are undercurrents of Islamic affiliations and apprehensive hostility towards India. So the reluctance to act decisively on Indian concerns regarding terrorism. Government of Bangladesh should realise that given the international campaign against terrorist violence, its own credibility and internal stability depends on putting a stop to subversive activities against India within its own territory. Bangladesh should also realise that India is in a strong and convincing position to take counter measures against terrorist activities sponsored by Pakistan from Bangladesh. Bangladesh should also take note of the fact that fragmenting North eastern states of India or the Indian Republic has been a continuing strategic objective of Pakistan's policies since early 60s. Bangladesh's being involved in such policies will unnecessarily identify Bangladesh with Pakistani policies which is not good for Bangladesh's security and Indo-Bangladesh relations.

One cannot wish these issues away. They have to be tackled in a practical and peaceful manner through political means. It is a pity that neither Government has come to grips with prospects of cooperation for mutual benefit potentialities of which are enormous in the sectors of trade, investment, technology, transit, energy and utilising the water resources.

Purposive action to translate these prospects into reality is stymied not due to functional or practical reasons. There is no progress because Bangladesh remains a prisoner in some respects to attitudes and perceptions of its Pakistani past. And India subject to:" we did so much for you and you have behaved in a negative and ungrateful manner," syndrome. Space does not permit the listing of a number of other controversies which afflict Indo-Bangladesh relations which really should not be points of contention. It is not only desirable but necessary that the two sit and reason together.

The 13th Non-aligned Summit in Kuala Lumpur : Formalities without Substance

The 13th Non-aligned summit ended in Kuala Lumpur on the 25th of February. In numerical strength the forum has a membership next only to the United Nations with 116 members. Malaysia has taken up the leadership of the movement as the host country of the summit for the next three years. There was high level participation in this summit, including from India and Pakistan.

With the end of the Cold War and related inhibitions fading away, observers were present from the major powers of the world. In formalities the summit was acknowledged as a major event on the international scene. But two questions remain unanswered. The summit was supposed to re-define the terms of reference and policy orientations of the movement collectively to sustain the relevance of the movement in changed circumstances in international politics. The declaration and resolutions of the summit on various issues gave no indications of such an exercise being undertaken seriously. One of course, takes note of the fact that many of the leaders did emphasise the need to re-define these terms and to work on new orientations. One has to recall the qualitatively transformed international situation in which the movement is sought to be sustained and revived, and also look at the manner in which the summit addressed macro-level issues affecting the global order, to make an assessment of the results of this Summit.

This summit took place after the USA's politico-military position as supreme power in the world has crystallised itself. It took place after the terrorist attacks on the US made international terrorism the top priority in the international agenda on security concerns. The summit was held when two major planks of the new global order, envisaged in the mid-90s of the last century have been fragmented and then displaced, namely, the collective international effort on moving towards non-discriminatory disarmament is now on the back burner, with the US not having any interest in the process and a number of countries, even signatories to the Non-Proliferation Treaty like North Korea, pulling back from their commitment to non-proliferation arrangements (the fact being that such countries never fully complied with the provisions of the Non-Proliferation regimes to which they had agreed).

Two vital ingredients of the global arrangements on economic and developmental issues envisaged in the agreements related to the WTO, and the management of Ecology and Environment covered by the Kyoto Convention stand either eroded or discarded, basically through certain initiatives taken by the US within the framework of its own perceived interests. The non-aligned summit followed the divisive sessions of the WTO on these issues at Seatle, Barcelona and Doha. The US-led campaign against international terrorism has been refracted through USA's diversified foreign policy agenda within the framework of its own nation-specific interests, as shown in President Bush's punitive concentration on Iraq.

The trans-continental cohesion in terms of shared concerns and objectives which characterised the NAM movement till the early 80s, is subjected to centrifugal influences of different regional groupings to which Members of the Non-aligned movement belong. These regional and sub-regional groups of Asia, Africa and South America have defined their compartmentalised economic, political and social interests and policies to meet them. More important among these groupings like ASEAN, have their own separate fora dealing with strategic and security issues. India is part of such arrangements with ASEAN. Individual members of the movement as well as their regional groupings have structured and are restructuring their own separate equations with the major power centres of the world, particularly with the US to meet their region-specific and country-specific concerns, priorities and interests, which naturally and logically preclude their joining in a collective approach within the framework of the Non-aligned Movement, even on issues where there may be some parallelism of concerns and interests applicable to the entire membership of the Non-aligned Movement. No member of the Non-aligned Movement will abide by the attempts at United non-aligned approach to deal with issues if such a commitment involves a contradiction between this approach and orientations of their regional and national policies.

These trends and factors influenced the deliberations of the summit at Kuala Lumpur leading to Resolutions and final Declaration which on all counts cannot claim the virtues of re-orienting the movement, re-defining its approach or promising an innovative or vigorous dynamics to the Movement.

The resolutions and the Declaration are anodyne and are, as always, master-pieces of consensual ambiguity. The Declaration and the Resolution of the Non-aligned Movement did not have the directness, the specificity or action-oriented decisions which characterised similar documents emanating from the meetings of G-7 (or G-8) or the ASEAN or the NAFTA. This is not a critical value-judgement on the Non-aligned Movement. When you have 116 members who unlike olden times have no integrated ideological roots, who have to deal with their separate interests, who have to sustain their patterns of relations with important powers amongst the advanced countries, it is natural and unavoidable that policy decisions and declarations reflect tenuous compromises.

Indian Foreign Secretary Kanwal Sibal and Minister for External Affairs Yashwant Sinha in the official level and Ministerial meetings preceding the summit drew attention to the contradictions in and incremental pressures on the Non-aligned Movement. Both of them stressed the importance of dealing with pernicious phenomenon of terrorism in principled, non-selective and non-discriminatory manner. They also emphasised the importance of dealing with developmental issue in the context of a crisis which has affected the WTO over the last 5 years. The policy pronouncements of Heads of State and Governments on these issues however proved the orchestra of Non-aligned to be a discordant phenomenon.

The Chairman of the Movement, Malaysian Prime Minister Mahathir Mohammed instead of taking note of the approach outlined by India and some other countries, proceeded to designate part of the anti-terrorist campaign as anti-Islamic phenomenon. President Pervez Musharraf of Pakistan indulged in perennial chant of the need to make distinction between terrorists and freedom fighters and pontificated on the need to remedy the root causes because of which people resort to terrorist violence. This philosophical approach had a clearly self-serving purpose of bolstering Pakistan's anti-India policies.

Discussions on the issues of Iraq, Palestine and other political problems were subject to the collective inhibition among the members of not offending the major powers beyond a certain threshold. It was recommended that USA's unilateralism should, to the extent possible, be covered by the fig leaf of action under the umbrella of the United Nations and its Security Council. Saddam Hussain has been given advice to unilaterally disarm himself and abide by Resolution 1441 of the Security Council, an advice which he is not likely to accept.

The declaration of the summit and the adjunct resolutions on all other major issues across the spectrum—from trade, technology, financial management, to environment and elimination of weapons of mass destruction were limited to an expression of idealistic and general aspirations and expectations. This was not surprising because in the New World Order, the members of the Movement are more anxious to maintain their regional and individual autonomies and deal with issues than be part of a united effort under the collectivity of the Non-aligned Movement.

Musharraf as expected raised the Kashmir issue. While being wholistic in the presentation of the case, he was accusatory about India. Prime Minister Vajpayee need not have reacted by refuting his arguments in detail. It would have been sufficient when he said that issues related to Kashmir have been part of the historical knowledge of the Movement. There was no need to waste time of the summit on an issue which should not have been raised and even when raised the movement has no locus standi to deal with the issue. They could then have gone on to say that India is more interested and more concerned with more objectives of the Movement in changed circumstances and wishes to focus on them. Musharraf's remarks on Kashmir should have been dismissed instead of being given importance which happened because of Atalji's detailed response.

There was also the interesting undercurrent of Prime Minister Dr. Mahathir Mohammed wanting to emerge as a major world leader and Pan-Islamist through the catalyst of the Chairmanship of the Non-aligned Movement. The substance and reality of his policies had always been rooted in nurturing of good equations with the United States, China and Japan. His public pronouncements many a time do not conform to the details of Malaysian policies.

What then is one to make of the 13th summit of the Non-aligned movement. In many ways it is fading away. It is being replaced by new inter-state arrangements. I recall a somewhat sceptical Foreign Office official from one of the Arab countries remarking to me during the NAM summit in Jakarta in 1992: "The movement is dying, perhaps even dead, but nobody wants to bury it".

This may not be entirely true, but one would do well to remember the distinction that Jawaharlal Nehru made between being non-aligned and being part of the Non-aligned movement. He was clearly of the view that remaining Non-aligned in the conduct of one's foreign and security policies would always be relevant as it ensures freedom of options. Being part of the movement is only relevant to the extent that the Movement can function in a united manner which is not the case.

Text of V.K. Krishna Menon Memorial Speech Delivered by Author at the Indian Society of International Law on 29th of March, 2003

I am grateful for the honour and privilege extended to me to deliver the 4th V.K. Krishna Menon Memorial Lecture. I cannot claim personal acquaintence with Mr. V.K. Krishna Menon, though I was witness to his functioning as senior leader of Prime Minister Jawaharlal Nehru's Government from 1958 to 1962. I had the privilege of listening to his lectures after he relinquished his position in the Government for nearly a decade. I have no hesitation in acknowledging that even the distant connections that I have had has left me with lasting impressions of his magnetic, intellectually vibrant and witty personality. He could be described as a curious and scintillating amalgum of the personality traits of Drydon, Oscar Wilde, Winston Churchill and Justice Oliver Wendel Holmes of the United States.

His was a many splendoured, multi-dimensional personality. In his life of nearly 4 score years, he was a freedom fighter, a journalist and polemical author, lawyer, a diplomat, a politician and a Cabinet Minister. He emerged on the national political stage transcending his origins in

Kerala due to nearly three decades in England. The second factor which contributed to his political and governmental role was his close friendship with Pandit Nehru. The third factor was that among the senior Congress leaders of the late 40s and 50s of the last century, he was one of the few who gave frank and objective assessments and advice to Jawaharlal Nehru, compared to most of Panditji's colleagues who tended to deliver their opinions to Nehru's inclinations. Krishna Menon was not subject to the emergent sycophancy in Indian politics. His contributions to India's foreign policy and defence arrangements have to be recalled and assessed in the context of his these personality traits.

His intellectual make up was deeply influenced by his education in England in the initial inter-war period after the First World War. Being an alumini of the London School of Economics, he was drawn into Indian struggle for freedom which ultimately led to his establishing the India League and what a galaxy of followers, he attracted, who became prominent in political, journalistic and governmental firmament. Suffice it to mention Dr. Shelvanker, P.N. Haksar, Indira Gandhi and Iqbal Singh who made India League under the guidance of V.K. Krishna Menon, an influential voice in England and Western Europe, advocating the cause of anti-colonialism and Indian freedom. The ideological and philosophical terms of reference constituting the foundations of his foreign and Defence policies were opposition to colonialism and all forms of discrimination. A deep conviction about the equality of states constituting the international community, a profound commitment to global peace rooted in inter-state cooperation and effective multilateralism. He believed that India has a special role to play in structuring the new world order which was emerging after the Second World War.

V.K. Krishna Menon, India's first High Commissioner to the United Kingdom and later on Nehru's Minister without Portfolio and Defence Minister is perhaps the most misunderstood Defence and Foreign Policy future in India's post-independence history. Certain aspects of his personality seen in the context of India's non-aligned foreign policy were deliberately mis-interpreted in an exaggerated manner by the power structures of western countries and the media both abroad and India, the Indian media blindly following the lead of the Western media in the matter. It is time to put Krishna Menon's contribution to India's Foreign and Defence policies in correct perspective (according to my assessment others may disagree for their own reasons). Krishna Menon was perhaps the most knowledgeable about international politics, great power equations and the chemistry of the phenomenon of imperialism, colonialism and resulting international economic arrangements amongst the first generation of Indian leaders during the beginning decades of India's existence as an independent country. He was the founder-member of the India League in England which functioned in tandem with the Indian National Congress in the independence struggle of India. He spent the inter-war and the Second World War period in England gaining first hand knowledge of the motivations of important world powers and the undercurrents influencing international power politics. He was also the founder-editor of the publishing house Penguins. Most importantly he had very close links with the Labour Party, originating in his connections with Fabian socialist leaders like Sydney and Beatrice Web, H.G. Wells, and so on. He became a close personal friend of Jawaharlal Nehru in the late 20s. It was a personal friendship transcending political considerations which lasted till Nehru's death in 1964.

Krishna Menon's intellectual make up was profoundly influenced by his academic background as a student of the London School of Economics. This mindset acquired additional qualities of sophistication and logical sharpness with his legal training as a barrister. More important than these academic and intellectual inhibitions or burdens of socio-cultural memories of living in a country under colonial ruled because throughout his youth and early adulthood, he lived in England and was capable of seeing Westerners in general and the British in particular, without the trappings of an Imperial power and without their having the advantage of treating him with racial superiority or disdain. He acquired the capacity to deal with the Western political and intellectual power structure objectively and on a basis of equality. Ideologically, his views and convictions were left of the centre. He was emotionally patriotic. He was deeply, and even mistakenly, conscious of his intellectual abilities and tended to be ascorbic and disdainful towards others who opposed him or, criticized him. His experience of European politics in the Inter-war period in terms of the rise of Nazism, Fascism and the Spanish civil war and the initial appeasement by the Governments of the UK and France convinced him that the western powers were at the most fundamental level insular and self-centred with no sensitivities for the principles of democracy, equality of economic opportunities and distributive justice. He was clear in his mind that India, even after becoming independent would have to be content with imperialistic and acquisitive motivations of important western powers. He was convinced that independent India should be Indo-centric, independent as well as economically and militarily strong to cope with the more established powers in international relations. He also believed that political stability, economic and military strength should be rooted, to the maximum extent feasible, to self-reliance. One of his initial contributions to India's foreign policy was his advising Nehru to change the structure of the Commonwealth by changing the status of the British monarchy from being the Head of State of all Commonwealth countries to being the Institutional head of a new Commonwealth organisation which would be a free association of member-countries which formerly belonged to the British Empire. It was on his advice that Pandit Nehru told British Prime Minister Attleee that India was going to declare itself a Republic and that India would remain a part of the Commonwealth as a Republic on the pre-condition of the status of the British Monarch being changed on the above lines. Had not Attlee agreed to this, the Commonwealth would have continued in a truncated form with only Australia, New Zealand and Canada constituting its membership. All the other African and Asian members of the Commonwealth would not have joined the association. Nehru invited Krishna Menon back to India in 1952 making him a member of the Cabinet as a Minister without Portfolio, he was also appointed the leader of the Indian delegation to the UN to deal particularly with the ambiguous and anti-India goings on at the UN on the Kashmir issue. As Minister without Portfolio he was the principal adviser on foreign and security policies to Jawaharlal Nehru.

It is pertinent to mention that the period between 1952 and 1962, was the period when India achieved its maximum influence in international relations. While Nehru was the architect of this achievement, Krishna Menon should rightly be considered the analytical adviser and executor of Nehru's foreign policy. It was during this period that India forced a strong Asian collectivity in international relations through the Colombo Conference in 1954, the Bandung Conference of Afro-Asian countries in Jakarta in 1955, which ultimately led the creation of the non-aligned movement in Belgrade in 1961. Krishna Menon assisted Nehru in transmuting his foreign policy orientations into an initial multilateral movement in which an overwhelming majority of newly independent countries of Africa and Asia which joined, the Non-aligned group of countries became powerful advocates of the political and economic aspirations of the developing countries of the world at the United Nations and its agencies. That the movement did not make an effective or tangible impact on international politics in the face of the military, economic, technological and political clout of the major powers of the world is a different matter, which proved that political influence not rooted in tangible ingredients of power has only limited effectiveness.

Krishna Menon played an important role in making India an impartial and respected mediator and interlocutor in resolving international crises. He was the behind-the-scenes negotiator at the Geneva Conference after the French defeat at Dien Bien Phu and the withdrawal of French Imperial Power from the countries of Indo-China. The international settlements arrived at Geneva lent political identity and tentative stability in the countries of Laos, Cambodia and Vietnam. Earlier, Krishna Menon had played an important role in structuring the management of residual problems of the Korean War which ended in 1954. India was designated the Chairman of the Neutral Nations Repatriation Commission to resolve questions arising out of the armistice agreement in Korea. Krishna Menon played an equally important and behind-the-scenes role in resolving the Suez crisis after the UK-French-Israeli invasion of Egypt consequent to President Nasser's nationalizing the Suez Canal. Krishna Menon's most important foreign policy achievement was his effective and articulate advocacy of the Indian stand on the Jammu and Kashmir issue at the United Nations. The Western Powers led by the United States and the UK were trying to convert the issue of invasion by Pakistan of Jammu and Kashmir into a bilateral issue between India and Pakistan being given the status of a legitimate disputant in the issue. Krishna Menon's well- researched, firm and articulated projection of Indian interests and policies countered the pro-Pakistani inclinations of the principal western powers on this issue, because by the mid 50s Pakistan had agreed to join the Western camp in the Cold War and had become a member of the US-sponsored system of military alliances aimed at containing the Soviet Union, China and "international communism." While being analytically thorough and meticulous in his policy articulations, Krishna Menon was ascorbic and sharp in refuting western arguments. He cut through their obfuscatory explanations defining specifically their motivations in terms of power politics and cold war objectives. When the British Permanent Representative and Ambassador to the UN satirically told Krishna Menon at a Security Council meeting that while the substance of what he said was questionable, he spoke English very well, Krishna Menon's response was that it was natural for him to speak English well, because he had learnt the language systematically, which was a foreign language for him, whereas the British Ambassador had acquired his linguistic capabilities in English through the unskilled and natural accident of being born as an Englishman. Obviously, this kind of repartee was not going to please his audience.

As an architect of foreign policy, Krishna Menon ensured that Indian policies were Indo-centric, realistic in terms of national necessity and clear in their objectives of safeguarding India's multifaceted national interests. He also ensured that India's foreign policy found a multilateral projection through the non-aligned movement and other multilateral fora of the developing countries.

It is as Defence Minister of India that he was dubbed a failure for not anticipating China's aggressive policies towards India and for having left the Indian Army ill-prepared to meet China' a aggression in 1962, which resulted in India's massive military defeat. In event-specific terms, this criticism is valid. His ideological yearnings prevented him from comprehending the aggressively nationalistic orientations of Communist China. He held on to the view that Pakistan was a greater military threat than China, in which he was wrong.

In overall terms, however, Krishna Menon laid the foundation of India's self-reliance in Defence production. There is ill-informed criticism that he spent the Defence budget on production of non-combatant logistic material. This is not true. It was during his tenure as Defence Minister of India that India signed agreements for defence supply and defence production with the former Soviet Union and other East European countries, because of which apart from purchasing defence equipment like aircraft, armour and ships, India was also assured of transfers of technology and indigenous production of these items. It was his policies and beginnings made by him which resulted in India today being capable of producing fighter aircraft, tanks, ships, heavy artillery and even missiles and satellites. The Indian army being defeated by the Chinese and his political miscalculation in which this debacle is rooted have obfuscated his sterling contributions to India's foreign policy and India's indigenous defence production capacities from public memory and public consciousness. It is time that the imbalance and the inaccuracy in judging his political role is redressed. He was profoundly patriotic and he had anticipatory vision about India's foreign policy and defence needs, and he was imbued with practicality and political realism.

History will judge him more fairly and objectively than his contemporaries who were victims of the pressure of negative events for which they blamed him.

Indo-Japanese Relations in Focus - Foreign Minister Yoriko Kawaguchi's Visit

India's relations with Japan were again in focus in India when Foreign Minister of Japan Her Excellency Yoriko Kawaguchi visited India between the 7th and 9th of January. This was in return to India's Minister of External Affairs Jaswant Singh's visit to Japan about a year ago.

Japan has always been an important factor in India's external relations specially since the mid-sixties of the last century.

The substance of this relationship was of course economic and technological. Japan has been a major donor of developmental aid (the top donor in the decade of the 90s of the last century), and among the top trading partners and foreign investors in the Indian economy. It is specially important to note that these investments have helped in developing the infrastructural sector of Indian economy in terms of shipping, ports, roads, bridges and transportation. Japan has also been prompt in sending assistance for disaster management of crises like the Gujarat earthquake in the year 2000.

There are certain historical dimensions which provide foundations for this substantive interaction between India and Japan. During the freedom struggle the Indian public rejoiced in the Japanese naval victory over the Russian Navy in 1907 as an expression of Asian resurgence. Whatever the clinical value Judgements of Japan may be during the Second World War large sections of Indian public opinion appreciated Japan's support to Netaji Subhash Chandra Bose's military campaign against the British by the creation of the Indian National Army; the dissenting opinion of the Indian Judge on the War Crimes Tribunal against Japanese accused, made a positive impact on Japanese public opinion. Justice Radha Vinod Pal is still remembered by old timers in Japan for his having refused to join the Judges from West European countries in his decision. Going beyond all this is the age-old cultural, religious links between India and Japan through the catalyst of Buddhism.

Whatever the long-term context of Indo-Japanese relations as detailed above may be, Japan's Foreign Minister Madam Kawaguchi's visit resulted in determining a new basis for Indo-Japanese cooperation and a new terms of reference in bilateral relations between the two countries.

Kawaguchi visited India in a politic-strategic context of twin dimensions. First, Japan over the last two decades has moved away from its politically insular orientations in external relations and has shown an inclination to assume political and strategic responsibilities as one of the important powers of the world, which Japan undoubtedly is. Secondly, Japan is agreeable to take on more activist role in economic development and political stabilization of the Asian region, particularly South East Asia and South Asia. Japan is also rapidly adjusting to the changing power equations in international politics after the disintegration of the Soviet Union.

India discerns the following ingredients in Japan's foreign and security policies :

Japan accepts its importance and role as a major Asian power and as a global economic power.

Japan's foreign policy objective is to maintain Japan's territorial integrity and safety and to sustain Japan's economic well-being and prosperity.

Japan considers the establishment of a stable political and security environment in Asia and the Asia Pacific Region as an important factor to meet the first two objectives.

Japan is willing to establish a network of bilateral and multilateral relations with all countries in the world particularly with countries in Asia, to further the objectives of stability and security for the states in this region.

Japan is willing to make contributions in terms of investment, economic and technological assistance for these purposes.

Japan is firmly opposed to the proliferation of all categories of Weapons of Mass Destruction.

There is an incremental willingness in Japan to be active in finding to crises and conflict situations. It is in this context that Japan is an active member of the ASEAN and the APC, as well as its security forums.

Japanese perception is that the present state of international relations is far from being in a security environment that ensures true peace free from threats of armed conflicts. The Japanese policy response to this situation is that Japan must take appropriate steps through diplomatic initiatives in stabilizing international relations by laying foundations for security through domestic political stability and enhancing self-reliance in defence capacities. This self reliance and the maintenance of US-Japan security arrangements are the twin factors on which Japan's, foreign and strategic policies are based.

In a Defence Policy Paper, of Japan's Self Defence Agency the Government policy on foreign relations was explained as follows: "On the diplomatic front, it is essential for Japan to take steps to prevent or resolve international disputes and confrontations, achieve economic development, promote arms control and disarmament and deepen mutual understanding and mutual confidence. This is necessary to create an increasingly stable security environment. The strengthening of Japan-US security arrangements is an anchor of Japanese foreign policy. Increasing bilateral cooperation with other countries and actively promoting regional cooperation in Asia, and global cooperation through the United Nations are the constituent elements of Japan's foreign policy."

Madam Kawaguchi had high level discussions in India with Prime Minister Atal Behari Vajpayee, with Minister of External Affairs Yashwant Sinha and the National Security Advisor to the Prime Minister Brajesh Mishra. As part of an effort to persuade India and Pakistan to re-start their dialogue, Madam Kawaguchi wished to visit Pakistan before coming to India. While India appreciated her intentions, it (India) advised that no purpose would be served by her visit to Pakistan at this point of time. India appreciated her accepting the Indian advice in the matter.

Madam Kawaguchi's visit removed last of the misunderstandings between Japan and India about India's nuclear weapons tests conducted in the summer of 1998. While there is no change in the basic policies of India and Japan on Non-Proliferation issues, it was significant that during Madam Kawaguchi's discussions, it was agreed that India and Japan should give primary attention to developing bilateral economic and technological cooperation and in forging political understanding to deal with the fundamental issues affecting regional security and stability. There was also agreement on sustaining, consolidating and increasing Indo-Japanese economic cooperation.

Madam Kawagachi also exchanged views with Indian leaders on developments related to negotiations to resolve the ethnic problem in Sri Lanka. She informed her Indian counterparts about missions being under, taken by Mr. Yasushi Akashi to help galvanise the economic dimensions of negotiations between LTTE and the Sri Lankan Government being brokered by the Norwegian Government. India appreciated being kept informed about Japan's interest and involvement in these negotiations. India, however, cautioned Kawaguchi that a solution to the ethnic problem is going to be a complex and long drawn out process and that too many external involvements may only result in one side or the other in the ethnic conflict exploiting such involvement to their advantage. India also appreciated the political and security concerns of Japan related to the

Northern sector of the Asia Pacific region. North Korea's threats to revive its missile and nuclear capacities, the security and strategic controversies related to Taiwan, the complex relations with China, were factors affecting Japan' external relations. It is to be noted that India shares Japan's concerns in these matters. There was complete agreement on strengthening the United Nation on working together to counter international terrorism and on the importance of strengthening the principles of democracy, good governance and human rights and international politics. India was supportive of Japan providing economic aid to Sri Lanka, including its Tamil regions to galvanize the process of reconciliation between Tamils and Sinhalese. India also took note of more orientations in Japan's foreign and defence policies.

The discussions with Madam Kawaguchi provided insights into the impact of Japanese policies in South Asia and South East Asia, Madam Kawaguchi's visit signalled the end of some distances which had developed between India and Japan between 1998 and 1999 due to India's nuclear tests. The visit generally brought back Indo-Japanese relations on track. This is the feeling in the Indian public opinion.

India's Foreign Policy Focus—Need for Attention to Neighbours Like Bangladesh

US military operations in Iraq, Prime Ministers Vajpayee and Jamali's interaction for normalising relations between India and Pakistan, and the visit of the US Deputy Secretary of State Richard Armitage and US Assistant Secretary of State for South Asian Affairs Christina Rocca have hogged both media and political attention in terms of India's external relations. In this pre-occupation, there is a general trend of neglecting India's relations with other important neighbours like Bangladesh, Sri Lanka, Bhutan, Myanmar, etc. An indication of this neglect in public perception is the visit by Foreign Secretary Kanwal Sibal to Dhaka (which took place in the fourth week of April), being more or less ignored both in reportage and analyses.

Sibal's discussions at Dhaka was the first high level interaction after a gap of time in a crucial political context. The meetings in Dhaka took place as Mr. Vajpayee was commencing his latest initiative on normalisation of relations with Pakistan, as the military operations in Iraq came to an end, and as mutually critical rhetoric about Bangladesh harbouring Pakistan-sponsored terrorists on its territory abated after reaching points of high controversy.

Sibal's visit also took place in the context of Begum Zia not having paid a single visit to New Delhi after she came to power this time in October, 2001. Mr. Vajpayee has not visited Dhaka at all. It is time to indulge in an over-view of Indo-Bangladesh relations at the end of more than three decades of Bangladesh emerging as an independent country. First, the important position which Bangladesh should occupy in our foreign policy scheme, and the reasons for it. Bangladesh is the third most populous country in Sub-continental Asia. Strategically it occupies an important position in the Northern segment of the Bay of Bengal and along the coastline from Cox's Bazar down to the western coastline of Myanmar. It is India's third largest trading partner with potentialities both as a market and as an area of investment and transfers of technology for mutual benefit. Bangladesh also lies athwart the North Eastern States of India and the rest of India.

Apart from Myanmar, and Manipur in India, there is Bangladesh's importance in terms of India's border security concerns in that region. Bangladesh is an important link in the land and land-based trading routes between South Asia and South Eastern countries stretching from Myanmar to Malaysia, including countries of the former Indo-China region. Bangladesh is a repository of natural gas reserves which could contribute to the energy security of India, after fulfilling of the needs of Bangladesh. All this is apart from a long-standing linguistic, cultural and religious commonalities between the people of the two countries transcending their respective national identities or recent history.

These factors plus the role that India played in supporting the liberation of Bangladesh should have resulted in a substantive and positive relationship between the two countries. This has not happened because of some atavistic elemental factors affecting Indo-Bangladesh relations. First, India expected general conformity pattern of gratitude from Bangladesh for India's support to that country's liberation struggle. Second, India though sensitive to Bangladesh's threat perceptions because of being surrounded on three sides by Indian States and the Bay of Bengal dominated by Indian Navy in the South, has not been responsive enough in political and security terms. Third, India has not been as forthcoming in meeting Bangladesh's economic requirements because of India's narrower and short term policy orientations on issues related to trade and transit.

Bangladesh's deliberately cultivating a closer relationship with Pakistan under successive regimes of the country since 1975-76 has not helped matters. In fact, developments became more complicated with

Pakistani Inter-Services Establishment, establishing a foothold for its anti-India activities in Bangladesh nearly a decade and half from the mid-80s of the last century, onwards. There has been delay in settling pending territorial issues with Bangladesh, like the exchange of border enclaves which have been pending almost since the time of India's partition. The demographic pressure on land in Bangladesh has perhaps unavoidably resulted in illegal migration of Bangladeshi's into India. Instead of tackling the problem on human terms of reference, both India and Bangladesh have taken a political and reductionist stand on this important issue. Bangladesh saying there is no illegal immigration and India claiming exactly the opposite and threatening to take punitive action against the phenomenon.

Foreign Secretary Kanwal Sibal must have broadly touched on all these factors affecting bilateral relations but the focus must have been on expanding bilateral economic relations, finding ways to expand mutual cooperation against international terrorism and for consolidating regional security, as well as to see the extent to which Bangladesh would be interested in cooperation in the energy sector with India. Geo-strategic and general political benefits of mutual cooperation, ensuring mutual security are too obvious and need no elaboration. It is in the economic and technological fields that India should be more forthcoming and generous while Bangladesh should discard its irrational inhibitions about economic cooperation with India. The volume of India's exports to Bangladesh is of the order of one billion dollars in terms of formal exchange of goods. If informal trade is included, India's exports to Bangladesh would be of the order of nearly 3 billion US dollars. Bangladesh is the third largest importer of manufactured goods from India. Though Bangladesh's exports to India have increased over the last 30 years. Bangladesh has an adverse balance of trade with India. Bangladesh's trade deficit with India is of the order which can be economically debilitating with the passage of time.

There are two broad steps which can be taken to remedy this predicament. First, India should extend unilateral free trade treatment to Bangladesh. Not only would this result in expansion of Bangladesh's exports to India but would also help in reducing the trade gap, and establishing strong and fair links between economies of Bangladesh and India. A positive political fall out of India playing a role in contribution to Bangladesh's economic strength and development are obvious. Though India has extended tariff concessions to Bangladesh off and on, this has been done piece-meal and in an inhibited manner which has only generated misunderstanding and apprehensions in Bangladesh. Government of India's approach of allowing transit facilities through India to Bangladesh has been conditional to Bangladesh giving reciprocal facilities to India through its territories in India's north-eastern States. Though this is fair demand, perhaps India could extend these concessions first to which Bangladesh could respond later after assessing the benefits of a mutually trustworthy economic relationship.

If Bangladesh gives up its political inhibitions and decided export its surplus natural gas to India it would be a major step benefiting Bangladesh and qualitatively reducing its adverse balance of trade position with India. Though India does not have any intention of making a demand on this subject or imposing on Bangladesh. Bangladesh would be the loser if it does not take an early positive decision in the matter. India is discovering new oil and natural gas fields on land and its coastal seas. Multilateral financial institutions like the Asian Development Bank are exploring oil and natural gas projects in Central Asia and West Asia targeting on Indian import market. India itself is investing in its energy security in countries as far away as Kazakhstan and Russian Federation, on the one hand and to Sudan, on the other. It is for Bangladesh to objectively calculate the implications of India moving away to alternate sources of energy. If this happens Bangladesh would be sitting on an asset which it would not be able to use as effectively as it can (if it does not move into the Indian market).

The problems of illegal migration and Pakistan-sponsored terrorist bases in Bangladesh need to be addressed not through polemics but through a rational and cooperative approach. Options regarding both these problems are available and have been widely discussed. It is time that governments of the two countries translate positive options into operation. One hopes Foreign Secretary Sibal's visit to Dhaka might have made a beginning in this direction.

Prospects of Peace in Sri Lanka—Still a Lot of Question Marks

Issues of sending troops to Iraq and Mr. Vajpayee's visits to Europe and China, Foreign Secretary Kanwal Sibal's visit to the USA, have dominated the foreign policy discourse in India during the last two months. Not only the media and public opinion, but even the Government seems to have given scant attention to the critical developments in the Sri Lankan peace process in recent weeks. The cease-fire which came into being 17 months ago early in 2002, is fraying.

Discussions between the LTTE and the Sri Lankan Government are stalled. It is significant that this impasse has occurred when both sides are about to enter into discussions on substantive issues to resolve the ethnic problem.

India has been kept informed by all parties involved in these discussions through direct briefings, except perhaps the LTTE. President Kumaratunga was here early in the summer. LTTE, Mr. Peiris was in Delhi early in June. Senior Member of Parliament from Eelam People's Democratic Party, Mr. Douglas Devananda, was here in July for discussions with senior Government officials and to inform them about the complexities which are affecting the ongoing discussions between the LTTE and the Government of Prime Minister Ranil Wickeremesinghe.

The exchange of views over the last year and a half remain inconclusive except for a temporary lull in military operations by both sides. This is nothing new. Such cease-fires between the LTTE and the Sri Lankan Government have occurred several times between 1983 and now. One hopes that the present impasse does not run into the pattern declining again into a conflict situation. One indulges in this apprehension because of a statement by the LTTE in the second week of July. The LTTE stated that while it desires peace, it has the capability and the will to go to war again.

Given the current stalemate and the maneuvea related to the negotiations between the Sri Lankan Government and the LTTE, it would be relevant to examine the basic terms of reference of the two sides animating their negotiating stances. While the LTTE has been consistent and open in its demands laced with strategic and tactical ambiguities, the Ranil Wickremesinghe's Government has a different set of objectives.

First the LTTE's Real and Substantive Objectives

The LTTE's basic aim is to create a sovereign Tamil state on the Island of Sri Lanka. The interim negotiating stances seem to be technical stratagems. Their is no articulation or commitment from the LTTE that it will accept the overall sovereignty and suzerainty of a Central Government in Colombo. When Mr. Anton Balasingham expresses the hope that Ranil Wickremesinghe will come out with innovative proposals to meet the Tamil aspirations, he in fact is demanding that the Sri Lankan Government accepts not just autonomous but also separate Tamil territorial entity in Sri Lanka with minimum linkages with the Central Government and Tamil areas which LTTE controls and dominates. LTTE cadres have transformed themselves from a guerilla force to almost a regular army with a land army, as well as a Naval force, namely the Sea Tigers of the LTTE. The LTTE wants to expand the cease-fire arrangements into a formal recognition of LTTE's jurisdiction in the Northern and Eastern provinces of Sri Lanka as well as over the adjacent seas. They have demanded that Sri Lankan Navy on the coast lines of Tamil areas, Administration, law and order and internal financial arrangements in Jaffna and to some extent in Trincomallee are being managed by LTTE cadres. The LTTE organised a passing out parade of its military cadres on 15th of April last with all the formalities which characterise a national army.

It is interesting that while the LTTE is demanding innovative proposals for meeting Tamil aspirations it has not spelt out what precisely its demands are. The LTTE is reserving the option of just accept or reflect any Sri Lankan proposal that may come up without making any clear and specific proposals on its own. More importantly, LTTE remains in its claim that it is the sole organisation representing Sri Lankan Tamils. LTTE refuses to recognise the role of remaining Tamil organisations which are participating in the democratic processes in Sri Lanka like the Eelam People's Democrative Party. In fact, Douglas Devananda, MP from the EPDP informed Delhi that LTTE continues its policy of eliminating leaders of other Tamil parties. There are reports that Tamil clergy is toeing the LTTE line on various issues. The fractiousness amongst the Sri Lankan Tamils is manifest in the statement of the EPDP that it considers the Liberation Tigers of Tamil Eelam, a liberation movement that has with time degenerated into a terrorist movement, that it is a fascist organisation which has harmed the Tamil cause by its actions over the last fifteen years.

Similar contradictions are afflicting the negotiating stance of the Sri Lankan authorities with the LTTE. President Chandrika Kumaratunga and the party which she leads under the umbrella of SLFP is highly critical and apprehensive about the concessions which Prime Minister Ranil Wickremesinghe has extended to the LTTE since the summer of 2002, accepting de facto jurisdiction of the LTTE in the Jaffna and parts of Eastern provinces, not questioning the LTTE projecting itself as separate entity with a national army, the acceptance of LTTE's demands to remove Sri Lankan Government authorities from Tamil areas or Sri Lanka, are considered concessions which could evolve into a break up of Sri Lanka. The Buddhist clergy in Sri Lanka is incrementally and openly becoming opposed to the Peace Initiatives in recent weeks.

Despite the good intentions animating the Norwegian facilitating initiative, it appears that Norway is more interested in getting some kind of a peaceful solution even if it erodes the unity of Sri Lanka substantially. The first example of this is the declaration of the Norwegian Government after the LTTE-Sri Lanka discussions at Hakone in Japan, wherein the Norwegian Government declared : "The parties reiterated their commitment to develop a federal system based on self-determination within a united Sri Lanka." The crux of the matter is how the LTTE interprets the concept of self-determination and how the Sri Lankan Government reconciles this interpretation with the federal system which it has in mind.

The Norwegian Sri Lanka Monitoring Mission which is supervising the cease-fire has not helped matters. Norwegian Government donated a separate broadcasting station to the LTTE which was to operate without the authority of the Sri Lankan Ministry of Information. General Tryggve Teleffsen has made a number of suggestions sustaining a cease-fire which if fully implemented make the LTTE a de facto sovereign authority. The suggestions made by him are worth quoting : "In the spirit of the cease-fire agreement, Government of Sri Lanka and especially the Sri Lankan Navy should recognise the LTTE Sea Tigers as a de facto naval Unit." This proposal would amount to Sri Lankan Government recognising the LTTE as a sovereign nation with a separate naval arm. Then comes the suggestion : "That as a confidence Building exercise Sri Lankan Navy and the LTTE Sea Tigers should allow observers from both sides on Board their respective naval vessels. The Sri Lankan Navy and Sea Tigers should agree on specific and separate areas for their naval exercises without interfering with each other. Both sides should agree to give safe and legal Maritime passage to each other for transporting personnel and non-military goods."

Ranil Wickremesinghe's Government is in a problematic predicament with such suggestions from Norway which indicates that either Norway does not understand implications of these suggestions on Sri Lankan sovereignty or the Norwegians are not averse to the LTTE gradually assuming a separate sovereign jurisdiction and identity.

The ground reality in Jaffna now is that more than half if not two-thirds population of Jaffna has migrated outside the peninsula, either going abroad or moving to other parts of Sri Lanka. While the ceasefire stumbles on, the LTTE continues to demand the removal of Sri Lankan army military camps from the North and the East. Sri Lankan Armed Forces are in a limbo and demoralised while the LTTE's political and military establishment seem imbued with the sense of confidence of having a range of options, to resort to, regardless of whether the negotiations succeed or fail. Tamil parties participating in the democratic processes have another apprehension. They feel that Ranil Wickremesinghe's objective is drag on these negotiations without letting them come to any conclusion till the next Presidential election which he propose to fight on the record of his efforts for peace. The theory is that if he wins the elections, he will pull back from negotiations and revert back to anti-Tamil campaigns. Tamil parties feel that the present ruling party, the UNP scuttling the constitutional proposals of the year 2000, a major opportunity for compromise, which was lost. The fact of the matter is that LTTE has transformed itself from a guerilla group under separatist political Movement into a semi-governmental authority with all the paraphernalia of sovereign jurisdiction. Political discussions remain stalemated and the fundamental contradictions which neither side seems to address for compromise is between Sri Lankan Government's basic conviction that country's unity should be preserved even if Tamil aspirations are not fully met, and the LTTE's view that Tamil aspirations be met unless a separate Tamil state is created, joining the Northern and Eastern Provinces of Sri Lanka.

India is supportive of the peace process. If it does not succeed, India will have to deal with dilemmas and the contradictions mentioned above.

7

Regional Challenges

Short-term Regional Challenges to India's Foreign Policy

As the year ends, the normal inclination is to review problems both domestic and foreign, which India faced during the year 2002, and the manner in which we coped with them. This introspection about the immediate past is no doubt relevant but the existentialist reality is that the past is done and over, and it would be more pertinent to make an assessment of the problems India would face in the coming year. There is no doubt that the impending domestic political predicaments would and should dominate our collective consciousness. Nine state elections are due during the year 2003. The year 2003 would also be the preparatory year for the next general elections in 2004. The chemistry and dynamics of these elections stand affected by the sweeping victory of the BJP in Gujarat rooted in the Party's advocacy of assertive Hindutva of a particular brand. There is and there would be sufficient cogitation about domestic prospects in the public discourse of all categories. So one focuses attention on the challenges that India faces in terms of its external relations in the coming year, a subject which is not prominent on the radar screen of the general public.

In general terms relations with our neighbours, relations with important power centres in the world and adjusting policies on matters of international concern would constitute the tasks ahead for India's foreign policy. It is the ingredients in these challenges which merit description and assessment. India's immediate neighbours (not unlike India) are going through a phase of ferment and political uncertainties which, in turn impinges on their policies and attitudes towards India.

The King of Bhutan is undertaking constitutional reforms to give more powers to Bhutanese Parliament and to convert the Monarchy into a constitutional monarchy. But he still has to cope with the twin problems of certain amount of disaffection among his Nepalese subjects in southern Bhutan and southern Bhutan being used as a haven by cadres of the separatist movements of the north east. Problems with the Nepalese are a factor of debate with India as well as Nepal. The disturbing presence of Indian separatist elements on its territory results in the dilemma of his having to give the Indian security forces unrestricted access to the Bhutanese territory which could effect his image in the Bhutanese population as a sovereign state. At the same time, these separatists could instigate disturbances in Bhutan affecting Government's stability. Bhutan would like to delineate its boundaries with China as early as possible but that exercise is linked with the Sino-Indian discussions on the boundary which remains a distant prospect. To some extent this complicates Bhutan's relations with China and with India both. Bhutan could also face the spread of the Maoist movement from Nepal into the State of Bhutan.

India obviously has certain responsibilities and role to play in relation to these issues which while safeguarding India's interests, would also be responsive to the requirements of Bhutan.

As far as Nepal is concerned, King Gyanendra is taking full advantage of the militancy of the Maoist Movement to consolidate his political power. The political parties of Nepal continue to be affected by factionalism, resulting in their inability to provide stable governments in Nepal. Apart from King Gyanendra taking advantage of the situation, countering Maoist violence has resulted in the armed forces emerging as the other centre of power in Nepal's politics even more than before.

India is helping the Government of Nepal in countering Maoist violence while parallely advising the King to appoint an interim government of representatives from the political parties. But the King does not seem to be amenable to this advice. His objective seems to be to revert back to the system of his father. This will complicate Indo-Nepalese relations which may be compounded by the continuing differences of opinion between Nepal and India on issues related to sharing of water resources, jurisdiction over Kalapani area, and so on.

Relations with Bangladesh have become tense over the last year and would continue to be so in 2003. The country has become a centre of anti-India terrorist organizations of India's North East. These have links with the Inter-Services Intelligence of Pakistan through the ISI's office attached to Pakistani mission in Bangladesh. India's formal communications conveying these concerns have been rejected by the Khalida Zia

Government, while other issues at dispute regarding migration, bilateral trade, transit facilities to India through Bangladesh to India's North-eastern states remain unresolved. The internal law and order situation in Bangladesh is becoming increasingly tense. Islamist parties like Jamaat-e-Islami are becoming more influential in Bangladesh politics. Khalida Zia being dependent on their support to remain in power. India's separatist cadres with bases in Bangladesh have created a situation where the Indian Border Security Force has been at higher levels of alert on the Indo-Bangladesh border in the second half of this year. India would have to cope with a tense phase in Indo-Bangladesh relations in the coming months.

Despite elections having been held in Jammu and Kashmir successfully and the establishment of some kind of a democracy in Pakistan, prospects of Indo-Pakistan relations remain tense. Public pronouncements by General Musharraf and the newly elected Prime Minister, Mir Fazalur Rehman Jamali indicate the following orientations in Pakistan's India policies. Pakistan does not consider the elections held in Jammu and Kashmir as legitimate. Pakistan continues in the assessment that the violence in Jammu and Kashmir is indigenous, is a freedom movement and is not cross-border terrorist phenomenon. Pakistan will continue to support the separatist movement in Jammu and Kashmir while denying that Pakistan is involved in operational and logistical support to crossborder terrorist activities. Pakistan wants India to resume bilateral dialogue without any pre-conditions. Pakistan has also indicated to the United States and other major powers that while being a partner in anti-terrorist campaign led by the United States, Pakistan is not willing to pull back from supporting the violent terrorist cadres operating in Jammu and Kashmir. The important political position which the Mutahida Majlis-e-Amal, MMA, has acquired in Pakistani politics would be a destabilizing factor both in Afghanistan and in Jammu and Kashmir. The stand-off with Pakistan would continue.

The three challenges inherent in the situation for India are of countering Pakistan-sponsored terrorism effectively, of convincing the major powers and international community about the rationale and legitimacy of the stand on the resumption of dialogue with Pakistan, and to cope with Pakistan's diplomatic and publicity offensive against India.

A solution to the ethnic problem of Sri Lanka is still far away despite reports about some kind of a breakthrough at Oslo in the talks brokered by the Norwegian Government. There would be difficulties about the extent to which the Sri Lankan Government would be able to delegate powers to meet what the LTTE calls full self-determination within the general framework of a united Sri Lanka. The Buddhist clergy, the Sri Lankan Army and President Chandrika Kumaratunga have indicated their reservations about the self-determination package being discussed. Political circles in Tamil Nadu, supportive of the LTTE want India to be more active in supporting the Tamil cause. LTTE's objective is to convert Northern and Eastern Sri Lanka into a de facto independent political territorial unit. This will not be acceptable to Sri Lanka. India would have to undertake a very difficult exercise in tight rope walking in dealing with the evolving Sri Lankan situation that is of being steadfast in supporting Tamil aspirations and to ensure that Sri Lanka does not get divided.

It is in this context that prospects of India's involvement with the SAARC has to be assessed. The scheduled summit of the SAARC to be held in Islamabad between 11th and 13th of January has been postponed because Prime Minister Vajpayee declined to attend the summit. SAARC is really in the doldrums. Even after 17 years, no substantive cooperation arrangements have become a reality. India would have to look for alternatives in regional cooperation policies. India should perhaps examine the possibilities of a closer pattern of relations with South East Asian countries and as far as South Asia is concerned, India will have to develop new frameworks for bilateral cooperation with countries in the immediate neighbourhood. Involvement with the SAARC may have to be replaced with expanded relations with South East Asia, China and Central Asia, as well as with Iran.

Iran has emerged as a major factor in India's foreign policy over the last 12 years, as an Islamic power, as a link between India and Central Asia, as a source of energy and as a balancing factor against adversarial attitude of Pakistan. President Khatami is coming to India as the Chief Guest during the Republic Day 2003. All this however should not make India ignore the fact that Iran considers its relations with Pakistan as an important part of its foreign policy scheme. Pakistan and Iran have even had a joint military exercise in December. The other factor to be noted is President Bush designating Iran as the next target of USA's anti-terrorist operations, claiming that Iran is also in the process of developing nuclear weapons. India will have to counter this insistently intrusive orientations in US Foreign Policy, while at the same time ensuring that substance of Indo-US relations do not get negatively affected - a very difficult task indeed.

India's relations with China can be described as being in a state of positive ambiguity. Prime Minister Vajpayee is likely to visit China in the summer of 2003 after the new leader Hu Jintao formally takes over as Head of Government.

Indo-China talks on the boundary question have made only marginal progress. Government of India remains reluctant to address the boundary question in any substantive manner because of its apprehensions of Indian public opinion not supporting such a move. (An assessment which is not correct). The Chinese are sitting pretty. They have no anxiety to discuss the boundary question. China has recently bought nearly 2 billion dollars worth of arms from the Russian Federation. China is consolidating its position as the most powerful military entity in the region, if one leaves Russia.

China's intensively assertive nationalism, its aspirations to emerge as a major Asian power and the undercurrents in its strategic posture to encircle India, are factors which India has to take into account in fashioning its China policy.

India's relations with the US and Russian Federation will impinge on India's regional equations. But then this dimension of foreign policy challenges requires a separate analysis. Suffice it to say that the year 2003 in many ways would be a test of India's adroitness in adjusting to and managing a highly complex regional political and security environment.

Visit to the Gulf—A Journal

The Zayed Centre for Coordination and Follow Up, a political and Strategic think-tank of the United Arab Emirates, chaired by the Deputy Prime Minister of the country invited me to participate in two Seminars in Abu Dhabi between the 11th and 15th of January. The first Seminar was not so much a seminar but a presentation made by me followed by an hour-long group discussion. The subject was "Conflicts in the Asian Continent with special emphasis on current developments in the situation between India and Pakistan." The second Seminar was on "International Terrorism, the Need for Rational Counter-measure in which representatives from the Arab League, from some of the Gulf countries and major Arab countries like Egypt and Saudi Arabia participated. I also addressed the meeting of the apex body of the Indian Associations in Dubai on the 14th of January.

[The subject of my speech was "Current Developments in India and India's Relations with the Countries of the Gulf."] Discussions in these seminars provided one with insights into the transitions which are taking place in the countries of the Gulf and equally importantly the analyses and assessments of analysts and intellectuals in the area about the theme on which these discussions were held.

Three fundamental political perceptions permeate assessments and prognosis about the political and economic situation in the area. First and foremost, ramifications of the Iranian and Afghan revolutions of 1979 and 1978 remained a factor influencing the evolving political situation. The power structures of the countries of the Gulf are incrementally conscious of the democratic impulses which characterise their respective countries. As a consequence of events in Afghanistan and Iran. Higher levels of education resulting in higher levels of political consciousness about global trends in politics and restructuring of States have created impulses in civil societies in these countries which desire greater participation in governance, and reduction of the role of the ruling families of these countries. What is interesting is that ruling power structures are responsive to these impulses. Processes of sharing power with citizens and subjects has commenced in a gradual manner, though this process may not conform to concepts of western democracies.

Secondly, there is an acknowledgement that extremist militant Islam and its manifestation in terrorist violence is not conducive to the stability, prosperity or well-being of the people of the Gulf countries. This acknowledgements has however generated some tense predicaments in the countries of the Gulf where the clergy and the militant Islamic elements interpret this rational perception as a surrender to the West and are inclined to agitation; a phenomenon which the Governments in the Gulf have to deal with.

An important side effect of these perceptions and extremist religious reaction to them is of all the countries of the Gulf having reservations about the prospects of military action led by the United States against President Saddam Hussain of Iraq. Though countries like Kuwait, Bahrain, and Qatar have reconciled them to the prospects of US force's operating from their countries and their coastal waters, both the general political support and operational cooperation of these countries in relation to the US are reluctant exercises without support among the people of the region.

The third perception and resulting prognosis is that the USA's macro-level politico-strategic objective is to have a long-term hold on, and access to the energy resources of the entire region stretching from Central Asia to the Red Sea. There is a feeling that the US aims at creating power structures in all the countries of the region which would support USA's objectives and strategic interests, and that the autonomy of the Governments of the Gulf, West Asia and Central Asia, to control and manage their enormous energy resources, is sought to be eroded.

The political situation in the Gulf seems subjected to two challenges; First, of sustaining their independence to the maximum extent possible from the framework of US objectives in the region, and secondly, to resolve the contradictions between the semi-feudal authoritarian rule and the democratic impulses in the countries of the area. It is significant to note that one consequence of these turmoil's and tensions is that the Gulf Cooperation Council has not been very active over the last 2 to 3 years when compared to the regional grouping's political activism and economic cooperation during the decade of the 90s of the last century.

My interaction with the leaders of the Indian community in the UAE was much influenced by the large-scale conference of Overseas Indians which was held in Delhi between the 9th and 12th of January. One does not have to describe and emphasise the important role that the Indian community plays in the management of the economies of the countries of the Gulf. There are between 1.5 to two million Indians in the Gulf, a fair segment of them are prominent entrepreneurs and have access to the highest levels of Governments in the countries where they reside. The points of significance which emerged from my discussions with them should be taken note of by the Government and people of India. There was collective pride about India's economic reforms and India's becoming a nuclear weapons power, but there was a feeling that India's pace of economic reforms lacked purposiveness and dynamism. There was both concern and anxiety about the rise of Hindu-Muslim antagonisms in India, under the present coalition government. Events in Gujarat and election results there were viewed with dismay given the Islamic countries in which these Indians are living. Leaders of the Indian community felt that Government of India has not been paying sufficient attention to India's relations with the countries of the Gulf over the last four or five years. The view was expressed that it was because of this lack of high level contacts and the unwillingness to maintain continuity in them which results in the governments in the Gulf countries not reacting promptly to Indian requests regarding repatriation of Indian individuals involved in terrorism and trans-border crimes. The assessment was that there are close linkages between Pakistan and Governments in these countries at the lower administrative levels. Only high level political contacts can neutralize

Pakistani influence.

The assessment was also that Governments of the Gulf at the highest political levels have no excessive inclination to side with Pakistan barring perhaps the Saudi Establishment. Uniform disappointment was expressed about the proceedings of the Pravasi Bharatiya Conference organised by the Government of India in Delhi. The view was expressed that the conference smacked of subservience to North America, Western Europe and England. The grant of dual nationality on a selected basis was strongly criticised. In fact, most of the leaders of the Indian community expressed the view that there was no need for granting dual nationality or Identity cards to persons of Indian origin. It would have been sufficient to liberalise visa facilities to Indians of various categories and to give them economic incentives to participate in the Indian economy. It was also said that the entire exercise was a partisan one, engineered by supporters of the BJP abroad. There was also criticism about the awards given to some of the Indians who came for the conference. They pointed out that many Indians who could claim great achievements and service to India from the Gulf were not taken note of. The majority of awards also went to people living in North America and in Europe. One of the community leaders told me that the whole show was a manifestation of India's submissive colonial psyche.

To get back to the seminars which I went to attend, certain macro-level political assessments expressed by participants from the Gulf are of interest.

- With the end of the cold war, Inter-state equations have become rooted in economic, military and technological factors unrelated to any ideology,
- Religion and ethnicity have replaced ideology as a factor in international politics.
- The effect of globalisation so far has been of a discriminatory division of economic endeavour with the poorer countries playing the role of labour and the richer countries assuming the role of management and controlling instruments of production.
- A lower priority is being given to the objective of social and distributive justice in the world economy.
- Old multi-lateralisms have been replaced by new regionalisms, trans-continental bonding of developing countries has faded away.
- The role of the United Nations has diminished.

- The role of the multi-lateral financial institutions has become more influential.
- Old style military alliances are being replaced by new security arrangements on the basis of regional security consultative mechanisms.
- The authority of the territorial nation-states and the concept of state sovereignty is getting reduced due to the impact of Information Technology and globalisation.
- Plural state structures are under threat by centrifugal forces, both internally and externally.
- Terrorism is a major factor in this phenomenon.
- The world politics is characterized by an intense competition to control technologies and to have access to energy and material resources.
- The United States has emerged as a unipolar centre of power which is sought to be balanced off by various countries by regional groupings and geo-strategic consultative arrangements.
- It may be stated after due assessment that India should re-invigorate bilateral contacts with the countries of the Gulf and make a conscious effort to foster cooperation with the collectivity of the Gulf Cooperation Council.

Iraq-Indian Perceptions and Predicaments

The US-Iraq confrontation, is reaching a crisis point. While the United State's policy pronouncements indicate a determination to launch military operation against Iraq, international public opinion as well as the major States are incrementally opposing the resort to military option because of their assessments regarding the critical consequences of an attack on Iraq. UN Security Council meetings during the second half of March would decide fundamental question regarding the role of the United Nations in dealing with macro-level international crisis.

Latest indications are that France would veto any resolution which authorizes military operations against Iraq. The other two permanent Members of the UN Security Council, Russia and China, are likely to abstain. The United States is finding it difficult to even muster the support of nine out of the 15 members of the Security Council for its military inclinations, though the effort to garner such support continues. Among the non-permanent members, Mexico and Pakistan are also likely to abstain,

President Bush in his public pronouncements between the 8th and 10th of March has announced that US will implement its military policies, even if there is no security council resolution. If this happens, the institutional marginalisation of the UN will become a manifestly confirmed fact.

Leaving aside the larger international implications of a war on Iraq, it would be pertinent to take note of Indian perceptions of the developing situation, the implications of the military action against Iraq on Indian interests and the lines on which India is reacting to the crisis.

Indian perceptions are subject to a complicated dichotomy. Saddam Hussain and his Government have had a record of friendly and cooperative relations with India. The Baath Party regime under him is perceived by large sections of Indian public opinion as secular, modern state. His Government has been one of the very few Islamic governments which have been supportive of India's stand on Jammu and Kashmir. Iraq is a major supplier of oil and energy resources to India. Iraq has also been a market for Indian technology and investments. Till the Gulf War a large numbers of Indians lived is Iraq, enhancing India's foreign exchange earnings. So there is a certain emotional sympathy and support for Saddam Hussain. While this is so, Saddam Hussain's repressive activities against his own citizens over the last decade and more, his launching wars against Iran and Kuwait and his systematic accumulation of all categories of weapons of mass destruction have affected his image and credibility in Indian public opinion. His wars against Iran and Kuwait have particularly contributed to this latter process. Even more pertinent is the fact that despite Saddam Hussain's disclaimers about not having weapons of mass destruction and his questioning the assessments of the Weapons Inspectors Hans Blix and Mohammed Elbaradei, there is sufficient objective evidence about stockpiles of nuclear weapons related material, biological, chemical and missile capabilities of Iraq. There are still about 59 locations widely separated through the Iraqi territory, where he has dispersed and stockpiled such material. His compliance of the stipulations of the UN Security Council resolutions has been selective, gradual and always subject to accelerated pressure. India also feels that he does not seem to be concerned about enormous sufferings the Iraqi people have gone through since the Gulf War and which they are likely to go through if the American military operations take place.

The likelihood is of not a most surgical or conclusive military operation but of a prolonged conflict in which common Iraqis would suffer. This is apart from the destructive consequeneces of military options which Saddam

Hussain may choose in response to the US attack. The military prospects are fraught with dangerous uncertainties. India, therefore, has complex of either choice of standing by Saddam Hussain who has been a friend or joining the mainstream of international action against him for the undoubtedly negative role he has played in de-stabilizing our region over the last two decades.

There is no need to recount the declared and undeclared objectives of the US in launching its military campaign. What is of importance is to assess the implications of direct relevance to India. The war will certainly disrupt energy supplies to India for some time which would negatively impact on all sectors of Indian economy. There may not be a major disruption of work and earnings of Indians living in the Gulf except those living in Iraq. But the ripple effect of critical response from public opinion in Arab countries, particularly in the countries of the Gulf will create tense situation for the large Indian community resident in the region. The impending change of regime in Iraq necessitates India being in a position to establish contacts with the new regime in Iraq and to be able to revive both political and economic relations with the new dispensation in Iraq. This necessity stands acknowledged by the Government of India and the Indian public opinion. Most important of all is the strategic and security implications of a successful military operation by the US against Iraq for India.

One must expect high level resentment among Islamic countries neighbouring India against the US reattaching in and higher levels of international terrorist activity because the networks led by Al Qaeda are still operating. This could subject Jammu and Kashmir in India to higher levels of terrorist attacks. It is to be noted that the national security objectives document issued by the White House in September 2002 clearly states that the US reserves its right to political and military intervention to meet three objective—Elimination of terrorism, elimination of weapons of mass destruction and savageness of military confrontation due to violations of human rights. It is not illogical to speculate that given the continuation of cross border terrorist acts in Jammu and Kashmir, the possession of nuclear weapons by India and Pakistan in the framework of an adversary relationship and the predicament of regarding human rights put forward by Pakistan, the US could generate direct military and political pressure on India and Pakistan. While the pressure on Pakistan could only be on the issue of terrorism, pressure on India would be to agree to a compromise on Kashmir which can be interpreted as the cause of terrorism and possibilities of nuclear confrontation between India and Pakistan, a compromise which could be detrimental to Indian interests.

On the other hand, India being supportive of the acquiescence of the major powers regarding the military option, resulting in a change of regime in Iraq, would ensure India's political and economic interests both regional and global in terms of future dispensations. While it is true that implications in terms of international law and the structuring of an international order based on unilateral superior force would be negative, India has to be realistic. The only feasible option available to India is not to confront the USA but to advise that whatever military action is taken it should be under the umbrella of the Security Council. Secondly, India should convey to the US that India generally understands the logic of US policies but as a friend, India must point out the macro-level institutional, political and economic consequences of unbridled unilateralism.

India should be candid and specific and categorical in cautioning the US about it and must also urge that Indian cooperation in the situation should result in the US safeguarding India's national as well as regional interests. It must also be stressed that if consequent to the Iraq operation, the US or any other country takes an initiative which are detrimental to Indian interests, political, strategic or territorial, India would firmly resist such initiatives.

India and Iran—President Khatami's Visit

President Khatami's visit to Delhi between the 25th and the 29th of January was a significant event not only in Indo-Iranian bilateral relations but also in terms of structuring a framework for regional stability and peace. That President Khatami was invited to become the chief guest at this year's Republic Day functions was a clear signal from India of the high importance that Delhi attaches or its relations with Iran, and its assessment that Iran is a vital player in regional inter-state relations and security arrangements.

President Khatami's visit and high level discussions here have to be assessed in the context of broad trends in Indo-Iranian relations over the last eleven years. India's relations with Iran were in doldrums during the late 70s and 80s of the last century because of the political uncertainties generated by the Iranian Revolution of 1979 and India's stand of the Russian intrusion into Afghanistan (generally supportive of the Russians), the same year. India's ambiguous approach on Saddam Hussain's mis-adventure in Kuwait and the consequent Gulf War contributed to distances between Iran and India. Indo-Iranian relations were revived when a conscious initiative was taken by the Congress Government between 1991 and 1996 to remove past misunderstandings and to develop substantive relations. Interactions between late President Shanker Dayal Sharma and the then Prime Minister, Shri P.V. Narasimha Rao with President Rafsanjani of Iran led to the revival and continuity in political contacts and incremental consolidation of economic relations. This included spheres of technology and information technology. During the decades of the 90s Iran agreed to give India transit facilities through its ports and its territories to the Central Asian Republics.

The only trauma which Indo-Iranian relations underwent in the recent past was the destruction of the Babri Mosque in December 1992 and the consequent Hindu-Muslim riots when a large number of persons of Iranian origin were affected, particularly in Maharashtra. Iran's critical response to these events in India however did not last for any significant length of time. High level Indo-Iranian contacts between 1993 and 1996 overcame the misunderstandings generated by the Babri Mosque incident.

The results of President Khatami's recent visit have to be understood in the context of certain complementarity of interests between Iran and India. First and foremost, Iran is isolated from the mainstream of the international Community since the Revolution of 1979 primarily because of USA's persistent hostility towards the current leadership and dispensation in Iran. So a substantive and feasible working relationship with a major democracy like India helps in reducing, if not eliminating this isolation. Secondly, India is a large potential market for Iran's hydro carbons energy resources. Third, Iran needs a wide range of manufactured and industrial goods as well as technologies and investments from India. Fourth, Iran giving transit trade facilities to India to reach out to Central Asia would benefit Iran also in terms of improving of its ports and transportation infrastructures. India has the second largest Shia Muslim population in the word, perhaps after Iran. So there is cultural and religious involvement animating Iran's policy towards India. Iran shares the concerns of India about a unipolar world dominated by just one power. The complementarity of interests of India in having good and substantive relations with Iran are: Iran is a major Asian power, more particularly, the major Islamic country, contacts with which could contribute to India's relation with other Islamic countries; Given the likelihood of continuing Pakistani hostility towards India, an equation with Iran is obvious balancing factor. Iran could become an important and long-term source of hydro carbon energy resources required by India. Iran is large market for Indian investments, technologies and exports.

Given the unlikelihood of India having access to Central Asia from Pakistan and Afghanistan, in the foreseeable future, Iran is most proximate route though which India can access Central Asian market for trade and a range of economic interactions. Iran is an important geo-strategic entity straddling the Gulf, an area of interest to India both politically and economically.

While this is the matrix of the mutuality of interests which influences the policies of Iran and India towards each other, one has to acknowledge that these potentialities are being realised with very inadequate speed and promptitude. It is obvious that President Khatami's visit was aimed at galvanizing bilateral relations. That India invited President Khatami to be the chief guest at the Republic Day, when Iran remains on the black list of the USA, being described as a member of what President Bush calls "An Axis of Evil" underlines the fact that despite India's desire to have friendly and cooperative relations with the USA, India is not going to compromise on its national interests and its freedom of assessments and options in dealing with important countries of our region. President Khatami was welcomed to India at a critical juncture in regional developments when the United States is poised to attack Iraq, an approach which is opposed by majority of the countries of the world, particularly of the Asian region. The credibility of present power structures of the Gulf has been under challenge due to the moral claims and democratic impulses generated by Iranian Revolution. Whatever isolation or criticisms Iran suffers from, the country is an harbinger of change in West Asia.

President Khatami and his delegation signed a number of agreements during their recent visit to New Delhi. These included agreements to expand economic and commercial relations, arrangements for certain categories of defence cooperation and the expansion of transit facilities from India to Central Asia from the ports of Chabahar and Bandar Abbas. There was not much progress on the possibilities of supply of gas from Iran through a gas pipeline running through Pakistan though the project is still on the drawing boards. Some tribal groups in Baluchistan (Mazaris and Bugtis) destroying gas pipeline in Baluchistan added to the apprehensions and uncertainties which the projected gas pipeline from Iran was being considered.

On the vital issue of Indo-Pakistan relations President Khatami took a detached and correct stand which is a marginal improvement on the generally pro-Pakistan stance which Iran used to take on the Kashmir issue.

On the whole, President Khatami's visit was assessed as an important step in the right direction regarding Indo-Iranian relations. But there is also a feeling that the visit did not result in any major initiative in terms of the potentialities that one anticipated.

What then are the concrete prospects of Indo-Iranian relations generated by interaction between the two countries during 1991-2003. There has been an expansion in Indo-Iranian relations in the economic field. There are distinct possibilities of Indo-Iranian cooperation in the spheres of developing and sharing energy resources and setting up power plants as also in expanding the railway systems of Iran. In the fields of petroleum, oil and fertilisers, Indo-Iran interaction can prove fruitful. Trading links between ports on the west coast of India and Bandar Abbas in Iran and from there through overland route to the Caspian coast and the north-eastern frontiers of Iran could provide opportunities for expanding contacts with the Central Asian Republics, an exercise in which Iran would be equally interested. This interest was manifested in the memorandum of understanding signed between India and Iran between 1992 and 1994.

Having taken note of these positive prospects, we must not under-estimate Iran's pronounced Islamic identity. We must not structure our relations with Iran on any expectation that it would become distant from Pakistan and other Muslim countries due to India's importance in its foreign policy. Iran's relations with other Islamic countries, good or bad, would depend on the manner in which the policies of countries such as Pakistan and Afghanistan and political developments in these countries affect Iranian interests. Subject to these considerations Iran will always remain an important point of interest in India's West Asian policies.

Colin Powell's Security Council Testimony-U.S. on the Brink – How should India React

US Secretary of State Colin Powell made an hour-long presentation of evidence about Iraq's continuing to possess and deploy weapons of mass destruction, to the United Nations Security Council on the morning of 5th of February. His presentation followed the Report of the United Nations Chief Weapons Inspectors Dr. Hans Blix and Dr. Elbaradei to the UN Security Council on the 27th of January. The reports of these two Inspectors on the work done by them since October last, were inconclusive. While stating that Iraq was generally cooperating they said they were not able to come to any definite conclusions about Iraq's culpability or otherwise.

Before assessing the evidence presented by Secretary of State Powell and reactions of the major governments, the situation on the ground as it has evolved over the last six months should be noted, especially because there is clear contradiction between the politico-military postures on the ground adopted by the United States and UK and the declaratory aspect of international policy that Iraq is being given an opportunity to prove its innocence. Developments confirming this contradiction are:

- Even as the Inspectors proceeded for the Inspections, senior government officials including Prime Minister Blair of UK, and US Secretary of State Colin Powell, declared that they would not be inclined to accept the conclusions reached by the UN Inspectors if those conclusions give Iraq a clean chit.
- Though the US–sponsored Inspection and reporting exercise under the umbrella of the Security Council Resolution 1441, was time-bound, accusations continue about Iraq hiding its stockpiles of weapons of mass destruction, keeping them away from their alleged normal places of storage.
- Iraq's denials have been branded as mendacities.
- Even before the first phase of the Inspections were underway President Bush had categorically affirmed that the removal of Saddam Hussain and change of regime in Iraq, are clear policy objectives. US Secretary of State Collin Powell invited Saddam Hussain to go into exile if he wants to save himself.
- President Bush also declared that the United States would use nuclear weapons against Iraq if Saddam Hussain's government uses any weapons of mass destructions against the United States and its allies in the eventuality of a military conflict; since such conflict is on the cards according to the Government of the US, the implications of this warning are clear.
- There has been a steady military build up by the Central Command of the US in the Gulf since late November.
- Forward operational bases have been established in Bahrain, Kuwait and Oman.
- Ships from the USA's 5th and 7th Fleets with enormous striking capacities are located in the Gulf and the northern reaches of the Indian Ocean and the Arabean Sea.
- British forces are part of this build up.

- By end January nearly one hundred thousand western coalition troops stand assembled at what one may call launching points.
- Official sources of the US have confirmed that US Special Forces and Para-military cadres of the Central Intelligence Agency have infiltrated into Northern Iraq, particularly, the Kurdish areas of Iraq.
- Various agencies of the US Government are in negotiation with anti-Saddam Iraqi group in Europe and North to establish an alternative government after Saddam Hussain's overthrow. There are even reports of President Bush considering a panel of senior US military officials out of whom the intention is to choose a US military Governor General of Iraq to manage the interim phase after the defeat of Saddam Hussain. The model and time-frame for this interim arrangement is to be patterned on the arrangements made in Japan after Japan's defeat in the Second World War, according to some think-tanks.

Back-room planners of the US Government are reportedly considering the option of bifurcation of Iraq and if necessary trifurcation of the country between areas inhabited by the Kurds, Sunnis and Shias.

While West European countries generally endorse the UN Resolution sanctioning Inspections and possible punitive action against Iraq, two major European Powers, France and Germany, are advocates of restraint before adopting the military option.

Meanwhile, Saddam Hussain remains firm in his denials about having nuclear weapons. He has rejected suggestions that he relinquish power and go into exile. In his public pronouncements since the middle of December, he has affirmed his determination to respond to any military operation against Iraq firmly.

It is in this context that one makes an assessment of the evidence presented by Colin Powell to the UN Security Council on Wednesday, 5th February. The evidence can be summed up as follows:

- Satellite and clandestine photographs of chemical and biological weapons, storage site with some equipment was shown. Photographs of metal tubes which were utilized to engineer gas centrifuges were in Iraq's possession.
- Iraq continues to have large stockpiles of chemical and biological weapons which remain in its possession after the Gulf War. These stockpiles were not destroyed by the Iraqis. Saddam Hussain refuses to give credible information about the whereabouts of these toxic

weapons. Saddam Hussain has not given up his nuclear weaponisation programme. He continues to clandestinely collect, the necessary raw material and equipment for this purpose (about which some more photographs were shown).

- Saddam Hussain has links with Al Qaeda since the mid-90s. Iraq with Saddam's support is home to radical Islamic group Ansar-a- Islam led by one Mullah Krekar. This group has links with Al Qaeda through a senior member of the Al Qaeda Abu Musah Zarqawi. Zarqawi has been a frequent visitor to Iraq to orchestrate terrorist violence.
- Saddam Hussain's Human Rights record is horrific and unacceptable. His political and military strategy in relation to Iraq's neighbours includes unhesitating use of weapons of mass destruction, weapons which he used against his own people in the past.

Powell stated that the sources of all this evidence are – high altitude satellites and airborne photography (signal intelligence), human intelligence based on information given by defecting Iraqi civil and military officers and scientists, some clandestine interviews and intercepted telephone and other category of messages.

The overall, reaction of the Member of the Security Council was that the evidence presented by Colin Powell was mainly circumstantial. There is no way in which the timing of the satellite photographs and images, or the communication intercepts could by determined, objectively. There was unanimity in the views of the three out of the five Permanent Member of the Security Council, China, Russia and France, that the Inspectors should be given further adequate time to examine the accuracy of the evidence presented by Colin Powell and to confront Saddam Hussain with this evidence. They also agreed that any action against Iraq, should be within the framework of the United Nations, and that the military option should be the last resort. Powell however indicated that the next Report from Hans Blix and Elbaradei is due on the 14th of February after which US would be inclined to take action, with or without support from the international community. This is a serious prospect.

India's reactions should be based on two considerations. First, how does the impending attack on Iraq affect Indian interests and regional politics. Second, what are the implications of this attack for the world order which is in the process of being re-fashioned under the leadership of the United States of America. First and foremost, unilateral military action against Iraq (even under the fig leaf of UN support, etc), under the US leadership is not going to be a positive development. The question, however is whether categorically opposing the US would prevent the prospect and how would this opposition affect Indo-US relations.

India's opposition cannot be preventive. Such opposition can however natively impact on India's relations with US, given the expanding economic, commercial, technological and even defence and political content of Indo-US relations, it would not be politic to confront the US in this matter. Whatever the past record of our positive relations with Saddam Hussain, it cannot be denied that Saddam Hussain has been a violent and de-stabilising factor in regional politics. His removal is more or less inevitable even if it takes some time. India should prepare the ground to have a good equation with the future dispensation in Iraq. The new regime in Iraq would be opposed to religious, extremism and terrorist violence.

A prospective working relationship with such a regime would serve India's interests in context of our concerns about religious extremism and violence. There would be temporary dislocation for the Indians working in Iraq and oil supplies from Iraq but things could come back to normal within six moths or a year, of the intended anti-Saddam Hussain campaign. In the interim, India can resort to purchasing energy requirements from international market.

There would be agitation and criticism from the Muslim citizens of India against the US military campaign. The campaign will also polarise international politics at the peoples level between Muslims and non-Muslims which could be a long-term destabilising influence. On balance therefore, India's stand should be practical and rooted in, recognized principles of international law. India could make the following points: (1) The latest evidence given by Powell merits detailed scrutiny and assessment; UN Weapons Inspectors should therefore be given sufficient time to verify the evidence and take necessary remedial action; (2) The military option should be the last resort. The aim should be to resolve the issue politically; (3) India should emphasise that the military option will primarily cause sufferings to the people of Iraq and not the Saddam regime; (4) It should be further underlined that military campaign will generate long-term antagonisms between Muslims and non-Muslims in the international community which must be avoided; (5) Whatever action is taken should be within the framework of the United Nations. Further steps should be considered by the Security Council only after receiving the Inspector's report and giving it due consideration; (6) It must be pointed out that whatever the immediate rationale and justification for a military campaign, it will create a dangerous precedent of unilateral and intrusive military policies questioning the sovereignty of nation-states; (7) Such a campaign will create a dangerous precedent in interstate relations, marginalising the UN, eroding the stability of national governments which may not be acceptable to one great power or the other, with important powers arrogating to themselves the right to determine the political dispensation and economic management of weaker countries. These should be basic considerations in coping with the evolving predicament of Iraq and the polices of the USA; (8) Our approach need not be confrontationist against the USA, but it should remain firm about the basic principles of international law and interstate relations.

Worldly Wise

Prime Minister Atal Bihari Vajpayee's three-nation tour of Germany, Russia and France in the last week of May has significance beyond discussions on specific issues which he held with the heads of State he met. The significance lies in the context of trends in international politics at this juncture. The significance also lies in the fact that Vajpayee is leading his coalition in the next general elections.

More immediate in the international context is the unilateralism of the US managing world affairs. The US-led campaign against terrorism has reached a watershed with the removal of Saddam Hussein's regime in Iraq and America's military presence in that country. This unilateralism has generated both concern and resentment among other major powers.

The situation is compounded by the fact that while the US has been militarily successful in Afghanistan and Iraq, it has not found it easy to stabilize the domestic political dispensation in these countries. The irony is that the peoples whom the US liberated from oppressive regimes are becoming increasingly resentful of American presence in Iraq and Afghanistan.

The fate of the Palestinian people hangs in balance with important powers trying to marginalise Yasser Arafat from the leadership of the Palestinian Authority.

The UN stands marginalized in dealing with crises and conflict situations due to some deliberate policy decisions taken by the US particularly since November last. There are fissures between the US and its West European allies on the management of European and global security. While the Europeans desire to move to more autonomous selective European security mechanism, the US has reservations about this move. There are indications that Washington may take intrusive political and diplomatic steps to bring about regime changes in Syria, Iran and Saudi Arabia. This has generated alarm and concern among Asian countries.

Here are some facts which lend credence to this alarm:

- Since October 2001, the US military presence has increased in India's neighbourhood.
- Bahrain, Qatar, Pakistan, Afghanistan, Iraq, Uzbekistan, Kazakistan and the Philippines.
- The US is showing greater political and strategic interest in Nepal and Bangladesh.
- India and Pakistan have taken tentative steps to resume a dialogue under gentle US pressure, regardless of denials of such pressure by the Indian government.

Out of the three countries visited by Vajpayee, his discussions with German Chancellor Gerhard Schroeder was the only substantive bilateral exercise. Meetings with Russian President Vladimir Putin, Chinese President Hu Jintao as well as the brief conversation with American President George Bush were influenced by the contextual trends mentioned above. The visit to St Petersburg was essentially for the public celebration of the city's 300th anniversary. The visit to Evian in France was to participate in the dialogue which French President Jacques Chirac organised side by side with the G-8 summit with a number of important African, Asian and Latin American countries, a dialogue which focused on macro-level global economic and security issues.

In cosmetic terms India's importance in global affairs was acknowledged by its inclusion in the list of countries invited to the G-8 summit, as well as Vajpayee being seated at a head table at the State banquet at St Petersburg alongside President Bush. Presidents of Russia and France signalled the importance they attach to India by these gestures. But this should not result in any illusion that India has arrived as a member of the Big League. It is India's potential that was given recognition, a potential that India has to fulfill in terms of its domestic and international performance.

The objectives of Vajpayee's visit and results of his discussions could be summed up as follows:

Vajpayee desired an assessment of reactions of leaders whom he met to the trends in international politics. It is significant that discussions were with the three major leaders of Europe – Russia, Germany and France -who have concerns about the emerging unipolarity in international politics, a concern which India shares. The possibility of India cooperating with these major powers to balance the US's unipolar influence without confronting Washington was an unarticulated objective.

Vajpayee desired to garner international support for the initiative that he has taken to normalize relations with Pakistan. He got such support in great measure. One, however, wishes that he had not made individual pleas to Chancellor Schroeder and President Bush to ask President Pervez Musharraf to stop cross-border terrorism. An important power like India does not have to plead in this matter. It would have been sufficient for India to mention its continuing concern about cross-border terrorism and to say India would be taking decisive action against the phenomenon, leaving it to the foreign leaders to tell Musharraf what they wanted, consistent with their own declared policies against international terrorism.

Nevertheless Vajpayee successfully utilized the opportunity to brief these leaders on India's Pakistan policies. His interpretations and advocacies were strengthened by the support he has got from major Indian political parties.

Vajpayee's clear articulation of India's views supporting the Kyoto Convention and on the shortcomings in the implementation of commitments underpinning the WTO agreements were timely and relevant.

External Affairs Minister Yashwant Sinha and Commerce Minister Arun Jaitley were on the Prime Minister's delegation. So were Principal Secretary to the PM Brajesh Mishra and Foreign Secretary Kanwal Sibal. It is logical to presume that these senior officers must have followed up prime minister discussions with their counterparts in the delegations at Berlin, St Petersburg and Evian.

This cycle of high-level discussions will be completed when Vajpayee visits Beijing on June 22. His preliminary meeting with President Hu in Moscow has prepared the ground. The briefing on these discussions from the Indian side again showed India's pathological anxiety to assert self-importance. The Indian side proceeded to aver that President Hu told Vajpayee that he attaches the highest importance to China's relations with India. Would it not have been better if the Chinese had mentioned this in their press briefings? If India is self-assured as an important power, it does need to mention assessments given by foreign leaders about its importance. Reticence rather than self- congratulatory assessments would have been better.

In overall terms, Vajpayee's recent tour and his impending visit to China are irrportant strategic and diplomatic initiatives to make a first-hand assessment of the developing international situation and to brief the leader of the major powers about the orientations of India's foreign and security policies. The visit also has implications in terms of domestic politics in that Vajpayee can claim a measured and planned approach in the structuring of India's foreign policy and its equations with important powers with domestic Indian audience.

Deputy Prime Minister L.K. Advani's visit to Washington will be an exercise in emphasizing to President Bush that while India has differences of opinion about a unipolar world with the US, India's approach is not confrontationist but animated by a conviction that relations with the US are an important factor in its foreign policy.

Factors which would determine the success or otherwise of this diplomatic exercise would include India keeping in mind the fact that despite differences with the US, France, Germany, Russia and China, it attached high importance to their relations with Washington. Second, India-US relations remaining stable and positive while India's overtures to these powers are nurtured as a calibrated foreign policy effort. A positive follow-through on the initiative to normalize relations with Pakistan would be a factor increasing India's credibility in the international community.

Moving forward in relations with China in a practical manner would be another factor that would strengthen India's position in global equations. These are the complex challenges which India has to cope with as a follow –up of Vajpayee's visit.

India's Role in Peace—making in Iraq—Complex Prospects

The US Government had asked the Government of India to depute a largish Indian military unit (approximately one Division), to Iraq to restore law and order. India's Cabinet Committee on Security discussed the proposal in the beginning of June and could not come to an agreement because non-BJP members of the coalition in the Cabinet Committee were opposed to the deployment of Indian troops in Iraq. The decision was deferred pending Deputy Prime Minister L.K. Advani's scheduled visit to the US between the 8th to the 17th of June.

US Defence Secretary Donald Rumsfeld and President George Bush repeated the request to Advani and implied that India's response to the US request would be a fairly substantive test of how meanigful an equation India wishes to have with the United States. Defence Secretary Rumsfeld decided to send a military mission led by Assistant Defence Secretary Rodman to Delhi on the 16th of June to give required clarifications about the conditions which would govern the deployment of Indian troops in Iraq. The team arrived in Delhi on 16th of June and has given clarifications. The Government of India is examining these and has raised three specific points for clarification. What would bc the Command Structure under which Indian troops would be functioning in Iraq; what is the likelihood of a legitimate and effective interim Iraqi Government coming into being in Iraq, and thirdly, what would be the role of the UN in overseeing activities carried out to restore peace in Iraq.

In the meanwhile, the main opposition party in India, Congress, in a letter to the Government on the 5th of June (from Mrs. Sonia Gandhi) objected to Indian troops being deployed in Iraq without the UN Umbrella. This was before Advani's departure to the US, and before the Pentagon team came to Delhi. Mrs. Sonia Gandhi met Prime Minister Vajpayee on 15th of June to re-examine Congress Party's policy orientations in the light of these developments and indicated that Congress's views, would be finalised only after the Government of India consults the Congress Party and other political parties after receiving clarifications from the Defence team sent by the United States. Mrs. Sonia Gandhi also suggested that India should finalise its decision on the issue in consultation with other Asian countries, neighbours of Iraq.

Since this meeting between Vajpayee and Mrs. Sonia Gandhi, the Government has announced that a final decision about deployment of Indian troops in Iraq and details thereof would be announced only after Mr. Vajpayee's return from his visit to China. A meeting of the Cabinet Committee on Security held on the 21st of June has left the decision to the Prime Minister.

There are reports that since 15th of June, the armed forces headquarters have been asked to initiate preparations for sending of one Division of Indian troops with requisite armour and air support as well as for deputing two field Hospitals with necessary equipment and medical personnel. These initial steps were the result of clarifications given by Assistant Secretary of Defence of the USA Mr. Rodman to the Government of India on the 16th and 17th of June in New Delhi.

Though details of the US clarifications have not been made public, indications are that US will deploy Indian troops in different areas of Iraq, subject to Indian consent. Secondly, Indian personnel will be functioning under the control of Indian Commanding Officers. Third, the seniormost

Indian Commander may be a member of the Co-ordinating Committee of Security and Military Affairs in Iraq.

Parallely, while these assurances are being considered adequate by the BJP, the NDA Govt has taken other steps to follow through the assurances given that the final decision will be based on discussions with Iraq's neighbours and on the basis of consultations within the country leading to a national consensus. Senior officials of the Ministry of External Affairs have proceeded to Jordan, perhaps even to Syria and Iraq, for consultations. The visit to Iraq would be to see if an invitation for Indian troops could be obtained from Iraq's interim authority which is being put in place. Iran and countries of the Gulf are being consulted through the diplomatic channels. N.P. Pakistan's promptly agreeing to send its troops to Iraq, responding to the US initiation, has increased BJP's inclinations to send Indian troops. The decision will be announced one way or the other, by the end of June or the first week of July. Nevertheless, it is necessary to take note of certain considerations which should influence Government of India's decision in this matter.

Public opinion in India views the issues related to deputing of Indian troops in Iraq as a matter of national concern. Above party politics, and that whatever decision is taken by India should be based on national consensus.

People of India wish to emphasise that they are not opposed to India cooperating with authorities and entities in Iraq, trying to restore security, stability and economic well-being of the people of Iraq.

Congress's opposition to sending of Indian troops to Iraq is based on the fact of the deployment being without any UN umbrella of the UN. Other reasons for this approach are : a majority of people of Iraq are resentful of the American military presence : no major power apart from the USA is sending troops for "peace-making operations" in Iraq; the terms of reference under which Indian troops will be deployed are not clear; Indian public opinion has general reservations about deployment of Indian troops in that country; the US-led Interim Authority in Iraq may delegate the controversial aspects of work related to maintenance of law and order to Indian troops which would subject India to criticism from the people of Iraq.

The Parliament and Indian people would like to be fully informed about these framework and terms of reference: details of the command and control structure of possible Indian troops deployment; who would the commanders of the Indian troops report to; where in Iraq would the Indian troops be deployed; the extent of autonomy and freedom of action that Indian troops will have in discharging their functions.

Would the Indian troops be engaged in "peace-making", coercive action or would they be engaged in "peace-keeping" tasks.

What is the Prime Minister's assessment of the US responding positively to India's broader regional political, security, and economic interests. What would be the implications against Indian interests if India does not send troops to Iraq. What is the Government of India's interpretation of UN Security Council Resolution 1483 legitimising US presence in Iraq. Does this Resolution provide any scope for a representative of the UN to play an overall supervisory or advisory role about managing the affairs of Iraq. What is the Government of India's assessment of reaction of Islamic countries about deployment of foreign troops in Iraq? How would it affect India's relations with these countries ?

There is general acknowledgement of high importance of India's relations with the USA but policy decisions on this issue and other such issues have to be primarily based on considerations of India's supreme national interests and the country's international credibility.

What has happened in Iraq in the meanwhile is tragic and will remain a matter of concern in the foreseeable future. US Government has had to undertake an extensive replacement future of personnel whom they had originally designated to take up interim authority in Iraq. Lt General J Gardner because of his previous role in the Middle East found himself unacceptable as the Chief Administrator. He has been replaced by Mr. Paul Bremer, a career diplomat. There have already been changes in American officials down the line with a larger number of civilian officers being posted in Iraq. US Government's attempt at establishing a credible interim government in Iraq has not succeeded so far. None of the political figures projected as possible heads of Iraqi (Challabi Pellachi, etc) are acceptable to Iraqi people. Shia population under the leadership of Shiite clergy is expressing incremental opposition to the US and western military presence in the country. Sunnis and Kurds have their own reasons for being disappointed with the political dispensation orchestrated by the US. The US Government has not been able to find an 'Iraqi Karzai' on the lines of which it succeeded in Afghanistan.

To compound all this, there are reports regarding the CIA's assessment that Saddam Hussain and his two sons are still alive and still in hiding in greater metropolitan Baghdad, and that they are being safeguarded by an underground anti-US militant movement. Prospects, therefore, are of political uncertainty and internal instability for some months to come.

India's decision on this issues has to be taken with caution and deliberation. It is important to keep in mind that there is growing resentment among the people of Iraq, over the manner in which US is managing affairs in that country since the removal of Saddam Hussain. India should not find itself in a position where its credibility with the people of Iraq stands diminished.

India can play an important role in reviving the education system of Iraq, regarding which India has decades of experience of assisting Iraq. Wherever possible or feasible, India can contribute to reviving the infra-structural spheres of Iraq's social and economic development programmes. The guiding principle for India's involvement in the reconstruction and rehabilitation of Iraq should be participation in these spheres which would directly benefit the people of Iraq, taking into account their sensitivities and aspirations resulting from the trauma of war.

Does a Pre-emptive Indian Strike on Pakistan Make Sense

Government of India's pronouncements on the doctrine of pre-emptive strikes against Pakistan is getting cariouser and cariouser. External Affairs Minister Yashwant Sinha quoting the Iraqi precedent, asserted more than once in the first fortnight of April that there is justification for India to take pre-emptive action against Pakistan as sponsor of cross-border terrorism. Defence Minister George Fernandes, first endorsed Sinha's statements and later on expressed the view that what Sinha said was not a policy statement or a formal declaration of intent by the Government. Fernandes went to the extent of saying that it was a casual remark by the Foreign Minister. Prime Minister Vajpayee in a public statement in Sikkim around the same time said that India does not believe in military solutions to disputes but India's policy is to find solutions through peaceful negotiations. Then there is the Deputy Prime Minister L.K. Advani who talked earlier more than once about right of reprisals and right of hot pursuit.

This reflects a kind of confusing and irrational impulsiveness which shows lack of gravitas on matters of high policy in the Government of India. The US has flatly questioned the Indian rationale for pre-emptive strikes. Secretary of State Colin Powell pronouncing that no parallels can be drawn between the situation in Iraq and the Indo-Pakistan face off on the Kashmir issue. Pakistan, as expected, has threatened not just firm but aggressive retaliation. Addressing a Formation Commanders, meeting on 8th April President Musharraf has said Pakistan's defences are impregnable. Pakistan Foreign Minister Khurshid Mehmood Kasuri went one step ahead by saying that India should not indulge in mis-adventures because Pakistan's missiles capacities are far superior to those of India.

The first point to be made is that excepting in exceptional cases no country announces its intentions of undertaking pre-emptive strikes, the rights of reprisals or hot pursuit in advance. The key factor in these exercises is surprise, speed and decisiveness. Secondly, before indulging in such assertiveness there should be careful assessment whether India has the capacity to undertake pre-emptive strikes without doing too much damage to itself. Thirdly, given the massive military presence of US in Pakistan, in the Gulf and in Iraq, as well as on the northern edges of the Arabian Sea and the Gulf, will the United States countenance such a strike against Pakistan? Which is considered an important ally in the current US operational strategies in the region.

Three further questions arise: can the US attack on Iraq be a model for India and Pakistan, secondly, to what extent can India's pre-emptive strike across the Line of Control be tolerated by Pakistan before it resorts to nuclear weapons. Third, what does India hope to gain by such military moves with its attendant risks. US attack on Iraq cannot be a precedent or model for India, primarily because the asymmetry in the military power equations between Iraq and USA. As such, USA has overwhelming technological operational and human resources superiority over the military resources of Iraq in all these respects. Secondly, Saddam Hussain was generally considered a perniciously violent influence in regional politics by countries of the region as well as by the important powers. Third, though there was no consensus on the manner in which the military operations were launched by the USA against Iraq, there was general agreement that Saddam Hussain's regime should be removed from authority. Fourth, no individual country or a group of countries, has the capacity or the political will to prevent the USA from carrying out its decisions on the ground notwithstanding political and diplomatic moves made through the United Nations to restrain the USA. Saddam Hussain's regime did not have the spontaneous or genuine support of the Iraqi people. Lastly, the Bush Administration had the will and resources to carry through its decisions regardless of objections from the national public opinion and world public opinion.

The Indian predicament is exactly the opposite of all the points underpinning and supporting the US attack on Iraq. The rationale of the US attack on Iraq may conform to India's predicaments and concerns vis-a-vis Pakistan, but it is not an operational model which India can follow.

As far as the threshhold up to which India crossing the Line of Control in pre-emptive military action without its resulting in nuclear war is concerned, prospects are not definable. They are both uncertain and unpredictable. Musharraf has stated that any Indian security forces move across the Line of Control will be considered sufficient justification for him to initiate nuclear retaliation. This is an exercise in psychological warfare and pre-emptive politico-diplomatic sabre-rattling. There is sizeable US military presence in the region, including Afghanistan and in Pakistan. If the Indian pre-emptive action across the LOC is in consequence of a major act of violence by Pakistan-sponsored terrorist, and if the operation is a brief surgical operation, and has the advantage of surprise without threatening Pakistani territory proper, it is plausible and reasonable to expect that the US will prevent Pakistan from getting into nuclear mode while parallely preventing India from larger military operations or nuclear weapons postures. If the suggested pre-emptive military action by India is prolonged and threatens the Government of Pakistan, the conflict can escalate into a nuclear confrontation despite the US military presence and pressure in our region.

The next question is what can India hope to gain from such an adventure given the attendent risks? A limited pre-emptive response to Pakistan-sponsored terrorism cannot and should not be described as an adventure. This is a long delayed and necessary response which India should have undertaken more than once after the Kargil conflict. If a short pre-emptive military operation is undertaken with careful planning and without our penchant for indulging in advance publicity and posturing, the gains could be :

- A clear signal to Pakistan that India will retaliate against the source of terrorist violence against the country.
- Secondly, it will affirm both our realisation and determination that India has to fight its own battles against terrorism without presuming on the participation or support by USA or other countries. This will result in the US not taking India for granted as a country which will abide by US advice even when its own interests are seriously threatened.

- Fourth, it could not only bring down levels of terrorism but reduce Pakistani support to such terrorist acts.

- The civilian population on the other side of the Line of Control in Pakistan occupied Kashmir will be less willing to support terrorists being launched from their side of the border against India.

- If India indulges in pre-emptive action, two risks are :

- Lose of support and some levels of cooperation with the US for a brief period, an attitude which will be shared by other countries.

The second more serious risk is a nuclear war. But that can be avoided if our pre-emptive actions are limited and brief in their time-frame.

If India deems it necessary to take pe-emptive action, it need not be linked to the US operations in Iraq. It should be an autonomous exercise based on ground realities and governed by careful and measured calculations.

Iraq-Responding to the Post-war Prospects from the Indian Perspective

The post-war re-organisation process of Iraq has commenced. US authorities organised a meeting on the 15th of April near Nasiriya under the Chairmanship of Lt. General J. Garner with various tribal leaders and Iraqi groups which were opposed to Saddam Hussain. If the US thought that there would be a spontaneous unity in Iraqi response to forge a political dispensation under US guidance, the expectation was premature. Representatives of major Shia groups from Southern Iraq boycotted the Nasiriya meeting. There is no agreement yet on who among the Iraqis should lead the new Iraqi Government. Differences continue between the US and major West European powers about the UN role for overseeing the re-construction and development of Iraq. Even Britain is not entirely in agreement with the US about the US wanting to give the United Nations only a secondary role in post-war economic management of Iraq. The conference of Arab Foreign Ministers in Doha in the second week of April, has expressed unhappiness about US unilaterally continuing in the post-war planning regarding Iraq. A suggestion from US that instead of the United Nations, the security back up for the new regime in Iraq should be provided by NATO has been opposed by France and Germany.

Prospects in Iraq therefore seem to be fraught with uncertainties. What could be Indian interests and objectives in the foreseeable future in this context ? First and foremost Iraq's territorial integrity should remain inviolate. Tentative suggestions about Iraq being politically re-organised as a "confederational democracy" portend a division of Iraq on ethno-religious lines, generating de-stabilising forces in the Gulf and West Asia. Second, Iraq's post-war government should be run by Iraqis themselves and not under the tutelage of any foreign power or powers. Third, reconstruction and economic revival of Iraq should be undertaken under the umbrella of the United Nations. Fourth, Iraq should not become (to the extent possible), an instrumentality for pure furtherance of US strategic policies in West Asia and the Gulf. An international collectivity and consensus has to be attempted to prevent this prospect. Fifth, project contracts and other economic agreements between India and other countries, on the one hand and the previous Iraqi government, on the other should be respected. The successor regime in Iraq should fulfil past obligations. This includes continuation of Indian projects and the repayment of dues to India from Iraq which amount to nearly two billion dollars. The assertive US presence in Iraq and other parts of West Asia should not result in a one-sided solution to the Palestinian problem favouring Israel. The question is how far the dominance of the US in the power equations in the West Asian region will allow these objectives to be met. This is going to be a difficult predicament because objectives of the US do not entirely mesh in with those detailed above. It is therefore relevant to examine prospects in the near future in the larger context of US policy orientations.

There are motivations beyond the logic articulated by President Bush in justification of his decision to go to war. These are inherent in the National Security Objectives Document issued by the White House in September, 2002. It asserts that world's stability, respect for democracy and human rights and an equitable economic order is dependent on the US retaining the supreme and powerful position in the international community. The US reserve the right to take pre-emptive and interventionist political and military action against the phenomenon of possession of nuclear weapons, existence of terrorism, real or potential, and disrespect for human rights and democracy, or possibility of nuclear confrontation due to inter-state disputes. (This could be an argument for US intervention in Kashmir dispute between India and Pakistan within the above terms of reference). The National Security Documents issued by the US since 1992 have repeatedly emphasised that USA's supreme international position depends on controlling the development and dissemination of sophisticated technologies, unhindered access to world's natural resources, particularly, energy resources and USA ensuring that no other country in the world emerges as a competing power against the USA.

This includes preventing the rise of any regional power which may potentially opposed US policies and interests.

More specific and unarticulated policy objectives are to have geo-political control of oil and natural gas resources stretching practically from Kazakhastan to Saudi Arabia. Secondly, to have enhanced strategic presence in the Gulf and West Asia by having influence in Afghanistan and Iran, general dominance of Central Asian countries and the Gulf, would be ensured. Similarly, American influence in Iraq will enable the United States to act against Iran, and if necessary, against Syria, and against militant terrorist groups operating in the Middle East politico-strategic dimensions of West Asia is linked to US plans and policies to stabilise the Middle East, and impose some kind of solution of the Palestinian issue, safeguarding Israel's interests.

It is pertinent to note that US mentions India as a possible significant strategic ally for international security and stability. In this context, a practical approach for India would be not to oppose the USA in its Iraq policies because it will not succeed and it will unnecessarily generate misunderstanding in the Indo-US relations which are of importance for India, at this stage. Equally important for India is to be in a position to have good working relations with new political dispensation which could come about in Iraq. This is important for obvious political and economic reasons in terms of countering militancy and terrorism and having access to longer-term energy supplies. This should, however, not make us ignore profoundly important precedents which are going to be established as a result of US actions.

The US assuming the right to bring about regime changes negates the right of peoples of different countries to decide on their own governments. The US serving the right to a pre-emptive action against weapons and defense capacities of foreign governments negates the fundamental sovereign right of nation-states to decide on their own defence and military capacities. US institutionally negating UN role in this case relegates the US to being just a debating society. Shorn of the responsibilities of ensuring or orchestrating collective international peace and conflict resolution. This is not just PAX Americana but the prospects are of a US Imperium—a prospect looked upon with concern by important countries like France, Germany, Russia, China and Iran. The remedy does not lie in confronting the US but to establish broad political and strategic understanding with these powers to temper the new hegemony in making.

INDO-PAK SCENARIO

8

Agra Summit and Musharraf

The Pakistani Approach to the Agra Summit

The Vajpayee-Musharraf summit at Agra would be coming to an end as this article is published. The results of the summit would be known only on Monday, the 16th of July. Whatever the results, they will have to be understood by us in India in the context of attitudes and policy orientations with which President Musharraf arrived in Delhi on 14th of July. So one focuses on providing a contextual analysis of Pakistani policies immediately preceding the summit which will remain relevant regardless of the results of the summit. First and foremost, certain presumptions and predications were articulated in the media about Pakistan responding to the Indian invitation which are not entirely valid. These predications were, Musharraf is coming to India because Pakistan is economically on the verge of bankruptcy and serious political instability. Second that after two years in power, he is genuinely interested in finding a practical compromise on the Kashmir issue and in normal relations with India in other spheres. This second predication is based on the view that Pervez Musharraf thinks that his credibility will increase if he comes to an agreement with India on Kashmir in a manner which is acceptable to Pakistan.

While it is true that Pakistan is in some economic difficulty, it does not seem to be a major impelling factor pushing Musharraf to the summit which is taking place now. Granted that Pakistan's GDP has come down from \$62.2 billion in 1998 to a little over \$50 billion in the year 2000, granted that 74 per cent of Pakistan's budget is frittered away in debt servicing and defence expenditure, true that Pakistan's industrial production and export have declined and that it's foreign exchange reserves stand at on all-time low of only \$1.5 billion or so, but the fact remains that Pakistan is sustaining an annual growth at the rate of 4 per cent per annum. It is generally self-sufficient in food, it can presume a continuing energy supply from the Gulf countries, particularly Saudi Arabia due to the Islamic connection. The most fundamental fact is that the United States and western democracies would do their utmost to prevent Pakistan from economic disintegration when the chips are down. Musharraf's assuming the Presidency just before coming to the summit in a manner underlines the fact that he was confident enough about support from all important segments of the Pakistani establishment and public opinion. Otherwise, he would not have taken the decision to elevate himself to the Presidency of the country. The Islam-pasand parties and pubic opinion in general have endorsed his coming to Delhi as shown in his consultation with these entities on the 24th of June because he has told them that his objective is to persuade India to compromise on Kashmir within the framework of Pakistani objectives. He has conveyed the méssage that this is what his expectation is.

Before coming to the governmental and pubic responses from Pakistan which preceded the summit, it is relevant to mention the initiatives taken by Vajpayee signalling its genuine desire to bring Indo-Pakistan relations back on track towards normalisation and cooperation. Between the 1st and 12th of July, India announced a series of unilateral initiatives. India offered 20 scholarships to Pakistani students to come and study in India in subjects of their choice including science and technology. India also offered to implement the provisions of the Indo-Pakistan cultural agreement signed in July 1989 to enhance people to people contacts. India announced that it will not capture Pakistani fishermen who stray into territorial waters of India during their fishing operations. India also announced a decision to release such Pakistani fishermen in Indian custody. India announced its decision to expand bilateral trade with Pakistan within the framework of the MFN status which India has granted to Pakistan several years ago subject to Pakistan reciprocating the gesture. India announced that it is liberalising its visa regime for Pakistani nationals to extend them greater facilities to visit India not only across the international frontier but also across the Line of Control in Kashmir. Government of India announced that visa issuing offices would be opened at designated points on the Line of control in Jammu and Kashmir and on the international frontier in Rajasthan and Punjab so that Pakistanis who desire to visit India or Kashmiris from Pakistan-held Kashmir desiring to visit Jammu and Kashmir do not have to go to Islamabad to get visa. It was clarified that India has taken the initiative despite possible adverse security considerations, to affirm India's desire to encourage people to people contacts and normal interaction between the two countries.

Prime Minister instructed the Director General Military Operations of India to proceed to Islamabad to have discussions with his Pakistani counterparts on expanding mutual Confidence Building Measures, including CBNs related to the nuclear weaponisation of India and Pakistan. India has also indicated its willingness to move forward in implementing agreements which have been reached on issues like Siachen, completion of the Wullar Barrage (Tulbul Navigation Project), delineating the boundary at Sir Creek, etc, taking into account developments after 1994. India's motivation in announcing these unilateral gestures was to convey two signals. First, that India is serious about finding a negotiated settlement of the Kashmir issue in its internal dimensions. That is why India announced unilateral ceasefires, a willingness to have discussions with all Kashmiri groups and appointed Mr. K.C. Pant as special representative of the Government to conduct these discussions. The unilateral initiatives announced in relation to Pakistan as detailed above were a continuation of this process conveying a signal that India aims at doing whatever is necessary to create an environment conducive to a rational discussion on Kashmir and other issues with Pakistan.

The Pakistani response to these moves were deliberately negative. First and foremost, there was no positive reciprocal response to the specific unilateral initiatives detailed above. In fact, the Pakistani foreign office reacted to the initiatives by saying that these gestures were a calculated attempt by India to shift the focus of the Agra summit away from the Kashmir issue. Musharraf himself repeatedly harped on the point in his interviews that he is coming to the summit to discuss only the Kashmir issue and to find a solution within the framework of the aims of Pakistan. He further announced that changing the status of Jammu and Kashmir is "the unfinished part of the partition". He went on to say that all other issues affecting Indo-Pakistan relations can be addressed only after a solution is found to the Kashmir issue from Pakistan's point of view, though he has no objection in discussing those issues with Prime Minister Vajpayee. The most important point he made was that his objective is to persuade India to find solution to the Kashmir problem within a definite time-frame. (which in fact sounds like an ultimatum to India). When queried by senior Indian journalists about what is the solution to Kashmir that he has in mind, he said that only acceptable solution would be to hold a plebiscite or a referendum in Jammu and Kashmir on the basis of the UN Resolutions of 1947/1948. He also conveyed to the Hurriyat in a formal communication that Pakistan would continue to give diplomatic, moral and political support in their struggle for self-determination of the people of Jammu and Kashmir. In other words, Pakistan would continue to support the secessionist movement by employing mercenaries, continuing cross-border terrorism and destabilising Jammu and Kashmir.

Pakistan's Commerce Minister Mr. Razak Daud who told a FICCI delegation from India only in June that he would like Indo-Pak economic cooperation to expand stated in the second week of July that no expansion of economic relations or giving India MFN status would be possible unless the Kashmir issue is resolved. In between government-backed trial balloons were floated by Pakistani media that Prime Minister Vajpayee may agree to withdrawal of Indian troops from Siachin; he may reduce the strength of the Indian security forces in Jammu and Kashmir, India might agree at the end of the summit to relinquish control over the Kashmir valley giving it some kind of an autonomous status while retaining Ladakh and Jammu Most extraordinarily India in a bold mo could allow Jammu and Kashmir a semi-independent status under some kind of a UN Observers' Group for a period of 15 years after which India and Pakistan would jointly agree to a referendum in the State for its future status.

This is both a pressure tactic and a ploy to tell the world that Pakistan has several suggestions to resolve the Kashmir issue to which India has not responded. The fact of the matter is that India would be absolutely justified in refusing any of these hair-brained proposals floated as trial balloons. There has been no signal from Musharraf acknowledging the serious implications of the nuclear weaponisation of India and Pakistan and the need to have discussions on nuclear risk reduction. To compound all this he has changed the composition of the original Pakistani delegation which was coming to the summit. He was planning to bring Foreign Minister Abdul Sattar, Finance Minister Aziz and Commerce Minister Daud. But the delegation which has come now consists only of Sattar, known for his negative attitude towards India. Finance Minister and the Commerce Minister have not come, a clear signal that Musharraf has approached the summit with a tunnel vision to discuss only Kashmir and is not even prepared to have exploratory discussion on possibilities of broader cooperation between the two countries which would create a positive environment and general mutual trust.

India was conscious of the importance of stabilising relations with Pakistan both in terms of regional considerations of peace and stability and in terms of the concerns of the international community. President Musharraf, in contrast, seemed to have the mind-set that he can use this factor as a leverage for propaganda and publicity purposes after the summit, is over.

India and Pakistan at the Threshold of Military Confrontation—Predicaments and Prospects

It has been a politically and militarily hot summer since the beginning of May as far as Indo-Pakistan relations are concerned. The expectation that political and military stand-off between India and Pakistan which commenced by attack on the Indian Parliament could be defused because of India's high military deployments and international pressure is not fulfilled. On the contrary, tensions have increased further. The terrorist attack on the Indian military residential camp at Kaluchak on the 14th of May and the murder of the moderate Hurriyat leader Lone on the 21st of May, have only exacerbated the situation. Certain policy decisions taken by the Government of India in the aftermath to the Kaluchak violence signalled perhaps an inclination to do something decisive in retaliation to Pakistan's insistent and increasing terrorist subversion against India.

In my last week's column on this subject I had analysed the undercurrents of US policies on the developing Indo-Pakistan tension. It is pertinent to make an assessment of General Pervez Musharraf's mind-set and his policy orientations and resulting actions therefrom. It is of primary importance to comprehend Musharraf's mind-set to the extent feasible, as separate from his public personna and pronouncements. His professional and psychological background is not just that of an army officer but that of a commando and Special Forces Officer. His psychological make up and mind-set is essentially aggressive, operation-uninhibited about taking risks and of an inner confidence about military victories. Add to this his deep ideological commitment to Jehad and making Pakistan the most influential Islamic country in South Asia and West Asia. He is permeated by the negative perceptions about India underpinning the partition and creation of Pakistan. Now as head of State and the Chief of the Pakistani Army, he controls the highest levers of power to determine Pakistan's India policies.

India should therefore have not any illusions about his willingness to have any reasonable compromises on issues at dispute with India. It would be relevant to mention that on returning from India after the Summit meetings with Atal Bihari Vajpayee in July 2001, he gave a private assessment to his inner circle that the Indian political leadership is indecisive and has no unity. He went on to give the assessment that the Indian armed forces though adequately equipped and well-organised, are not backed up by assertive political will and therefore its morale is not very high. The state of morale has also been affected by prolonged ambiguities and covert military operations in which Pakistan has engaged it over the last decade and more. He has come to the conclusion that if a war occurs, Pakistan could certainly match India effectively, if not defeat India. One learnt about this assessment from one's acquaintances in Pakistan from the period when I was High Commissioner in Islamabad.

The consequent decisions which have characterized Pakistani policies clearly reflect these assessments of Musharraf. It would be enough to re-count the more recent ingredients of Pakistan's India policies, that is, since his January 12 speech which was hailed precipitatedly by the international community as a turning point where he was supposed to give up terrorist subversion against India. But the substance of Pakistan's policies since January completely disprove this perception.

- Despite his announcing opposition to all forms of terrorism he continues to maintain the distinctions between the general phenomenon of terrorism and the terrorist violence in Jammu and Kashmir. He continues to assert that the violent movement by the Jehadis in Jammu and Kashmir is an indigenous freedom struggle to counter Indian obstinacies.
- Though he banned organisations like the Lashkar-e-Toiba and Jaish-e-Mohammed and arrested large numbers of their cadres, he has released them all. The Government of Pakistan justified this decision by saying there was no evidence against these cadres. The leaders of these cadres are in comfortable house arrest. Their communication facilities and their arms and movements have not been subjected to any restrictions.
- In fact, Pakistan has encouraged these terrorist organisations to continue their operations against India under new nomenclatures.
- The High Command of the Pakistan armed forces and the Inter-Services Intelligence have continued to infiltrate terrorist cadres into Jammu and Kashmir from Pakistan occupied Kashmir. With the onset of summer this infiltration as well as terrorist violence has increased.
- The attack on the Indian residential military complex of Kaluchak and the killing of Lone clearly indicate that the planning of and support to terrorist activities will continue from Pakistan.
- Pakistan government's immediate objective is to subvert the preparations for State Assembly elections in Jammu and Kashmir due

in September and to ensure that the elections are not held.

- The expulsion of those leaders of Hizbul Mujahideen like Abdul Majid Dar from the organisation by its Pakistan-based Chief Salahuddin, who were inclined towards a dialogue and were opposed to foreign Jehadi cadres operating in Jammu and Kashmir, is clear indication that Pakistan does not want any internal reconciliation process to succeed in Jammu and Kashmir.
- It is also significant that Lone's murder followed his having discussions with political leaders from Pakistan-Occupied Kashmir in Sharjah and Dubai. Indian intelligence agencies have clear evidence that his assassination plan was orchestrated by the Inter-Services Intelligence, details of which have been reported in the media.
- Musharraf also has to divert Pakistani and Pushtun cadres of Al Qaeda who have escaped from Afghanistan to some enterprises away from Pakistan proper as otherwise they will create major domestic problems for Musharraf, apart form creating difficulties for him in his relations with the USA which are based on his commitment to neutralize these Jahadi cadres. So he has targeted Jammu and Kashmir.
- The alienation of Jammu and Kashmir from the Indian Republic by parallel violent and political means remains the macro-level political objective of Musharraf's India policies.

The inescapable conclusion is that while Musharraf cooperates with the USA in its campaign against terrorism, he will continue to nurture and sustain terrorist violence against India. The objective is to generate such pressure through these means that it compels India to come to the negotiating table on his terms.

To ensure international support to this undeclared objective, he is utilising two leverages. First, the Indian military build up and diplomatic pressure, is used by him as an argument and a threat to Pakistan from which the US and Western democracies should save him. Secondly, he harps on the likelihood of his being compelled to use nuclear weapons against India which will lead to India retaliating with nuclear weapons, a situation to which the major powers of the world would be totally opposed, both at the political and military level. His strategic anticipations appear being fulfilled as shown in the high level diplomatic pressure being generated on India by the United States and the U.K. US Deputy Secretary of State Richard Armitage and British Foreign Secretary Jack Straw are visiting India later this month. Both the Russian President Vladimir Putin and the Chinese leadership have officially advised India to remain restrained, giving the assurance that these powers would exert more pressure on Pakistan to pull back from supporting the Jehadis.

Prime Minister Vajpayee's statement at Kupwara to the army Jawans that India would take decisive action against Pakistan has evoked assertive and smug response from Musharraf. Apart from affirming Pakistan's capacity and will to retaliate effectively he has re-affirmed the nuclear threat. It is clear that the US and the western powers have a limited objective of preventing an Indo-Pakistan war. They do not assign the necessary high priority which India has of countering Jehadi terrorism against Indian security. Nor do they seem inclined to acknowledge link between Pakistan-sponsored terrorism and the resulting politico-military pressures which India is trying to generate against Pakistan. This attitude of the major powers reduces India's options. First, it is clear that India would have to carry on its campaign against terrorism in Jammu and Kashmir on its own, barring general political sympathy and concern from the major powers. Secondly, India should structure its Pakistan policies clearly on the predication that any decisive military option chosen by India would attract opposition from the USA and major powers as well as the United Nations.

India faces a very complex challenge of sustaining its credibility as a country capable of taking decisive action against Pakistani mischief despite high international opposition.While at the same time ensuring that domestic processes of election and reconciliation are successfully carried out. While we are mounting diplomatic, political and limited military pressure on Pakistan, the litmus test would be our being able to effectively neutralise Pakistan's current long-term intentions. Given developing circumstances, there does not seem to be any alternative to act decisively in operational terms against Pakistan's activities in Jammu and Kashmir.

Continued Pak Terrorism – Kashmir – International Pressure – Difficult Choices for India

The massacre of innocent civilians by Pakistan-based terrorist groups Jaish-e-Mohammed and Lashkar-e-Toiba (as assessed though not announced by the Government of India), in a manner disrupted the second phase of diplomatic pressure on India and Pakistan, to prevent a sub-continental conflict; which was underway since the end of May and beginning of June. The telephone calls from Bush, Blair, Putin, followed by visits of Foreign and Defence Ministers of practically all the major powers of the world to New Delhi and Islamabad between end-December and May, had produced some results. President Musharraf made his policy speech on May 27 reaffirming his determination to fight terrorism in all forms and stating that he will not allow Pakistani territory to be used by any entity or any individual, for terrorist actions anywhere. There was some reduction in military skirmishes and firing on the Line of Control. India restored over-flight facilities for Pakistani aircraft in Indian airspace, withdrew parts of its naval forces from the Arabian Sea back to their home ports. This indicated that India might be willing to restore full diplomatic relations.

It was in this context that the second phase of generating pressure on India and Pakistan commenced in the beginning of June because western democracies became optimistic about pushing India and Pakistan towards the negotiating table from the position of military confrontation. The reason for this optimism was the restraint which India continued to show due to international pressure even after the terrorist attack on the family camp of Indian security forces at Kaluchak on May 14. This second cycle of diplomatic persuasion is aimed at persuading India and Pakistan to take some further steps to normalise relations and to initiate procedural measures for a bilateral dialogue. British Defence Secretary Geoffrey Hoon, Mr. Chris Patten of the European Union and Sir David Manning, special envoy of British Prime Minister Tony Blair, visited India in June and July. British Foreign Secretary Jack Straw and US Secretary of State Colin Powell will be visiting New Delhi in the second half of July. They will continue their discussions with external affairs Minister Yashwant Sinha at Brunei in August during the meeting of ASEAN Foreign Ministers. US Deputy Secretary of State Richard Armitage has scheduled his visit to Islamabad and New Delhi in September. The expectation of moving India and Pakistan further on steps at normalization have gone off the spin with the Qasimnagar massacre. Though all the major western countries have condemned this incident, they still advocate restraint on the part of India. There is no categorical affirmation of the links between the Government of Pakistan and terrorist violence in Jammu and Kashmir even after the Qasim Nagar incident.

While generally supporting the Indian decision to hold elections in the state of Jammu and Kashmir, there is skepticism about India's ability to ensure free and fair elections. Unpublicised foreign advocacies continue that India should allow institutional foreign observers to oversee this election which India has rejected.

India's post-Qasim Nagar policy stances merit a nuanced assessment. New Foreign Secretary Kanwal Sibal speaking at the CII early in July voiced India's disappointment about US and western powers being hesitant to accept Pakistan's responsibility in supporting terrorism in Jammu and Kashmir, even before the Qasim Nagar incident on the 14th of July. Deputy Prime Minister L.K. Advani made two significant points in Parliament on the 16th of July while making a statement on the Qasim Nagar incident. First that India is clear in its perceptions that other countries would react to India's predicaments in Jammu and Kashmir on the issue of terrorism not on objective proof or on merit but within the framework of their own interests. Second, that India is progressively coming round the view that despite the international campaign against terrorism, India would have to fight its own battle against terrorism directed against the country. This undercurrent of distances between the United States and India finds further expression in differing assessments about levels of terrorism in India, between India and western powers. The Government of India's assessment is that intrusions have not been reduced and that covert support for this subversion from Pakistan continues. The US State Department spokesman Boucher asserted on the 15th of July that there is a tangible reduction in infiltration from Pakistan into India (this is after the Qasim Nagar incident).

An important point to note is that neither Advani nor other senior government figures have categorically affirmed Pakistan's involvement in the Qasim Nagar incident. There have been only hints about it. The reason for this is that if the Government of India confirms Pakistani involvement, Parliament and public in India would generate pressure on the Government of India to take operational steps against terrorists across the Line of Control which the Government may not be willing to do, given the international diplomatic pressures and the larger implications of such action in terms of general military confrontation with Pakistan. It is clear that the Government of India is on the defensive about taking operational steps against Pakistan. Another reason for Indian reticence is that any military operation would put the scheduled election process in Jammu and Kashmir into a spin, delaying them. Such a situation would make serious negotiations which are now underway between the Government of India and Kashmiri political Groups to ensure a free and fair election in the state of Jammu and Kashmir problematic. The positive results of these negotiations so far in the Government of India's assessment should not become infructuous. The National Conference Government is not averse to President's rule being imposed on Jammu and Kashmir for the elections, as stated by Omar Abdullah. The Government has nominated former Law Minister Arun Jaitley as special envoy to discuss the autonomy package for Jammu and

Kashmir with leaders of all Kashmiri groups. Dr. Farooq Abdullah has welcomed this initiative. Barring hard-core anti-India elements there are incremental signals that various political groups in Jammu and Kashmir may be willing to participate in the elections.

The political situation in Jammu and Kashmir is at a critical point with possibilities of normal political processes being restored. India does not want this opportunity to be lost.

In contrast, Pakistani policies reflect a more sophisticated adversarial approach towards India. Pakistan also condemned the Qasim Nagar incident tongue in cheek but did not comment on the involvement of Pakistan-based terrorist groups in the act. Musharraf claims that he has succeeded in reducing military tension and infiltrations into India. The later part of the claim is not borne out by facts. More importantly, Pakistan terrorist campaign has adopted additional objectives. First to prevent and scuttle all developmental activities in Jammu and Kashmir by terrorising technicians and workers coming from other parts of India, to work on such projects (Most of those killed in Qasim Nagar were labourers from outside the State). Secondly, to undertake a systematic ethnic cleansing of Jammu to push out the Hindu population and increase the number of Muslims in the region. Third, to push out the professional middle class Muslims from Jammu and Kashmir who are supportive of India, and fourthly, to foment communal tensions between Muslims and Buddhists in Ladakh. Pakistan is implementing these policies under the pretence that it has nothing to do with terrorist subversion in the state and that incidents of violence are indigenous by socalled freedom fighters.

Parallely, Pakistan continues to argue that India is not responding to the positive steps that it has taken against cross-border terrorism. Pakistan wants India to come in for a dialogue without in any way reducing its proxy and violent pressure on India.

India has the extremely difficult challenge of taking some tangible action against Pakistan-sponsored terrorism while the world insists that India remain restrained. At the same time India has to revive the normal political processes in Jammu and Kashmir within the framework of its new initiative to include all segments of political opinion in this exercise. India has only one option. It has to fulfill both these tasks without being over-concerned about external advocacies. India must show its capacity to walk alone down the path which meets its clearly defined national interests in this respect.

Defusion of Indo-Pak Tensions – Only Tentative Beginnings

The visits by senior political figures from the Governments of the major powers of the world to India and Pakistan, are a matter of political attention and much public and media discussion. The visits of British Foreign Secretary Jack Straw, US Deputy Secretary of State Richard Armitage and US Defence Secretary Donald Rumsfeld between May and June have been acknowledged as high points of diplomatic pressure exerted on India and Pakistan to de-escalate the political and military confrontation. While there is acknowledgement that there is a marginal de-escalation in terms of ground realities, there is a consensus that the situation still remains dangerous. The objective here is to recall the promises inherent in President Musharraf's policy statements, compare them with the realities of Pakistani policies and to make an assessment of how far the beginnings of the defusion of tensions will transform itself into some kind of normalcy devoid of apprehensions about a military conflict which remain a matter of concern. It is not President Musharraf's responses to the US-led campaign against international terrorism that concerns India. It is the extent to which his joining the campaign against terrorism has resulted in Pakistan pulling back from his adversarial violent and intrusive activities against Indian security that concerns India. So one focusses only on his public pronouncements.

President Musharraf's policy statement to the people of Pakistan and the international community on June 12, has been interpreted by international community as signifying a radical change in Pakistan's policies towards extremist, religious and terrorist groups. The main points which he made in his January 12 speech were that Pakistan rejects and condemns terrorism in all its forms and manifestations and that Pakistan will not allow its territory to be used for any terrorist activity anywhere in the world. He went on to state that no organization will be allowed to engage in terrorism in the name of Kashmir and that anyone involved in any terrorist act would be dealt with sternly. He promised further that any Pakistani, individual or group or organisation involved in terrorism within Pakistan or outside Pakistan would be subject to strict action. He proceeded to announce the banning of the Lashkar-e-Taiba, the Sipah and Jaish-e-Mohammed, and said that any organisation or individual would be subject to punitive measures if found inciting violence inside Pakistan or outside the country. He added that he will not allow the misuse of mosques for militant or terrorist activities.

He also assured his audience that any Madrasa indulging in subversion, militant activity or possessing weapons will be closed.

In a statement made on May 22nd (following a joint meeting of Pakistan Cabinet and the National Security Council), he repeated the assurance that Pakistan will not allow its territory the country or any territory whose security is the responsibility of Pakistan to be used for any terrorist activity anywhere in world and that no organisation in Pakistan will be allowed to resort to terrorism in the name of Kashmir. In his speech of May 27th he again reiterated the assurance of Pakistani soil not to be allowed to be used for terrorism against anybody. And then added the assurance that no infiltration is taking place across the Line of Control. He went on to say that Pakistan will not allow export of terrorism anywhere in the world from within Pakistan. It must also be noted that he condemned the December 13 attack on the Indian Parliament and the attack on India's military camp at Kaluchak.

The point to examine is how these policy pronouncements transmuted themselves into operational policy decisions and the extent to which they are reflected in ground realities. Musharraf detained the leaders of the terrorist groups which he had banned in January and arrested about 2000 cadres belonging to these groups. But by the end February, beginning of March, all of them including the leaders of the terrorist groups have been released. Training of terrorist cadres continues in training camps in locations in Pakistani Punjab and in Pakistan-occupied Kashmir. The logistical and communications linkages between the ISI and Pakistani army units, on the one hand and terrorist cadres on the other, continue. The pattern and number of infiltrations from Pakistan into India across the Line of Control, have been at the same level this winter (even after his January 12 speech) as before. The terrorist training and launching camps which were closed briefly after the January 12 speech have been re-opened and re-located in other parts of Pakistan and Pakistan-occupied Kashmir, in the Northern areas, in the Punjab and the North-West Frontier Province. There is a confirmed estimate of 70 to 75 such camps continuing to be active. India also has information that Harkat-ul-Mujahideen and Lashkar-e-Taiba cadres returning from Afghanistan due to the US anti-terrorist campaign in that country, are now located in Pakistan-occupied Kashmir, proximate to the Line of Control. There are atleast 12 launching camps being used for funnelling terrorists across the Line of Control into India in Jammu and Kashmir. The estimate of the Indian security forces is that there are about 3000 to 3500 militants under training in Pakistan to continue terrorist subversion in India. Internationally banned terrorist group are becoming re-active under new names. For example, the Markaz-Dawa-Wal-Irashed which as been banned by the US and other western democracies has actively re-incarnated itself under the new name Jamat-ul-Dawa. There were some un-confirmed reports that President Musharraf had instructed commanders of the 10th Corps of the Pakistani army deployed in Pakistan-occupied Kashmir and Northern areas to pull back from giving logistical and tactical support to militants groups who were functioning under the umbrella of the Pakistan armed forces and the ISI, and there was an assessment in the western media that levels of infiltration into India had come down. This is not the case so far.

Rates of infiltration diminish due to two reasons. First, the normally bad winter weather conditions. The second, large-scale deployment of the Indian armed forces and more intense patrolling on the Line of Control by the security forces after the attack on the Indian Parliament.

An objective assessment of whether Pakistan has stopped support and taken measures to prevent infiltration can be made only by observing the situation on the ground till the middle of September. Till mid -June there are no indications of any reduction in attempts at infiltration or terrorist attacks on civilians and no-combatant dependents of the police and security forces in Jammu and Kashmir. This situation is to be viewed in the context of Pakistan's basic orientations towards India in the recent past.

There can be no doubt that Pakistan has been using terrorism as an instrument of state policy waging a low intensity covertly planned conflict against India particularly over the last two and half decades. This policy is predicated on Pakistani calculation that as long as the levels of intrusive terrorist violence remains short of a threshold, Pakistan could inflict damage upon India without attracting any punitive action against itself. There is also the Pakistani assessment that important powers would be willing to tolerate the situation in Jammu and Kashmir (indirectly accepting the theory that in violence there is some kind of a freedom struggle) as long as this terrorist violence does not expand into a general conflict between India and Pakistan, and its effects do not spread to other parts of the world.

During the 80s, Pakistan actively supported separatist terrorism in the Indian State of Punjab. From 1989-90, the focus of Pak-sponsored terrorist activities shifted to Jammu and Kashmir. Pakistan has been the architect and source of logistical support to terrorist acts in other parts of India. The bomb blasts in Mumbai in March 1993, the hijacking of the Indian Airlines aircraft from Kathmandu to Kandahar in December, 1999, the more recent attacks on the Red Fort, the Chambers of the Jammu and Kashmir Legislative Assembly and later on Indian Parliament were incidents in which militants with close links with ISI were involved. There are confirmed reports that ISI of Pakistan is orchestrating anti-India terrorist activities from Nepal and from Bangladesh in the North Eastern States of India.

India's high alert, diplomatic, political and military response to Pakistan since mid-December 2001, is a consequence of cumulative impact of Pakistan's unremittingly subversive orientations against India. When faced with the prospect of punitive action by India, Pakistan resorted to nuclear blackmail. President Musharraf and senior officials have more than once threatened the use of nuclear weapons against India, if India undertook any military action against the terrorists located in Pakistan occupied Kashmir. The world has responded to this blackmail. Hence the instant pressure on India to remain restrained, to de-escalate its military posture and to quickly resume the dialogue with Pakistan. There are reasons to be skeptical about Musharraf's assurances about adjuring terrorism as instrument of policy. He has only talked about taking effective and restrictive measures against Pakistan individuals and organisations located in and operating from "Pakistanis territory" (both in his January 12 and May 27 speeches). He continues to assert that there is no Pakistani sponsored infiltration across the Line of Control and he sticks to the argument that "Azad Kashmir" is not Pakistani territory and that terrorists operating from that area are indigenous freedom fighters. There is no dilution in this stand taken by Musharraf and his predecessors. Whereas the objective reality is exactly the opposite. There are reasons therefore to be sceptical about Musharraf fulfilling his promises till he proved his assessment wrong through the situation on the ground in Jammu and Kashmir.

Despite this India has restored civil aviation facilities to Pakistan, it has pulled back its Navy from the Arabian Sea. There are also reports of restoration of diplomatic contacts at the levels of High Commissioners. India's reactions are based on two considerations. India wishes to be responsive to the international community's apprehensions and advice. Secondly, India wants to give time to President Musharraf to translate his pronouncements into actual decisions implemented on the ground. External Affairs Minister Jaswant Singh aptly summed up the likely orientations of India's Pakistan policies when he stated on May 28: "All that he (Musharraf) has to do is to abjure violence, stop infiltrations across the Line of Control, disband terrorist training camps, cease providing support to terrorists and their organisations give up terrorism as an instrument of state policy and hand over the 20 criminals, a list of whom has been given to Pakistan-based on incontrovertible evidence."

India will respond to international suggestions and advice upto a point but de-escalation and moving towards dialogue and normalization will ultimately depend on President Musharraf translating his promises into ground realities. India's insistence on this general requirement is logical and valid, given the realities of Pakistan's India policies, even after Musharraf's speech of January,12.

Musharraf's Regional Diplomatic Initiative-A Calculated Move

Pakistan President Pervez Musharraf visited Bangladesh, Sri Lanka, with a brief stop-over in China in the last week of July and the beginning of August. This on all counts is a measured diplomatic initiative by General Musharraf with objectives falling into two categories. The first category of objectives is in terms of broad politico-strategic interests of Pakistan. The second category of objectives was country specific in relation to Bangladesh, Sri Lanka and China. The broader political and strategic aims of the visit were determined by the immediate context of regional security and political developments from Pakistan's point of view. Musharraf has stabilised and legitimised his political position as the Pakistan Head of State (regardless of the criticism against the referendum which he held to confirm himself in power). He has also completed the necessary procedural steps to hold general elections in Pakistan on his terms. He is considered as a major positive factor in the campaign against international terrorism by United States and the Western Democracies. He also seems to have put in place both domestic arrangements and international equations aimed at the economic survival of Pakistan. His interaction with the leaders of the major powers and all regional powers in the Islamic world seem to confirm his incremental acceptability in the international politics. There is only one aberration in this apparently positive secenario for Pakistan, namely his inability to bring in substantive or quantitative change in Pakistan's India policies. The reasons for this are clear. He is already on the defensive against segments of Pakistani public opinion who are critical of his joining the anti-terrorist campaign led by the United States, performing a complete U-turn in Pakistani policies supporting the Taliban and Al-Qaeda, etc. The bonafides of his move towards holding general elections are under doubt, both at home and abroad. Despite his joining the USA and other Western democracies in their anti-terrorist campaign they continue to pressurise him to pull back from supporting separatist terrorist activities in Jammu and Kashmir.

Since coming to power in 1999, his interaction with the Chinese leadership has been less than satisfactory and with other South Asian leaders have remained minimal. The Almaty conference on Asian Security and the Ministerial meeting of the A.R.F., the Asian Security Forum, have resulted in implied criticism about his India policies and his not fulfilling the promises which he made about eradicating terrorism in his speeches of January 12 and May 27, 2002. His objectives at the macro-level therefore seem to be to intensify Pakistan's relations with important South Asian countries like Bangladesh and Sri Lanka to touch base with the Chinese leadership to brief them about his latest regional policy objectives and to seek Chinese support for Pakistan's regional Policies. To be precise, the objectives of this category consist of ensuring that Pakistan does not get isolated on the issues of terrorism, relations with India and in regional equations. Secondly, to seek support for Pakistan's India, specifically Kashmir policies. Third, to seek Chinese support in dealing with India as well as the uncertain political situation in Afghanistan, and fourth, to augment economic and technological relations with all these countries.

Specific objectives of his official perigranation to Bangladesh, Sri Lanka and China merit an assessment in terms of the declared results. His visit to Bangladesh was replete with important political undertones. He is the first military head of State and government from Pakistan to visit Bangladesh after Bangladesh's liberation. In contrast to Zulfiqar Ali Bhutto's visit to Dhaka in July 1974, Musharraf officially regretted the tragic violence in Bangladesh preceding and during liberation war. (he of course did not specifically mention the Pakistani army as perpetrators of this violence which he regretted). Zulfiqar Ali Bhutto had not expressed any regret and it is with great reluctance and in a very casual manner that Bhutto visited the Martyrs' Memorial of Freedom-Fighters at Savar, near Dhaka. Bhutto had demanded that his visit to the memorial should be a private one and there should be no military guard of honour, etc. Musharraf apparently has closed this feeling of bitterness in the Bangladeshi psyche. This is not to say that the people of Bangladesh generally did not have reservations about the Commander-in-Chief of the Pakistani Army coming to their country and expressing sophisticated and reticent regret.

While this may be so, there has been a new foreign policy and political dynamics in Bangladesh-Pakistan relations since the advent of military rule in Bangladesh. This dynamics is positive and has been an incremental phenomenon, responsive to Bangladeshi threat perceptions and Bangladeshi interests, a phenomenon which has been utilised by Musharraf. India looms large in Bangladesh's foreign and security policies as a potential threat. India is too over-arching and too proximate. Therefore, Bangladesh needs to counter-balance the potential threats that it perceives. (Right or wrong), with equations with countries like Pakistan which have an equally, if not more tense relationship with India. Compulsions born of history and Bangladesh's geo-strategic location have transcended the memories of India's support to Bangladesh's freedom struggle. Bangladesh, therefore, believes in cultivating close relationship with Pakistan to redress over-arching geographical presence of India. Pakistan is equally and intensely interested in creating a sub-continental balance of power vis-à-vis India. These orientations of Pakistan and Bangladesh foreign policy underlined Musharraf's visit. The two agreements signed during his visit on cultural and technological cooperation serve two purposes. First, the cultural agreement by implication makes Pakistan acknowledge the separate ethno-cultural identity of Bangladesh, while at the same time it would emphasise and give substance to links between Bangladesh and Pakistan as Islamic countries, a measure which would counter the influence of "Hindu India". The agreement on technological cooperation is an umbrella under which Pakistan can be of assistance to Bangladesh not only in terms of technologies aimed purely on economic purposes, it would provide an umbrella for defence supplies cooperation between the two countries. There are defence technology capacities in Pakistan which Bangladesh cannot get from other countries unless it is willing to pay very high prices.

Both Pakistan and Bangladesh have agreements with the United States for location of US forces in their respective territories. This results in an unarticulated security arrangement also. No overt political or security agreement was signed as this would have evoked a critical response from India which Bangladesh wants to avoid. Musharraf's visit was an important event adding substance to Pakistan-Bangladesh relations.

As far as Sri Lanka is concerned, Pakistan-Sri Lanka relations, particularly economic and security relationships, have been close and substantive from 1977 till today except for a gap of 3 years between 1987 and 1989. Sri Lanka-Pakistan trade is substantive, Pakistan has been a reliable and steady supplier of defence equipment to Sri Lanka over the years. Sri Lanka, military and para-military personnel have been and are trained in Pakistan. The Sinhalese also consider Pakistan as a more reliable friend against Tamil separatism when compared to India because of India's social, ethnic and linguistic linkages with Sri Lankan Tamils . Sri Lanka is aware that no durable solution to ethnic conflict can be achieved without the support of India, but at the same time the Sri Lankan government legitimately feels the need for other sub-continental actors supporting them against excessive Tamil demands. Musharraf's visit has been fully responsive both to specific needs mentioned above and the general orientations of Sri Lanka's security and foreign policies. It is clear that Musharraf stressed the need of smaller countries of South Asia having a close and positive relationship with each other to counter the asymmetric influence that India can generate. There are reports that in his high level discussions he hinted at this prospect being more specific under what is called "A Hindu Nationalist Government."

As far as China is concerned, the visit was too brief. The most important signal Musharraf gave by stopping over in China is that Pakistan considers China as its most reliable friend not only in terms of bilateral political, economic and defence cooperation but also in terms of structuring a regional security environment in Central Asia and South Asia. There are also reports of Musharraf having requested the Chinese to facilitate Pakistan's membership of the ASEAN Security Forum, ARF. There was also a message that Musharraf's closeness to the United States would not be at the cost of any dilution of Pakistan's relations with China.

Musharraf's visits to Bangladesh, Sri Lanka and China are a timely and measured diplomatic initiative. It is obvious that India should monitor Pakistan's relations particularly with Bangladesh and Sri Lanka in the coming months, to see that these equations do not militate against Indian interests in these countries and India's relations with China.

The Almaty Conference – Indo-Pakistan Tensions

The conference on International Cooperation and Confidence Building in Asia Measures convened by Nursultan Nazarbaev, President of Kazakhstan, concluded on the 4th of June. What was supposed to be a summit meeting of the major Asian powers focusing on macro-level security issues was overshadowed to some extent by the tensions generated by the current Indo-Pakistan confrontation and resulting stand off.

Nursultan Nazarbaev's initiative was primarily to deal with developments related to Asia's security after the ouster of the Taliban from Afghanistan and to chart out a role for Asian countries to deal with problems arising out of international terrorism and the relative political uncertainties affecting most Asian countries. The impact of deliberations at the conference has to be assessed in two dimensions. First, the decisions taken regarding multi-lateral inter-state cooperation in the region in the spheres of security, political interaction and economic efforts. The second dimension is that of examining the manner in which these deliberations and the high level discussions held between Heads of Government on the tense situation in the South Asian sub-continent.

There are reasons for India to be satisfied about the collective decisions taken at the Almaty Conference as reflected in the Almaty declaration and agreement. The final documents of conference clearly acknowledge the threat posed to international security by extremism and terrorist violence. There is also the collective decision to take individual as well as collective initiatives to counter the phenomenon of international terrorism. The Almaty documents stressed the importance of preventing the disintegration of pluralistic societies and the States, of the need to collectively ensure the stability of states in the region, of the relevance of increasing mutual economic and developmental cooperation, and to work together against externally-sponsored subversion, are points responsive to India's concerns and interests. These are equally supportive of Indian policies on these issues. It was equally significant that barring the protagonists in the sub-continental crisis, India and Pakistan, none of the other world leaders expressed value judgments on the Indo-Pakistan stand off. It was, however, gratifying for India that in the major policy statements clear opposition was expressed to cross-border terrorism and subversion of state structures particularly democratic state structures. It must be mentioned in paranthesis that the outcome of the conference on Asian Security organised by the International Institute of Strategic Studies London and that of the Almaty Conference, both reflected an understanding of Indian concerns and by implication, India's security predicaments.

It is the second dimension of the Almaty conference mentioned earlier which is of more direct interest to India. General Musharraf, contravening normal conventions at multi-lateral conference of not raising specific bilateral issues, raised the issue of Kashmir at the conference. His policy stance at the conference was inevitable and unavoidable from his point of view. He had to prove to his domestic constituency that he has not and he will not succumb to the incremental international pressure generated on him to stop being supportive of the phenomenon of terrorism, even though the other leaders did not openly state the ground reality that Pakistan remains the refuge of Al-Qaeda and other extremist religious terrorist cadres and organisations, all the other leaders were aware of this fact and in discussions on the margins of the conference, must have urged him to fall in line with the general orientations of the international community to take decisive steps against terrorism within the framework of assurances which he has given in his public pronouncements on January 12 and May 27 this year. He also had to project Pakistan's image of being part of the mainstream of international attitudes on this issue. At the same time he had to project himself as a reasonable leader willing to negotiate with India without eroding his image as tough Head of Government capable of coping with any challenges that he may face from India or due to international pressure. His remarks about a strong and determined reaction if any war is imposed on Pakistan reflected this latter point.

Prime Minister Vajpayee's response was equally firm, clear and categorical. The two main points made by Mr. Vajpayee were that India would resume a dialogue with Pakistan only after there is clear and verifiable evidence that Pakistan has stopped supporting cross-border terrorism, and secondly that once this happens India would be willing to have negotiations with Pakistan including on the issue of Jammu and Kashmir. Mr. Vajpayee also implied that if cross-border terrorism did not stop, India retains all relevant options to counter this pernicious phenomenon.

The expectation that the general objective of this high level summit of encouraging cooperation and forging meaningful confidence building measures would generate political pressures on both the leaders, leading to a thaw in the sub-continental situation was not fulfilled proving that speculative media anticipations and interpretation were just a wishful thinking. Both Vajpayee and Musharraf met Russian President Putin and Chinese President Jiang Zemin separately. There were anticipatory assessments that these meetings, particularly the meeting between Putin and the sub-continental leaders may result in some kind of a breakthrough. There were reports about President Putin extending an invitation to both Musharraf and Vajpayee to come for talks under Russian auspices (like the Tashkent meeting of 37 years ago in 1966) to Moscow. In actual fact no such formal proposal was made. President Putin only offered to help in the matter if both the leaders were agreeable. Both Putin and Jiang Zemin advised India and Pakistan to act with restraint and de-escalate the situation. Putin, of course, was more direct in underlining to Musharraf that an Indo-Pakistan dialogue can be resumed meaningfully only if Pakistan stops supporting cross-border terrorist subversion against India. Jiang Zemin articulated the traditional Chinese stance about the need for India and Pakistan to resolve the Kashmir issue, which is an inheritence from the colonial past. But interestingly, he emphasised that terrorism violence is not the means to solve this problem. There was a suggestion from Musharraf to Putin that an Indo-Pakistan dialogue may be organised in Moscow with Russia as the go-between and that he will be willing to come to Moscow. The Indian response to this suggestion was that while India welcomed Russian concerns, in resolving the issue, it did not need to go to Moscow for such a meeting. The meeting could be held either in Pakistan or in India. Mr. Putin was practical and realistic. While he has agreed to receive President Musharraf in Moscow, he was not inclined to pressurise Mr. Vajpayee to come to Moscow. In the event, the result was that Musharraf would have discussions in Moscow and Putin may continue the process when he comes for an official visit to India later this year.

Given this context, the Almaty conference made only a marginal impact on the current state of Indo-Pakistan relations. Both Musharraf and Vajpayee acknowledged on their return in Islamabad and New Delhi that the deliberations in and outside the conference in Almaty did not change the Indo-Pakistan stand off materially. The results of Almaty conference from India's points of view would be summed up as follows:

The decisions of the conference as embodied in its final documents shared India's concerns and India's stand on cross-border and external subversion. None of the participants, Heads of States or Government showed any inclination to mediate between India and Pakistan resuming a direct dialogue as early as feasible. There was an agreement among them that such a dialogue can be resumed only if there is tangible proof on Pakistan pulling back from its support to cross-border terrorism.

Both in the conference and in bilateral meetings the advice to India and Pakistan was to rapidly de-escalate the military confrontation because of the danger of such confrontation leading to a military conflict which could escalate into the use of nuclear weapons. The important powers did not take sides on the substantive issue of Kashmir. Even Russia was comparatively impartial emphasising that the problem should be resolved by the initiation of and continuation of a political dialogue.

In bilateral discussions Musharraf was given clear enough messages that he has to do something more to fulfill the general assurances about countering terrorism based in Pakistan, which he has given to the international community.

India's participation in the Almaty conference has ensured that India will have an active and substantive role to play in future security and confidence building arrangements in Central Asia and South Asia. The conference was also significant in that Prime Minister Vajpayee met the Chinese President Jiang Zemin for the first time in his capacity as head of the Indian Government.

What India should monitor now is the political and diplomatic moves that Russia, USA and China undertake to follow up on the discussions held between Vajpayee and the leaders of these countries. Hopefully, Musharraf may ultimately respond to the pressure of important powers on him to abandon his adversarial stance atleast terms of sponsoring terrorism if not on the Kashmir issue. India should also anticipate incremental pressure to de-escalate the military situation and to resume the dialogue with Pakistan.

The coming six weeks to two months would be characterised by critical developments. India has to cope with the challenge of remaining firm about her security interests and territorial integrity while at the same time preventing a war with Pakistan to the extent feasible. President Musharraf has a special responsibility in this regard because if he sponsors or connives at further terrorist incidents, India's option to remain retrained will decisively diminish.

9

Pakistan Tensions Uncertain Political Prospects

Elections in Pakistan-Implications-Regional and for India

President Musharraf completed his promised electoral exercise in Pakistan over the last weekend (10th to 13th October). Constitutional amendments which he introduced in the 1973 Constitution had a singular substantive political objective, that of consolidating his hold on the power structure of Pakistan. The political and orchestrated judicial decisions which he took also had the same objective. Results of the elections are as expected, except for the People's Party of Pakistan still emerging as a significant segment of the National Assembly despite all the discriminatory restrictions placed on it. Musharraf prevented Nawaz Sharif and Benazir Bhutto from coming back to Pakistan and leading their parties in the elections by threatening drastic political action and imprisonment against them. Restrictions which he introduced in the electoral laws about eligibility for fighting elections further debilitated established and old political parties.

The election results have radically changed the political landscape of Pakistan. The Muttahinda-Majlis-e-Amal, a coalition of extremist Islamic parties supportive of the Taliban and Al-Qaeda, has emerged as the largest group of Members of National Assembly party winning 77 seats. The Muslim League and Benazir Bhutto's People's Party of Pakistan have emerged as the next two largest groups in the National Assembly. The MMA has also absolute majorities in the Provincial Legislative Assemblies of the North-West Frontier Province and of Baluchistan. The Muslim League (Qaid) has swept the polls in the Legislative Assemblies in Punjab. The MQM, the Muslim League (Qaid-e-Azam) and People's Party of Pakistan have emerged parallely victorious in the Legislative Assemblies of Sindh. One has reports that Muslim League (Qaid-e-Azam) is not averse to forging equations with the MMA for the formation of the Central Government of Pakistan.

Some analysts have expressed the view that President Musharraf is perturbed and in difficulties because of the emergence of MMA as the most influential political group in the Central legislature. This is a somewhat simplistic analysis based on the presumption that this group of Islam-pasand parties being opposed to Musharraf cooperating with the US, in its anti-terrorist campaign, will create domestic political difficulties for him. Such analysis has brought special attention to the anti-US rhetoric of the MMA and its demand that America troops should be withdrawn from Pakistan and Afghanistan. This analysis is valid only to a limited extent. The more plausible and logical reality could be that Musharraf himself orchestrated the victory of Islam-pasand parties in the politically sensitive provinces of North West Frontier and Baluchistan, with two objectives. Provincial Government formed by the MMA being in power in these two provinces bordering Afghanistan will enable Musharraf to tell the Americans that while he wishes to cooperate in the anti-terrorist campaign, the elected Government will put restraints on his extent of cooperation. So he ensures some kind of security for escaping Taliban and Al-Qaeda which leads on to his second motive that is a signal to the internal opposition to him in Pakistan that he is cooperating with the US only under overwhelming compulsion and that where possible he has allowed the Islamic groups to come into power which has never happened before.

One would do well to remember that in all the elections between 1988 and now, Islamic Parties barely got five or 4 per cent of the votes and never won a significant number of seats in the National or Provincial Legislatures. While Musharraf's pro-Islamic credibility gets a boost in NWFP and Baluchistan, he has ensured a hung National Assembly where no single political party has a sufficient majority to form the Government. It will be a coalition Government which will be dependent for its survival on Musharraf. That Musharraf has decided to play an assertively intrusive role in the electoral process was proved by the fact that he made some significant amendments to the original legal framework order which included all the major constitutional amendments which he initiated over the last five and a half months since April. He introduced these further amendments literally a few hours before voting for the general elections commenced in Pakistan on October 10. Musharraf stipulated in the new amendments to the legal framework order that Member of the Legislatures elected as independents could join any political party within three or four days of the official declaration of results. This led to the Muslim League (Qaid-e-Azam) gaining support of independents after the elections and managing a majority.

The second Musharraf amendment debars permanently any individual from being elected a member of any Legislature of Pakistan if he/she is disqualified under any law in force at the time, an amendment obviously debarring Benazir Bhutto and Nawaz Sharif permanently from politics. By the third amendment Musharraf extended the tenure of the existing judges of the Supreme Court and the High Courts of Pakistan who have supported him since he took over power by military coup. Another provision he made was that each political party which has got more than 5 per cent of the total number of seats in the Legislatures can claim the reserved seats in each legislature for that party proportionately. This means that political parties which have gained sufficient membership in the legislatures will proportionately lay claim to the 60 reserved seats for women in the National Assembly, 66 seats in this category in Punjab, 29 in Sindh and 22 in the NWFP. So would 11 women seats in Baluchistan go to the MMA. The ten reserved seats for non-Muslims in the National Assembly, 8 in Punjab, 9 in Sindh and three each in NWFF and Baluchistan would also be dispensed in the same manner enhancing the strength of MMA and the Muslim League (Qaid-e-Azam) with some marginal benefits to the PPP.

Most of the foreign observers have refrained from giving any categorical confirmation about the elections in Pakistan having been fair or transparent. There was a priori acceptance of the fact that elections were being held under the Terms of Reference formulated by General Musharraf. But the most telling criticism came from Mr. John Cushnahan, the leader of the Foreign observers team from the European Union who released the contents of the reports on Saturday, the 12th of October. The report states the Pakistani elections are deeply flawed due to the constitutional changes made by Musharraf in August. The report goes on to state that these changes could lead to the concentration of power into the hands of a single individual who can dismiss the elected Governments and institutionalise the role of the military in the Government. The report concludes that changes altering the 1973 constitution of Pakistan has converted the parliamentary Government into a Presidential form of Government headed by General Musharraf.

This is going to be a factually correct assessment because Musharraf and the National Security Council chaired by him, would emerge as the final arbiters of political dispensation in Pakistan in the foreseeable future.

The implications of this development should be a matter of concern to India, and the international community. Governments formed by a coalition of extremist Islamic political groups linked to the Taliban and Al Qaeda would create hurdles in the campaign against terrorism in Afghanistan. In fact, this may result in increasing strength and capacities of elements in NWFP and Baluchistan and southern Afghanistan wishing to de-stabilise the Karzai Government. The security prospects in Afghanistan will become more uncertain and dangerous. There are distinct possibilities of MMA Government in NWFP becoming more active and supportive of Pakistan-sponsored terrorist subversion in Jammu and Kashmir.

Given the links between Taliban and Al-Qaeda cadres with MMA and given the involvement of Taliban and Al-Qaeda in drug trafficking, the prospects of increased narco-terrorism can be ruled out. This will have negative ramifications both in Afghanistan and for India. Benazir Bhutto's statement from London saying that she will ask her party to cooperate with President Musharraf signals Musharraf consolidating his position at the Head of Pakistani power structure for some time to come. It is obvious that India will be under greater pressure to resume dialogue with Pakistan. Challenge to our foreign policy should be fashioned in the context of negative prospects which one discerns in post-election Pakistan.

Pakistan – Uncertain Political Prospects

Nearly five weeks have gone by since the general elections were held in Pakistan for what general Musharraf called restoration of democracy in that country. The Pakistan National Assembly is subject to a hung verdict. No political party has got a majority. The MMA (Muttahida Majlis-e-Amal), the Muslim League (QA) and People' Party of Pakistan have emerged as parties capable of playing a tangible role in Pakistani politics under its current term of reference. Attempts at forming a coalition government have not succeeded, though options of a coalition between the MMA and the Muslim League (QA) were first explored. This was followed by negotiations for the same purpose between the PPA and the MMA. The failure of these discussions led to General Musharraf calling an informal meeting of the Apex political entity, the National Security Council. There was speculation that he might impose martial law and then call for another general election in a couple of months' time.

At the time of writing this article, it has been announced that the National Assembly of Pakistan has been convened for its inaugural post-election on the 16th of November, the expectation being that a new coalition

Government of Pakistan could emerge by the third week of November. The creation of such a Government is going to be a complex task. Maulana Fazlur Rehman, the chief of the Jamiat-e-Ulema Islam, has been projected as the Prime Minister by the MMA. Chaudhary Sujat Hussain, former Finance Minister and Minister of Interior under Nawaz Sharif Government, is being projected as the most acceptable candidate by the Muslim League (QA), Qazi Hussain Ahmed and the perennial leader of the Restoration for Democracy movement in Pakistan Nawabzada Nasrullah Khan are trying to broker an agreement while former President Farooq Laghari, as Chief of the National Democratic Alliance is waiting perhaps to emerge as a compromise candidate to head the Government. The PPP guided from abroad by Benazir Bhutto is playing a curious game of shifting orientations. Benazir has publicly indicated a willingness to cooperate with General Musharraf to establish a Government and run it. Her party has negotiated with the MMA as well as Muslim League (QA), alternatively to create a coalition government.

I mentioned the terms of reference of functioning of a coalition government earlier. These go beyond the election results in Pakistan and maneouvrings of Musharraf and the political parties. Regardless of what kind of a Government comes into being, the ingredients of Pakistani politics in the foreseeable future have to be noted. Foremost, is the fact the General Musharraf intends to remain dominant in every aspect of political processes in Pakistan. He will be successful in this exercise as far as he retains the support of the military establishment of Pakistan. Second, he has isolated all the important political parties of Pakistan and their leaders. Consequently, new political groups and entities have emerged either independently or by splinter groups separating themselves from the main political parties. The polities of Pakistan do not seem to have any desire to adhere to any ideological roots in their political activity, across the spectrum. Their approach seems to be motivated by a desire to adjust to political dispensations being structured by General Musharraf. Though critical of the constitutional amendments carried through by General Musharraf, the political parties and the political classes in Pakistan seem to be reconciled to functioning under the new constitutional arrangements.

It is clear that Islam-pasand parties, for the first time seem to have displaced the moderate and liberal political parties like the Awami Party and the PPP particularly in the sensitive states of North West Frontier Province and Baluchistan. Given the relative strength of the MMA members in the National Assembly they are bound to play an influential role in Pakistani politics and policies in the foreseeable future.

There is limited accuracy in the conventional wisdom being touted about, that the emergence of the MMA as an important factor in Pakistani politics is a set back for General Musharraf. A more rationale and plausible assessment would be that Musharraf orchestrated the elections in a manner where factions of the Muslim League and the PPP amenable to him would find reasonable representation in the National Assembly while Islam-pasand parties would replace the liberal and democratic parties opposed to his assumption of power. Another motive of his enabling the MMA emerging as important political factor was to signal to the opposition in the Pakistani domestic politics that despite his having had to toe the US line in its anti-terrorist campaign, he still remains committed to the ideology, the fervour and the causes of Islam. It is also clear that no coalition Government in Pakistan can last for long unless it has the support of the MMA in one form or the other. MMA forming provincial Governments in North West Frontier Province and in Baluchistan is on the cards. The cadres of this party will also dominate the politics of northern areas and Pakistan occupied Kashmir in the coming months.

Given the prospects of a tenuous coalition Government coming into power , Musharraf's personal authority and influence will remain supreme. The only institution which will dominate the governing processes would be the National Security Council the substance of power will rest with the Pakistan Army High Command. Given this scenario, the implications could be a matter of concern in terms of regional security and stability. The US campaign against terrorism in Afghanistan and the Northern portions of Pakistan have been acknowledged less than successful by General Meyers, the Chairman of the US Joint Chiefs of Staff in an address to the Brookings Institution in Washington earlier this month. US defence and intelligence authorities acknowledge that the Al-Qaeda and Taliban cadres have escaped in sufficient number to re-group to continue their terrorist acts internationally as well as in the South Asian region. The MMA in power, and with influence, will give covert support to these terrorist cadres. The US response to these prospects and reports about Osama bin Laden being still alive has been that the terrorist campaign is not aimed at one single individual and that it will continue on all fronts. The incoming Government of Pakistan under Musharraf's overall guidance will have to cope with incremental de-stabilisation of Afghanistan and disruption of return to democracy in Jammu and Kashmir. Musharraf's likely advocacy to the US would be that he will not let the MMA disrupt or diminish his support for the US-led anti-terrorist campaign. He will also argue that while he will try to control the MMA activities in Jammu and Kashmir, US should take note of the fact that main separatist groups in Jammu and Kashmir did not participate in the recent elections there and therefore the violence in Jammu and Kashmir has to be assessed on a different criteria. Musharraf has also indicated his general support for the diplomatic and impending military campaign by the US against Iraq.

Domestically Pakistani democracy stands truncated for the time being a view generally expressed in the Pakistani media. Economic management and governance would be a complex task for Musharraf as he will finalise formulation and implementation of policies on the basis of bargaining with the political parties coming into the coalition Government. That Musharraf's predicament is being dealt with sympathetically by the US is indicated by the USA's very temporised, measured and non-committal response to the emergence of extremist Islamic political groups entering the power structure of Pakistan.

Pakistan economy will continue to get inputs from Saudi Arabia and other Gulf countries because there is a convergence of interests of Musharraf, on the one hand and the power structure of the States in the Gulf region, on the other. The shared phenomenon on which this convergence of interests rests is the fact that as in Pakistan so in the Gulf, genuine representative democracy could be a threat to Musharraf as well as the ruling classes in Gulf countries.

Adversarial policies towards India will be continued by Musharraf while he publicly pleads for resumption of dialogue with India. He will receive Incremental support on this second point from the major powers. The twin challenges to India's Pakistan polices is to structure timely and effective response to Pakistan's adversarial policies while at the same time formulating tactical moves to resume contacts with Pakistan, not that these contacts will lead to immediate results but because such contacts will sustain international support for India and could be long-term basis for coming to terms with Pakistan.

Keynote Address

The theme is : can we live in peace with Pakistan. The issue can be examined in two facets : the normative facet, what should be and the existentialist facet, what is. Then we can come to certain conclusions but no final consensus can be developed because there are both positive and negative dimensions of our predicaments with each other. I would like to go beyond the facts, episodes, issues and the current events to the fundamental or elemental factors affecting our relationship. Everybody may not agree with me but these are my perceptions.

Let me begin by ruminating on the historical aspects of our existence as two countries. If you carefully examine the origins of bifurcation of India, I think the freedom struggle mindset of the Congress was as much to blame as the Muslim League, leading to the partition of India. Roughly till 1933-35 the Muslim league did not consider the objective or determination to get Pakistan a realistic ambition. You go back to conceptual history; Chowdhary Rahamat Ali's Memorandum on the creation of Pakistan, the first party to reject it as utopian and chimerical was the Muslim League. He submitted his memorandum immediately after the failure of second Round Table Conference in 1931. He only put the proposal forward as a suggestion. I am not saying Congress should have abdicated its right to be representative as a national party with claim to represent all communities of India, but if there was another organisation, which wanted a certain exclusivity to represent certain part of the Indian civil society, so be it. I don't have to dilate on the obstinacies of the Muslim League, which resulted in Pakistan, but the more important thing is that though we keep saying that we accept Pakistan and its existence, the Pakistanis are not convinced that we are and we have recognized it, despite Atalji's visit to Minar-e-Pakistan in Lahore in Feb.1999. While we in formalistic political statements say that partition is a fact and India has no desire to undo it etc, we talk of Akhand Bharat whenever we can. Even in the nationalistic, secularistic lexicon, in sort of deeper theoretical analyses we still articulate the view the partition of India was an aberration. Factually it may be correct but you must think about the impact of this on the Pakistani psyche. Add to that the frustrations of Pakistan. Territorially it is truncated and moth eaten Pakistan said Mohammed Ali Jinnah. They wanted to redress the balance of territorial inadequacy by indulging in skull-duggeries against us four times on Kashmir. They were frustrated. They got defeated. So there is that sense of frustration. Then you have asymmetry between India and Pakistan not on only in terms of territory, demographic, technology, military capacity, economic diversities, but there is asymmetry in terms of political life and political achievements, in terms of institutional democracy, in terms of our Constitution which has been in place for some years, in terms of stability of political regimes and all such asymmetries result in complexes and threat perceptions, which may be wrong. But we must accept that they exist.

This point is very nicely brought out by two statements of two Pakistanis. Approximately six years ago, my friend and colleague Mani Shankar released a book of his of collections of notes, which he wrote as

Consul General in Karachi. He invited Riaz Khokhar, the then High Commissione of Pakistan, in India to be on the dais. It was our Indian audience in the Hall at IIC. The opening sentence of Khokhar, though it was a conciliatory book towards Pakistan, was "I want to begin by telling this audience, in no circumstances should any body think that Pakistan considers India as a model for its political organization". There was no provocation for him to say this. The second statement was on 19 Jan 1997, when Rajiv Gandhi Foundation had organised seminar on Indo-Pak relation on a very high level, with participation from various political leaders, various parties of India and from Pakistan, personalities such as Mehboob-ul-Haq, former foreign Minister of Pakistan, Lt. General Sahibzada Yakub Khan former Foreign Minister, and so on.

The summary of the seminar was being discussed in the final session, and as usual an attempt was on to sort out and present a picture of consensus and optimism about the future, when Lt. General Khan intervened in the debate and said that "all this is very well and that is how it should be done. This is the normal procedure, but let us be realistic. I want to tell this audience that there is a deep line of hatred and suspicion in Pakistan about India. Unless you overcome it all this kind of positive statements have no meaning." He said in 1997 and in the last five years what has happened? This is where I go into three aspects of the fundamental aberrations in Indo-Pak relations. First and foremost, the mind set of people of India and Pakistan. I do not think the common citizen of Pakistan and common citizen of India entertain structured antagonism towards each other. As in the world of common people, they are concerned with their immediate well- being, political stability and anxiety that they should not be subjected to unexpected sudden violence. Relations between India and Pakistan are viewed as something to be managed by Governments. The expectation is that they will ensure that these do not go out of control. This attitude is there even when there are moments of high crisis.

Two recent episodes are the Kargil war and the attack on Indian Parliament leading to the imminence of war. It is interesting while Indian reaction was, they have attacked the Parliament, hit them. Do something. We can't go on making speeches; it is time to send the message. When actually the tension built up, I was fascinated. Lots of people, knowledgeable people would say : what would happen if there was nuclear bombing all over. Don't you think we should not be adventurous? I presume that was the view in Pakistan also. Having said this, there is dichotomy or difference between the mindset of people of India and the

Pakistani people's mindset. I divide Indian mindset geographically. In north India there are segments of public opinion, which chant the mantra : we are the same people we speak more or less the same language. It is a great pity that partition took place.

Ok, we are separate but we must have good relations. What I call the Kuldeep Nayar doctrine of lighting candles at the border. On the other side it was most of the time "*candle bujhao*". But it is there people from south India do not have any such hang-ups. Pakistan is these if it becomes nasty we must be firm about it; but there is no emotional complication on the partition, which is there in the north. I lived for four years in Pakistan. I have a lot of friends amongst not only what I call the native Pakistanis, not the frontier Punjabis or Sindhis; I have lots of Muhajir friends. It is funny, after 55 years of independence they are still called Muhajirs. People from Bihar, Tamil Nadu, U.P., Kerala. Even they don't have this feeling which people in north India have that we are the same people. The limit of their positive thinking is : we were part of some kind of background so there is no point in fighting. But they don't say we are the same people. The most important example of this is a conversation I had with leader of the MQM, after I returned from Pakistan when I was Foreign Secretary. I met the person in London. He had read some newspaper commentaries by some brilliant strategists in India : We must cultivate MQM to breakup Pakistan. So he said "*Dixit Bhai sahib yeh yaad rakhiye ke humare dil me bahut khalish hai*. We are very upset with Government in Pakistan on how they treat the Muhajirs. But why do you forget that we are Pakistanis?"

He did not believe in the kind emotionalism, which I mentioned. So there is a sense of separateness, because of which they feel endangered because of our large looming presence. I am not saying the solution is breakup, I am not saying that we pander to that feeling but we must remain conscious of this. While they have their sense of separate identity and certain apprehension, I don't think they believe in adversarial approach in the operational sense. This is where lies the difference among the people particularly of Pakistan and its power structure. General Malik will be talking about the mindset of military but the mindset of powers that be is an absolutely different mindset in Pakistan. Indian mindset has certain angst : the power structure mindset, that OK, we reluctantly agreed to partition. They have created a separate country but they still have territorial claims, that they still bother us and we have to deal with it rather firmly. The sort of feeing that while one must respect Pakistan's existence, and so on, it is in the interest of India that Pakistan's adversarial attitudes are countered by certain strategic insistence on keeping it on the defensive—

I am not giving a value judgment whether it is right or wrong, I will give that value judgment towards the end of my presentation. There is also resentment about anything that Pakistan does to strengthen itself, whether it is the equation with US or equation with China, whether it is links with Islamic group of countries, its being considered an important Islamic country always bothers us. It comes out in subconscious and other analysis. In our power structure, it includes not just the Government relations, but also amongst what I call "strategic thinkers of India". As for mindset of the Pakistani power structure, less said the better. At least our power structure can have tenuous claim that it represents the people of India more genuinely than the Pakistani power structure. It is a very narrow power structure even when it assumes the democratic garb. It is still a very feudal power structure and their survival in power depends on an adversarial stand against India. They have gone to the extent of generally projecting an ethos and the philosophy where they feel that Pakistan's very existence depends on questioning the authenticity and the credibility of the Indian polity. Indian elections are a farce! Indian democracy is a sham! Indian secularism does not exist!

In 1993, Gohar Ayub the son of Air Marshall Ayub Khan in a press conference in Delhi, where he had come to participate in Inter Parliamentary Union, stated that peace can come to the South Asian subcontinent only when India breaks up and I am convinced that India will break up. Therefore there is nothing really in the chemistry of Indian polity, which cement to ensure the permanent unit. This claim was repeated perhaps two weeks ago by the present minister of information and broadcasting of Pakistan, who said that, this is a country full of castes and communal strife. Within each religion there are contradictions and it is only a matter of time, before India breaks up, so Pakistan should not worry. We are cohesive, Islamic etc. There is certain blandness because there are 70 or so subsects of Islam in Pak, which constantly give them high blood pressure. This is a country, which bombs its own people in Baluchistan because they dissent. This is a country where the Kadiyanis have been ex-communicated. But they still have this feeling. The combination of feudal mindset and the nexus between feudal industrially or economically well to do and the armed forces, whatever the Government, ensures the survival of the power structure.

So till power structure of Pakistan really undergoes profound and qualitative change, I do not expect positive relationship between India and Pakistan. It is not articulated very much apart from this dream about divided India being the only solution. The power structure has certain items on the agenda which is not articulated very much, except in the case of Kashmir. The other arguments about Kashmir do not interest me as much as their repeated chanting of "Takiya kalam" that Kashmir is the unfinished art of the partition. This fascinates me, Religion, territorial claims, Human rights, plebiscite, whatever in terms of historical arguments that from their point of view they can voice. But Kashmir is unfinished part of agenda. It raises in my mind an entire gamut of questions, which in analysis implies that not just Kashmir but the series of repartitions of India is political strategic ambition of Pakistan. Read the unfinished part of the partition with that India cannot remain united, cannot live together. Link them together and what is the picture that emerges? That is one aspect. Then there is feeling, especially among the military figures : the separation of Bangladesh has to be avenged.

Very few people know about the oath taken by the cadets in military academy in Kabul when they became commissioned officers after the passing out parade. The oath does not specifically talk about the separation of Bangladesh but says that the defeat of 1971 has to be avenged to restore the honour of Pakistan. So, I come to the final stage : what should be what is? In terms of geographical, economic and long-term political well- being of peoples of India and Pakistan, a normal peaceful relation which is not just necessary but imperative. Osmosis of events and historical forces has instead put us in an adversarial predicament, where such a relationship though desirable has not occurred. The situation today is not only an adversarial relationship but also policy pronouncements from both sides where General Musharraf says that Kashmir is unfinished part of the partition, India is a threat to Pakistan, etc. At the same time at a drop of the hat he says that elections in Kashmir are a farce. I will teach India a lesson. On our side, instead of making graduated calibrated response, we paint ourselves into a corner in adversarial attitudes towards Pakistan. I am not saying that we should not retaliate. In fact, I am an advocate for structured responses where it is necessary. If within a week or ten days of attack on Indian Parliament we had done a strike across the line of control —this is my considered opinion—nobody could/would have questioned us. I do not think Pakistan would have resorted to the nuclear option. In fact, we could have told General Musharraf that you are against terrorism, you say you have nothing to do with what's happening in Azad Kashmir. So we will help you to fight terrorism. Since you cannot fight them, we'll help you to fight. He would have no answer except perhaps a political answer. Instead of that what do you do? You deploy half a million troops on the border, you in one go withdraw your high commissioner, ban over flights, suspend the train and bus services and after that what are the options left? And then we will not talk. You put yourself in a position where moving back is not possible. You see when you take a final stance of assertive negotiation in terms of techniques straight away, then you are closing your ways of pulling back. You have put your feet forward then removed them. This is what we have done. And this has given Pakistan a chance to tell the world : look ok, we are at fault; something happened, we are not in control of things, but these chaps refuse to talk, they refuse to respond. Specifically on the Kashmir, I am sure Shri Jethmalani will be able to tell you much more, I am clear in my mind that Akhand Bharat is not the solution. This is not on, Kashmir has a requirement of a solution, which is responsive to the cross section of public opinion of that state of India. You have to be innovative, bold, compromising where necessary. Perhaps the bottom line is : no territorial alienation of Jammu and Kashmir, which is a part of India, to any other country. But rest, there are options available. You should not put yourself in a strait jacket. If you do not find any solution responsive to the aspirations and the angst of the people of Jammu and Kashmir, your adversarial relationship with Pakistan will continue of course, but you will also be nurturing internal centrifugalism in the Indian Republic. It is therefore necessary that we look at with a greater sense of concern and urgency at the Kashmir issue. I have a theory that if you somehow find a solution to the Kashmir issue, its ramifications, its cascading impact to some extent will move Indo-Pak relations to normalcy, over a period of time and not immediately. Having said all this what is my "Bhavishya Vani", my astrology? I do not think in the short term, I am giving a period of 10-20 years, we can have normal relations with Pakistan. We are going to have a difficult adversarial relationship, not only because of our limitations but also I do not see any easy change in the power structure in Pakistan. The situation will not change and as long as it, remains as it is the relationship will be negative and adversarial. In the interim, what should our approach be? It sounds simplistic, but I am clear in my mind, that when they bother us, physically threaten us in terms of territorial integrity and security, our response should be decisive and effective, the signal should go that we will reach out if you harm us and you will be subject to equal disadvantages. While doing this we must create and consciously nurture capacity for political flexibility. Keep the doors open for talks. But let not that door being kept open give the impression that we shall not keep our powder dry. It has to be a combination of these two approaches and I think we shall make occasionally, deliberately even if it is not so, certain distinction between our public pronouncements and policy stances between the people of Pakistan and the Government. It is necessary that, you generate that internal contradiction, which in fact is an objective reality in that country. We do not do that, we just paint them all with the same brush. That is not sophistication, that is not understanding.

Musharraf's Reality Check on India's Pakistan Policies

General Pervez Musharraf has one utility for India which cannot and should not be denied. Since becoming a player in the power structure of Pakistan from late 1998 onwards, he has repeatedly performed the task of giving us in India, and the world at large clear assessments about the efficacy or otherwise of India's Pakistan policies. His assessments have mostly been about the inefficacy of India's policies. One has to accept fair levels of accuracy in his assessments even if one dismisses 50 per cent of what he says attributing it to his prejudices and misunderstandings about India.

The latest example is his public pronouncements to Pakistani Air Force Officers on the 29th of December where he said that India was compelled to act with complete restraint against Pakistan during the year 2002 because of Pakistan conveying clear signals both to India and major powers of the world that the slightest aggressive military action by India, even only if it was to cross the Line of Control, would have immediately attracted a nuclear retaliation from Pakistan which India did not have the capacity or the stomach to face.

Indian official spokesperson has given the usual and expected response about Musharraf being highly provocative, about his heading an irresponsible Government, etc, accompanied by an appeal to the international community to take note of his assertively adversarial stance about India.

The basic predicament and image of India which emerged as a consequence, is that of a state not having been able to give tangible and effective response to the calculated provocations by a smug adversary.

One must go beyond this most recent statement of Musharraf about Pakistan's successful politico-military strategy vis-à-vis, India being anchored in its nuclear capacities, to understand the continuity as well as objective of Musharraf's policies (or even Pakistan's India policies rooted in its nuclear capacities). President Zia-ul-Haq had conveyed Pakistan's intention of exercising the nuclear option to the then Indian Ambassador to Islamabad S.K. Singh in the mid-80s during Operation Brasstacks. Senior

Governmental figures threatened to use nuclear weapons against India during the Kargil conflict. Being confident about Pakistan's nuclear weapons capacities, Musharraf was opposed to initiatives regarding normalization even before the Kargil conflict as Chief of the Army Staff. He was not supportive of Vajpayee's visit to Lahore in February 1999. Soon after overthrowing Nawaz Sharif, Musharraf publicly asserted more than once that Pakistan had to pull back from the Line of Control during the Kargil conflict only because of US pressure, otherwise Pakistan would have liked to take the conflict to its victorious end by whatever means possible.

Earlier in December 2002, addressing a group of civilian officials and politicians in Peshawar, Musharraf asserted that he had achieved political and military victory against India despite India's massive military build up against Pakistan without firing a single shot, while at the same time making India spend nearly eight billion dollars on a futile military exercise because Indian military build up did not in any way dilute Pakistan's policy of full support to the separatist movement in Jammu and Kashmir.

There are fairly reliable reports that after returning from the failed Agra Summit in July 2001, Musharraf gave informal briefings to senior retired military colleagues in which he gave the categorical assessment that India was a soft and fragmented state which cannot take any effective action against Pakistan and that it was a matter of time before Pakistan's Kashmir policies succeed.

Musharraf's objectives in this pattern of statement and claims are clearly the following. First, he is conveying a message to India that in any emerging conflict situation between the two countries, Pakistan will not be inhibited in using its nuclear weapons in the light of its declared option of first use. Secondly, the same message is conveyed to major powers and international community with the additional objective of generating pressures on them to restrain India through diplomatic, political and economic means. Thirdly he is conveying an assurance to his domestic audience, particularly to the military establishment and Islam-pasand parties that despite his line with the US against the Taliban and Al-Qaeda under unavoidable compulsions, he has not changed his strong and firm anti-India policies particularly on the Kashmir issue and more importantly he is not going to change this policy because he can sustain this policy due to his nuclear weapons capacities.

The absence of any critical response from the major powers of the world to his assertions about using nuclear weapons has also given him the handle to convince domestic political circles that the world is supportive of Pakistan's nuclear strategies and capacities. Pakistani experts have not hesitated to point out that there has not been any effective political criticism or pressure on Pakistan about its developing nuclear and missile technologies and weapons systems in collaboration with China and North Korea. In general terms, Musharraf has achieved his objectives and fulfilled his motivations, more or less.

Twin dimensions of a consequence to this state of India-Pakistan confrontation require an examination. First, to what extent Indian claims of having succeeded in its exercising a coercive diplomacy in the year 2002, and secondly what should be the Indian response to Musharraf's politico-strategic posture based on his nuclear and missile capacities.

It is clear that in substance India's extensive exercise in coercive diplomacy had only minimum and marginal success. The massive deployment under "Operation Parakaram" only resulted in some piecemeal cosmetic public pronouncements by Musharraf. It did not translate into any reduction of cross-border terrorism engineered from Pakistan, nor did the various political and military steps that we took, lead to any change in Musharraf's subversive anti-India policies. Even more unfortunate is the fact that while our assertive but cosmetic military posture resulted in high political pressure being exerted on us to remain restrained, there was no parallel operational pressure on Musharraf to control the Inter-Services Intelligence and its cohorts from acting against India. The key argument in their advice for restraint for us was exactly the point being asserted now about Musharraf; if India takes any effective action it will result in a nuclear war. There are some reports though Indian military establishment was poised to launch operations against Pakistan in mid- January 2002 and then again in mid- June , pressure from the United States and its allies compelled us to remain inactive, giving substance to the rationale being articulated by Musharraf since October 2002. The inescapable conclusion is that neither our diplomacy nor our military posture served our interests in any meaningful manner. The more important issue is to structure our response to Musharraf's postures and possible international attitude towards Musharraf's policies.

First and foremost, we must fashion our military and strategic doctrines in relation to Pakistan on a categorical acceptance that Pakistan will resort to weapons of mass destruction against India at any movement where it feels, not only its existence is threatened but where it feels that even its image or military credibility is challenged. Once we become conscious of this as fulcrum of our defence policies, India should first consolidate and then augment its nuclear weapons and missile capacities which would clearly signal a devastating retaliation against Pakistan, a signal which should be tangible enough for Pakistan to take note of.

Given this requirement, it is imperative for India to purposefully follow through negotiations on missiles and related technologies which it is having with Russia, Israel and the United States. Elements of these negotiations are in the public knowledge. Government of India can expect full public support for these negotiations. Recently retired Chief of the Army Staff, General Padmanabhan had asserted in January 2002 that Pakistan will face decisive distractive consequences if it resorts to nuclear weapons. He has generally reiterated this assessment in recent weeks. While India may have a capacity which he asserts, reports during the last week of December indicate that India still has to put in place its Higher Strategic Command Structure.

Four years have passed since India's nuclear weaponisation. Pakistan already has National Command Authority dealing with its nuclear weapons and missiles. India cannot afford any more delays in the matter.

It is equally important that Government of India conveys to the US and other major powers of the world that given Musharraf's declared claims, assertions and intentions, regarding his nuclear weapons capacities, the world should not expect India to remain restrained in face of structured and continuous provocations by Musharraf. India should do something pre-emptive on the ground to stress this message to the Chancellories of power. At some point Musharraf's bluff would have to be called. That point may not be too far because at certain thresholds in political affairs, reason has to be replaced by use of a structured force as the final arbiter of resolving issues.

10

The New Phase

The Line of Return

With the electoral process in Jammu and Kashmir nearing completion the Indian government will have to undertake two exercises : one, commence a dialogue with the elected representatives about the future political dispensation in J&K. Two, engage Pakistan in a dialogue on the Kashmir issue. It is in this context that one takes note of media reports in Pakistan and abroad about the possibility of Pakistan agreeing to the resolution of the issue on the basis of converting the Line of Control into an international border.

The Pakistan newspaper *News* reported in the last week of August that idea was gathering momentum. There was speculation that the US is supportive of the proposal. The media, in India and abroad, indulged in much speculation that Musharraf would discuss this proposal with US President George Bush, followed by discussions between Bush and India's prime minister while both Musharraf and Vajpayee were in New York for the UN session.

A number of political and strategic analysts contributed to this misplaced optimism. When questioned about these reports at a press conference in New York, Musharraf posed a curt and abrasive counter-question: "Do you think I am a fool to think about such a solution?" He added that his policy on Kashmir has not changed and that he will raise the issue in every forum and on all available occasions. Vajpayee was equally categorical in rejecting the idea of LoC as solution later at a press conference in New York.

It is worthwhile to examine why the suggestion has cropped up again. But first, the history. The origin of the LoC lies in the Karachi Agreement of July 17, 1949 in which the ceasefire line was drawn up at the end of the Indo-Pakistan war in 1948. This agreement was signed by Indian and Pakistani military commanders as well as representatives at the UN Commission. The line commenced from Manawar in the south (south-west Jammu) to Khot in the North upto a map grid reference point NJ 9842 from where it lies, in the language of the ceasefire-line agreement, "thence north to the Glaciers". During the 1965 war, the line was violated but at the end of the war, India and Pakistan agreed to exchange prisoners captured by either side across the line, reverting the ceasefire line to status quo.

At the end of the1971 war, however, both sides decided to keep the minor territorial gains that they had made across the ceasefire line under the Simla Agreement. So Indira Gandhi and Zulfiqar Ali Bhutto decided to delineate the ceasefire line and to re-designate it as 'Line of Control'. This was agreed upon in accordance with paragraph 4(ii) of Simla Agreement. The re-delineation and the change in the nomenclature of the line signified an important political transition from the cease fire line being a military line separating the two armies, to a line demarcating a political divide which was to evolve into an international boundary between India and Pakistan. Bhutto had agreed to this argument. This new LoC defined in December 1972 was cartographically demarcated in detail.

The present LoC has a length of about 740 km from the international border in the south upto the grid reference NJ9842 in the north. The legality of this line was accepted by Pakistan for nearly 28 years. It is only during Pakistan's invasion across the LoC in Kargil in 1999 that the Pakistani Army headquarters and the Pakistan Foreign Office started indulging in the patently mendacious argument that it was not fully demarcated, its delineation was ambiguous, etc. Pakistan wanted to regress from the political legitimacy of the LoC to make it a temporary ceasefire line, the validity of which could be challenged by Pakistan.

With this background in mind, Indira Gandhi advocated a permanent settlement of the Kashmir issue on the basis of the LoC to Bhutto in 1972 in Simla. Bhutto agreed but pleaded for time to make a formal announcement requesting that the suggestion should not be incorporated in the Simla Agreement. That Bhutto was serious is indicated by the fact that he merged the northern areas and made them a centrally administered territory of Pakistan soon after the Simla Agreement. He only resiled from assurances given to Mrs Gandhi when he found her inmeshed in domestic crisis in 1974-75. The Indian side has informally raised the question of resolving the Kashmir dispute along the LoC more than once between 1983 and

1991. Musharraf does not like the proposal regarding permanent solution. Pakistan is convinced that J&K are alienated. Secondly, he says that the Indian armed forces would not be able to hold on in the face of the prevailing situation.

Calling on Neighours

Pervez Musharraf visited Bangladesh and Sri Lanka with a brief stop-over in China in the last week of July and the beginning of August. This is a measured diplomatic initiative by Musharraf with the objectives falling into two categories. The first category of objectives is in terms of the broad politico-strategic interests of Pakistan. The second was country specific in relation to Bangladesh, Sri Lanka and China.

The political and strategic aims of the visit were determined by the immediate context of regional security and political developments from Pakistan's point of view. Musharraf has stabilised and legitimised his political position as Pakistan's head of State. He has also completed the necessary steps to hold elections in Pakistan on his terms. He is considered a major positive factor in the US-led campaign against international terrorism. He also seems to have put in place both domestic arrangements and international equations aimed at the economic survival of Pakistan. His interaction with leaders of the major powers and all regional powers in the Islamic world seems to confirm his incremental acceptability in international politics.

There is only one aberration in this apparently positive scenario for Pakistan: Musharraf's inability to bring in substantive change in Pakistan's India policies. He is already on the defensive against segments of Pakistani public opinion critical of his joining the anti-terrorist campaign, performing a complete Uturn in Pakistani policies supporting the Taliban, Al-Qaeda, etc. The *bona fides* of his move towards holding general elections are under doubt both at home and abroad. The US and the West continue to pressurise him to pull back from supporting separatist terrorist activities in Jammu and Kashmir.

Since coming to power in 1999, Musharraf's interaction with the Chinese leadership has been less than satisfactory and those with other South Asian leaders minimal. The Almaty conference on Asian security, the ministerial meeting of the ARF, the Asian Security Forum in Brunei have resulted in implied criticism about his India policies and his not fulfilling the promises he made about eradicating terrorism in his speeches of January 12 and May 27, 2002.

His objectives at the macro-level, therefore, seem to be to intensify Pakistan's relations with important South Asian countries like Bangladesh and Sri Lanka, to touch base with the Chinese leadership and to seek Beijing's support of Pakistan's regional policies. This is to ensure that Pakistan does not get isolated on the issues of terrorism, relations with India and in regional equations. His second objective was to seek support for Pakistan's India (specifically Kashmir) policies. Third, to seek Chinese support in dealing with India as well as the uncertain political situation in Afghanistan. Fourth, to augment economic and technological relations with all these countries.

Musharraf's visit to Bangladesh was replete with important political undertones. He is the first military head of state and government from Pakistan to visit Bangladesh after Bangladesh's liberation. In contrast to Zulfiqar Ali Bhutto's visit to Dhaka in July 1974, Musharraf officially regretted the tragic violence in Bangladesh preceding and during the liberation war. (He, of course, did not specifically mention the Pakistani army as perpetrators of this violence.)

Bhutto had not expressed any regret and it was with reluctance that he visited the Martyrs's Memorial at Savar near Dhaka. Bhutto had demanded that his visit to the memorial should be a private one and there should be no military guard of honour. Musharraf apparently has closed this feeling of bitterness and Bangladesh generally did not have reservations about the commander-in-chief of the Pakistani army coming to their country.

While this may be so there has been a new foreign policy and political dynamics in Bangladesh-Pakistan relations since the advent of military rule in Bangladesh. This dynamics is positive and has been an incremental phenomenon, responsive to Bangladeshi threat perceptions and interests. India looms large in Bangladesh's foreign and security policies as a potential threat. Therefore, Bangladesh needs to counter balance the potential threats it perceives with equations with countries like Pakistan.

Compulsions born of history and Bangladesh's geo-strategic location have transcended the memories of India's support to Bangladesh's freedom struggle. Dhaka, therefore, believes in cultivating close relationship with Pakistan to redress the over-arching geographical presence of India. Pakistan is equally interested in creating a subcontinental balance of power vis-à-vis India. These orientations of Pakistani and Bangladeshi foreign policy underlined Musharraf's visit.

The two agreements signed during his visit on cultural and

technological cooperation serve two purposes. First, the cultural agreement by implication means Pakistan acknowledge the separate ethno-cultural identity of Bangladesh, while at the same time emphasises links between Bangladesh and Pakistan as Islamic countries - a measure that would counter the influence of 'Hindu India'. The agreement on technological cooperation is an umbrella under which Pakistan can be of assistance to Bangladesh for defence supplies. There are defence technology capacities in Pakistan which Bangladesh cannot get from other countries unless it is willing to pay very high prices.

Both Pakistan and Bangladesh have agreements with the US for location of American forces in their respective territories. This results in an unarticulated security arrangement also. No overt political or security agreement was signed, as this would have evoked a critical response from India which Bangladesh wants to avoid. Musharraf's visit was an important event adding substance to Pakistan-Bangladesh relations.

As far as Sri Lanka is concerned, Pakistan-Sri Lanka relations particularly economic and security have been close and substantive since 1977- barring a gap of three years between 1987 and 1989. Bilateral trade is substantive. Pakistan has been a reliable and steady supplier of defence equipment to Sri Lanka over the years. Sri Lankan military and paramilitary personnel have been and are trained in Pakistan.

The Sinhalese also consider Pakistan as a more reliable friend against Tamil separatism because of India's social, ethnic and linguistic linkages with Sri Lanka Tamils. Sri Lanka is aware that no durable solution to ethnic conflict can be achieved without the support of India. But at the same time Colombo legitimately feels the need for other subcontinental actors supporting them against excessive Tamil demands. Musharraf's visit has been fully responsive both to specific needs and the general orientations of Sri Lanka's security and foreign polices. He stressed the need of smaller countries of South Asia having a close relationship with each other to counter the asymmetric influence that India can generate.

As far as China is concerned, the visit was too brief. The most important signal Musharraf gave by stopping over in China was to stress that Pakistan considers China as its most reliable friend not only in terms of bilateral political, economic and defence cooperation, but also security environment in Central and South Asia. There are also reports of Musharraf having requested the Chinese to facilitate Pakistan's membership of the ASEAN Security Forum, ARF. There was also a message that Musharraf's closeness to the US would not be at the cost of any dilution of Pakistan's relations with China.

Musharraf's visits to Bangladesh, Sri Lanka and China are a timely and measured diplomatic initiative. It is obvious that India should monitor Pakistan, relations particularly with Bangladesh and Sri Lanka in the coming months to see that these equations do not militate against interests in these countries and relations with China.

The Pak MMA Factor

The results of Pakistan's general election have not only radically changed the political landscape of that country but they will also have long-term implications for India and the region.

The emergence of Muttahida-Majlis-e-Amal (MMA), a coalition of extremist Islamic parties supportive of the Taliban and Al-Qaida, as a sizable group in the National Assembly with 45 seats and its victories in the North West Frontier Province (NWFP) and Baluchistan assemblies, where it has secured not only for Pakistan but India and the entire region as well.

Contrary to the views expressed by some analysis that MMA's victory has perturbed President Pervez Musharraf himself orchestrated the victory of these 'Islam-pasand' parties in the politically sensitive NWFP and Balochistan, with two objectives. MMA governments in the two provinces bordering Afghanistan will enable Musharraf to tell the Americans that while he wished to cooperate in the antiterrorist campaign in Afghanistan, the elected government will put restraints on the extent of his cooperation.

Thus, he ensures some kind of security for the Taliban and Al Qaida have been escaping from the US led military operation in Afghanistan. He could also cite the election results to tell the US that he is cooperating with it in the war against terrorism under overwhelming compulsions and internal opposition to him.

It may be recalled that in all the elections from 1988 onward. Islamic parties barely got five or four per cent of the votes polled and never won a significant number of seats in the votes polled in the national or provincial legislatures. While Musharraf's pro-Islamic credibility got a boost in NWFP and Baluchistan, he has ensured a hung National Assembly where no single political party has a sufficient majority to form the government. It will be a coalition government which will be dependent on him for its survival.

The largest group is the pro-Musharraf Pakistan Muslim League-Quaid-e-Azam (PML-QA) with 77 seats in the 272 member house followed by former Prime Minister Benazir Bhutto's Pakistan People's Party with 63. That Musharraf has decided to play an assertively intrusive role in the electoral process was proved by the fact that he made significant amendments to the original legal framework Order (LFO) which included all the major constitutions amendments that he had initiated since April.

He introduced further amendments literally a few hours before voting in the general election commenced on October 10. Musharraf stipulated in the new amendments to LFO that members of the legislatures elected as independents could join any political party within three or four days of the official declaration of results.

This led the PML-QA gaining support of independents after the elections. The second amendment debars permanently any individual from being elected a member of any legislature in Pakistan if he/she is disqualified under any law in force at the time, an amendment obviously debarring Benazir Bhutto and former Prime Minister Nawaz Sharif permanently from politics.

By the third amendment Musharraf extended the tenure of the existing judges of Pakistan's Supreme Court and the high courts who have supported him since he took over power in a military coup.

Another provision he made was that each political party which has got more than five per cent of the total number of seats in the legislatures can claim the reserved seats in each legislature for that party proportionately.

This means that political parties which have gained sufficient membership in the legislatures will proportionately lay claim to the 60 reserved seats for women in the National Assembly, 66 in this category in Punjab 29 in Sindh 22, in NWFP, and 11 in Balochistan.

The 10 reserved seats for non-Muslims in the National Assembly eight in Punjab, nine in Sindh and three each in NWFP and Baluchistan would also be dispensed in the same manner enhancing the strength of MMA and PML-QA with some marginal benefits to PPP.

Most foreign observers have refrained from giving any categorical confirmation about the elections in Pakistan having been fair or transparent. There was a prior acceptance of the fact that elections were being held under a terms of reference formulated by Musharraf.

But the most telling criticism came from John Cushnahan, leader of the foreign observers team from the European Union. His report states that the Pakistani elections were deeply flawed due to the constitutional change made by Musharraf in August.

The report went on to state that these changes could lead to concentration of power into the hands of a single individual who can dismiss the elected governments and institutionalise the role of the military in the government. The report also said the changes in the 1973 Constitution of Pakistan had converted the parliamentary form of government into a Presidential one headed by Musharraf.

This is factual assessment because Musharraf and the National Security Council chaired by him would emerge as the final arbiters of political dispensations in Pakistan in the foreseeable future. The implications of this development should be a matter of concern to India and the international community. Governments formed by a coalition of extremist Islamic political groups linked to the Taliban and Al Qaeda would create hurdles in Afghanistan.

In fact, this may result in increasing the strength and capacities of elements in NWFP and Baluchistan and southern Afghanistan wishing to destabilise the government of President Hamid Karzai in Kabul.

The security prospects in Afghanistan will become more uncertain and dangerous. There are distinct possibilities of an MMA government in NWFP becoming more active and supportive of Pakistan-sponsored terrorist subversion in Jammu and Kashmir.

Given the links between Taliban and Al Qaeda cadres with MMA and given the involvement of Taliban and Al-Qaeda in drug trafficking, the prospects of increased narco-terrorism cannot be ruled out. This will have negative ramifications in both Afghanistan and India. Benazir Bhutto's statement from London that she would ask her party to cooperate with President Musharraf signals the military ruler consolidating his position at the head of the Pakistani power structure for some time to come. It is obvious India will be under greater pressure to resume dialogue with Pakistan in the aftermath of the elections. New Delhi's response to this important challenge to its foreign policy should be fashioned in the context of negative prospects that are discerned in post-election Pakistan.

Musharraf will Continue to Call the Shots

Regardless of what kind of government comes into being in Pakistan, Pervez Musharraf, who took a fresh oath as President for a five- year term intends to remain dominant in every aspect of national politics.

He will be successful in this exercise so long as he retains the support of the military establishment.

Musharraf has already isolated all the important political parties and their leaders. Consequently, new political groups and entities have emerged either independently or as splinter groups, breaking away from the main political parties. The political parties of Pakistan across the spectrum do not seem to have any desire to adhere to any ideological roots. Their approach seems to be motivated by a desire to adjust to political dispensations being structured by Musharraf.

Though critical of the constitutional amendments carried through by Musharraf, the political parties and the political classes in Pakistan seem to be reconciled to functioning under the new arrangements.

It is clear that Islamist parties for the first time seem to have displaced the moderate and liberal political parties, like the Awami Party and the Pakistan People's Party (PPP) particularly in the sensitive states of North West Frontier Province and Baluchistan.

Given the relative strength of the Muttahida Majlis-e-Amal (MMA) member in the National Assembly they are bound to play an influential role in Pakistani policies in the foreseeable future.

There is limited accuracy in the conventional wisdom being touted about that the emergence of the six party Islamic alliance MMA as an important factor in Pakistani policies is a setback for Musharraf. A more rational and plausible assessment would be that Musharraf orchestrated the elections in a manner where factions of the Muslim League and the PPP amenable to him would find reasonable representation in the National Assembly while Islamist parties would replace the liberal and democratic parties opposed to his assumption of power.

Another motive of his enabling the MMA to emerge as an important political factor was to signal to the opposition in the Pakistani domestic politics that despite his having had to toe the US line in its anti-terrorist campaign, he still remains committed to the ideology, the fervour and the causes of Islam.

It is also clear that no coalition government in Pakistan can last for long unless it has the support of the MMA in one form or the other. MMA forming provincial government in NWFP and in Baluchistan is on the cards. The cadres of this party will also dominate the politics of Northern Areas and the Pakistan-controlled part of Kashmir in the coming months.

Given the prospects of a tenuous coalition government coming to power Musharraf's personal authority and influence will remain supreme.

With the National Security Council expected to dominate the governing processes, the substance of power will rest with the Pakistani Army high command.

Given this scenario, the implications could be a matter of concern in term of regional security and stability. The US has acknowledged that its campaign against terrorism in Afghanistan and the northern regions of Pakistan has been less than successful. The US defence and intelligence authorities acknowledge that Al Qaeda and Taliban cadres have escaped in sufficient numbers to regroup to continue their terrorist acts internationally as well as in the South Asian region.

The MMA, with power and influence will give covert support to these terrorist cadres. The US response to these prospects and reports about Osama bin Laden being still alive has been that the terrorist campaign is not aimed at one single individual and that it will continue on all fronts.

The incoming government of Pakistan under Musharraf's overall guidance will have to cope with incremental destabilisation of Afghanistan and disruption of return to democracy in Jammu and Kashmir. Musharraf's likely advocacy to the US would be that he would not let the MMA disrupt or diminish his support for the US-led anti-terrorist campaign.

He will also argue that while he will try to control the MMA activities in Jammu and Kashmir, US should take note of the fact that main separatist groups in Jammu and Kashmir did not participate in the recent elections there and therefore the violence in Jammu and Kashmir has to be assessed on a different criteria. Musharraf has also indicated his general support for the diplomatic and impending military campaign by the US against Iraq.

Domestically Pakistani democracy stands truncated for the time being, a view generally expressed in the Pakistani media. Economic management and governance would be a complex task for Musharraf as he finalises formulation and implementation of policies on the basis of bargaining with the political parties coming into the coalition government.

That Musharraf predicament is being dealt with sympathetically by the US is indicated by Washington's very temporized measured and noncommittal response to the emergence of extremist Islamic political groups entering the power structure of Pakistan.

Pakistan's economy will continue to get inputs from Saudi Arabia and other Gulf countries because there is a convergence of interests.

Musharraf will continue his adversarial policies towards India while publicly pleading for resumption of dialogue with India. He will receive incremental support on this second point from major powers.

The twin challenges to India's Pakistan policies is to structure timely and effective response to Pakistan's adversarial policies while at the same time formulating tactical moves to resume contacts with Pakistan, not that these contacts will lead to immediate results but because such contacts will sustain international support for India and could be long term basis for coming to terms with Pakistan.

India and Pakistan – A Further Slide Down

In the ongoing adversarial Tamasha between India and Pakistan, another contretemps occurred in the second week of February. The acting High Commissioner of Pakistan Jalil Abbas Jiliani was declared persona non grata and expelled from India for having allegedly given some money to a couple of Hurriyat workers in support of their subversive activities against India. As expected, government of Pakistan reacted by expelling India's Acting High Commissioner Sudhir Vyas along with four other officials of the Indian High Commission in Islamabad. The declared details about the incident are in the public knowledge. What is more important is to examine whether the decision taken by the government of India was a measured one based on incontrovertible evidence or did the government's decision have other orientations and motivations. Even more important is to assess the implications of this latest bout of diplomatic confrontation.

The information put out by the Government of India about the decision to expel Jilani so far indicates that the evidence about Jilani's giving money to the Hurriyat workers is mostly circumstantial. The first question needing an answer is how is it that a senior diplomat of the experience of Jilani personally decided to get involved in such a transaction when Indo-Pakistan relations are highly tense and even more relevantly when the Pakistan High Commission is under general and constant surveillance by Indian authorities. Secondly, the Hurriyat cadres who went into the High Commission must be aware of this surveillance. In spite of it what made them indiscreet or non-challant enough to go in and carry the money out. The lady from the Hurriyat instead of being taken into custody soon after getting out of the High Commission was only arrested a kilometre or two away. If she was to be caught red-handed, why not near the Pakistan High Commission. Our police authorities say she mentioned money being given to her by Jilani. But according to newspapers she did not mention Jilani by name in her statement, when she was produced in court. The case gets curiouser when one takes note of the fact that a senior Delhi Police official stated in a Press Conference that the lady Ansum Jamrood was to take the money and deliver it to some contact in Bangkok. If the money was to be used from Bangkok, could not the Pakistan embassy in Bangkok disburse the money instead of this being done by the Pakistan High Commission in New Delhi.

Then again senior diplomats and heads of mission normally do not get directly involved in such intelligence operations. It is highly unusual for a head of mission himself to get personally involved in such transactions, unless there is physical, electronic or photographic information about Jilani actually giving the money to Ms. Ansum Jamrood. The evidence remains circumstantial unless our authorities have some incontrovertible proof. The point being made is that these questions need to be answered by the Indian Government–both to our Parliament and to our public to confirm the logic of the decision. The same question would have to be answered because they would be posed by foreign governments who would be concerned and interested at the heightened Indo-Pakistan tensions resulting from this decision. If the evidence we have is incontrovertible then the action taken against Jilani and four of his colleagues expelling them, one accepts that it was both inevitable and unavoidable. It must be kept in mind that Pakistan has given no specific reasons for expelling our Acting High Commissioner and four of his colleagues. Pakistan would however not have to face the type of questions which have been mentioned above about our decision. They would just have simple answer that they have made the retaliatory diplomatic move.

Another worrisome aspect of our decision in this matter is that of the entire exercise being orchestrated and controlled by the Home Ministry, and police authorities. There was no, or very little consultation with the Ministry of External Affairs or perhaps even the PMO before the decision was finalised. One has been told by reliable sources that the Ministry of External Affairs came to know of the incident and follow up action first on the television. The first statements about the incident and follow up action being considered were made by Joint Commissioner of Police, and so on. One cannot escape the conclusion that the Ministry of External Affairs stood marginalized. Instead of the spokesmen of the Ministry of External Affairs being the principal articulator of the details of the incident and the action which followed. So the question arises whether the Home Ministry is becoming principal determiner of India's foreign policy Agenda.

The implications of this recent development in our bilateral relations are:

- India has given the signal that it has now reached a decision to take to decisive and drastic actions against Pakistani diplomatic links with separatist elements in Jammu and Kashmir and other parts of India, regardless of the status and rank of the Pakistani officials involved.
- An equally clear message has gone to Hurriyat and other such groups that they would now be subject to more drastic remedial action by the Government of India about their networking with Pakistani authorities.
- India-Pakistan relations have deteriorated further which will make the resumption of bilateral dialogue more difficult.
- Major powers of the world, particularly the United States of America, would react to this development critically and would interpret it as India's unwillingness to make some moves to restore some normalcy in Indo-Pak relations.
- Musharraf will utilize the incident to increase hostile and subversive activities in India and to launch a diplomatic offensive against India on the basis of this incident.
- It will increase his ability to assuage the Islam-pasand parties of Pakistan who are critical of his siding with the USA in its anti- terrorist campaign.
- While Pakistan is isolated to some extent as a state harbouring terrorists, Pakistan's credibility as an ally of the USA undiminished. Given this fact the United States will generate pressure on Musharraf's behalf on India to resume the dialogue with Pakistan without pre-conditions.
- As always the large Muslim citizenry of India will again get concerned about heightened levels of Indo-Pakistan hostility.
- With the United States planning military operations against Iraq, high levels of Indo Pakistan confrontation will be considered by the US and its allies as a factor disturbing the USA's anti-terrorist and anti-Saddam campaign. This would be so in the context of government of India having reservations about USA'S impending military plans against Iraq.
- Sustaining levels of positive equations with the USA will be an important task for India's foreign policy in the coming weeks. As far

as Pakistan is concerned some serious thought should be given to additional options in the linear logic of expulsion of Acting High Commissioner Jilani. Government of India should examine freezing bank accounts and other assets of the Hurriyat and other separatist groups operating in India, particularly those with links with the ISI.

India should consider declaring Pakistan a terrorist state taking the legal implications into account, a step we have not taken. We have limited ourselves to advocating that Pakistan be declared a terrorist state to other countries. Consideration could be given to closing down diplomatic missions of Pakistan in India and India in Pakistan, for a brief period. Interest sections of both countries could continue to function in friendly embassies in each other's capital to maintain minimum levels of contacts.

India's Pakistan policies should have two macro-level ingredients. First to respond decisively in terms of retaliatory action against any further major terrorist violence organized by Pakistan in India. Secondly, we must think about commencing a dialogue at some appropriate official level with Pakistan in some third country by the autumn or winter of this year. A complete break down of communications in relations with Pakistan is not a practical predicament either for India or for Pakistan. There is one more serious, and to some extent introspective question which both our Parliament and our public opinion should consider. Is Government of India's present orientations in its Pakistan policies only connected with the foreign policy move or the most recent decisions motivated by considerations of domestic politics and the general elections which are just a year away. There is speculation about this in the Indian public opinion.

Does a Pre-emptive Indian Strike on Pakistan Makes Sense

Government of India's pronouncements on doctrine of pre-emptive strikes against Pakistan is getting curiouser and curiouser. External Affairs Minister Yashwant Sinha quoting the Iraqi precedent asserted more than once in the first fortnight of April that there is justification for India to take pre-emptive action against as sponsor of cross-border terrorism. Defence Minister George Fernandes first endorsed Sinha's statements and later on expressed the view that what Sinha said was not a policy statement or a formal declaration of intent by the government. Fernandes went to the extent of saying that it was a casual remark by the foreign minister. Prime Minister Vajpayee in a public statement in Sikkim around the same time said that India does not believe in military solutions to disputes but India's policy is to find solutions through peaceful negotiations. Then there is the Deputy Prime Minister L.K. Advani who talked earlier more than once about right of reprisals and right of hot pursuit.

This reflects a kind of confusing and irrational impulsiveness which show lack of gravitas on matters of high policy in the Government of India. The US has flatly questioned the Indian rationale for pre-emptive strikes. The Secretary of State Colin Powell, pronouncing that parallels can be drawn between the situation in Iraq and Indo-Pakistan face off on the Kashmir issue. Pakistan as expected has threatened not just firm but aggressive retaliation. Addressing a Formation Commanders meeting President Musharraf has said Pakistan's defences are impregnable. Pakistan Foreign Minister Khurshid Mehmood Kasuri went one better by saying that India should not indulge in mis-adventures because Pakistan's missiles capacities are far superior to those of India.

The first point to be made is that excepting exceptional cases no country announces its intention of undertaking pre-emptive strikes, the rights of reprisals or hot pursuit in advance. The key factor in these exercises is surprise, speed and decisiveness. Secondly, before indulging in such assertiveness there should be careful assessment whether India has the capacity to undertake pre-emptive strikes without doing too much damage to itself. Thirdly, given the massive military presence of US in Pakistan in the Gulf and in Iraq as well as on the northern edges of the Arabian Sea and the Gulf, will the United States countenance such strike against Pakistan? This is considered an important ally in the current US operational strategies in the region.

Three further questions arise: can the US attack on Iraq be a model for India and Pakistan, secondly, to what extent India's pre-emptive strike across the line of control be tolerated by Pakistan before it resorts to nuclear weapons. Third what does India hopes to gain by such military moves with its attendant risks. US attack on Iraq cannot be a precedent or model for India, primarily because the asymmetry in the military power equations between Iraq and USA. USA has overwhelming technological operational and human resources superiority over the military resources of Iraq in all these respects. Secondly, Saddam Hussain was generally considered a perniciously violent influence in regional politics by countries of the region as well as by the important powers. Third, though there was no consensus on the manner in which the military operations were launched by the USA against Iraq there was general agreement that Saddam Hussain's regime should be removed from authority. Fourth, no individual country or a group of countries has the capacity or the political will to prevent the USA from carrying out its decisions on the ground notwithstanding political and diplomatic moves made through the United Nations to restrain the USA. Sadam Hussain's regime did not have the spontaneous or genuine support of the Iraqi people. Lastly, the Bush Administration had the will and resources to carry through its decisions regardless of objections from the national public opinion and world public opinion.

The Indian predicament is exactly the opposite of all the points underpinning and supporting the US attack on Iraq. The rationale of the US attack on Iraq may conform to India's predicaments and concerns vis-à-vis Pakistan but it is not an operational model which India can follow.

As far as the threshold upto which India cross the Line of Control in pre-emptive military action without its resulting in nuclear war is concerned, prospects are not definable. They are both uncertain and unpredictable. Musharraf has stated that Indian security forces move along the Line of Control will be considered sufficient justification of him to initiate nuclear retaliation. This is an exercise in psychological warfare and pre-emptive politic- diplomatic sabre- rattling. There is sizeable US military presence in the region including Afghanistan and in Pakistan. If the Indian pre-emptive action across the LOC is in consequence of a major act of violence by Pakistan-sponsored terrorists and if the operation is brief surgical operation, and has the advantage of surprise without threatening Pakistani territory proper, it is plausible and reasonable to expect that the US will prevent Pakistan from getting into nuclear mode while parallely preventing India from larger military operations or nuclear weapons postures. If the suggested pre-emptive action by India is prolonged and threatens the Government of Pakistan, the conflict can escalate into a nuclear confrontation despite the US military presence and pressure in our region.

The next question is what can India hope to gain from such an adventure given the attendant risks? A limited pre-emptive response to Pakistan-sponsored terrorism cannot and should not be described as an adventure. This is a long delayed and necessary response which India should have undertaken more than once after the Kargil conflict. If a short pre-emptive military operation is undertaken with careful and calibrated planning and without our penchant for indulging in advance publicity and posturing, the gains could be:

- A clear signal to Pakistan that India will retaliate against the source of terrorism violence against the country.

- Secondly, it will affirm both our realization and determination that India has to fight its own battles against terrorism without presuming on the participation or support by USA or other countries. This will result in the US not taking India for granted as a country which will abide by US advice even when its own interests are seriously threatened.
- Fourth, it could not only bring down levels of terrorism but reduce Pakistani support to such terrorist acts.
- The civilian population on the other side of the Line of Control in Pakistan Occupied Kashmir will be less willing to support terrorist being launched from their side of the border against India.
- If India indulges in ore-emptive action, two risks are:
- Loss of support and some levels of cooperation with the US for a brief period, an attitude which will be shared by other countries.

The second more serious risk is a nuclear war. But that can be avoided if our pre-emptive actions are limited and brief in their time-frame.

If India deems it necessary to take pre-emptive action, it need not be linked to the US operations in Iraq. It should be an autonous exercise based on ground realities and governed by careful and measured calculations.

Road Map for Indo-Pakistan Dialogue

The tense relations between India and Pakistan are the most important negative factor affecting South Asian security. I have no intention of going into the history of Indo-Pak relations or the rights and wrongs of the attitudes and issues involved. The last six weeks have seen a revival again of some positive initiatives by leaders of India and Pakistan to recommence an effort at normalization of relations between the two countries. The initiative is both logical and necessary given the following factors.

- the confrontation between India and Pakistan constitutes an unacceptable trend, draining away resources which can be devoted to the more important and urgent tasks of development and economic well being of the people of India and Pakistan.
- the confrontation contributes to centrifugal impulses disrupting the harmony and cohesion of civil societies in both countries
- the phenomenon of terrorism and ethnic religious extremism has to be

stemmed by cooperation between India and Pakistan in such a manner that the latter is persuaded to not only stop whatever residual support is being provided by its agencies but also that it takes all other steps to discourage this. This poses a danger to the unity, and territorial integrity of both countries.

- India and Pakistan having become nuclear weapons powers continuing confrontation between the two countries has dangerous implications.
- the international community in general and the major powers in particulars are more directly and incrementally concerned about hostile relations between India and Pakistan.

This adversarial relationship constitutes a hurdle against India and Pakistan becoming full participants in the mainstream of economic and technological developments in the world, preventing them from achieving their undoubted respective potentialities.

Positive trends in operational terms which could contribute to a process of Indo-Pakistan dialogue and some preparatory steps which would help the initiative : India should accept that issues related to Jammu and Kashmir constitute a core issue in Indo-Pak relations. There can be an agreement that this is a core issue but from different points of views to Pakistan and India.

There should not be too much focus on procedural details about the agenda for bilateral talks. The previous discussions about having 'composite approach' and priorities, of one item or the other, has proved to be empty and detrimental factor against meaningful discussions. The agenda would cover all issues affecting Indo-Pakistan relations which have been a part of the discussions since 1983.

The prioritization of different items on the agenda should be worked out at official level discussions, but the prioritization should not inhibit either side from having parallel discussions on various items.

The framework for discussions need not be based on one specific agreement or specific series of meetings of the past. The framework should be extracted from the positive elements of previous agreements, meetings and summits on which there is a general consensus between India and Pakistan. In fact, both sides should undertake a specific exercise for this purpose and work out such a consensus.

The process of reviving the dialogue should be gradually spread over perhaps a period of one year or 18 months. The engagement should be devoid of hype and should display perseverance by both sides. Senior middle level officers should commence the process. Moving on to Foreign Secretary level talks and then graduating to political levels. A summit meeting should take place only when prospects of agreements are clearly on the anvil. The process leading to the summit should be demystified. It should be acknowledged both by India and Pakistan that J&K is more than a territorial dispute for both countries and therefore a profound political approach transcending the attitudes and advocacies of the past has to be adopted.

Some points of detail which should characterise policies of India and Pakistan are :

India should not hesitate to acknowledge that to some extent, the disturbances inside J&K are a result of alienation of people from the Government of India and the Government of Jammu and Kashmir.

Pakistan should acknowledge that there has not been just political and diplomatic but material support to the separatist agitation from Pakistan. There is no point in resisting that this is not so.

In fact, I would venture the opinion that the credibility of the indigenous separatist movement in J&K since 1989-90 has been eroded by active participation from Pakistan in that violent agitation. This kind of acknowledgement would clear the air for meaningful discussions.

As far as the issue of trans-border terrorism across the Line of Control, it is a major concern of India. There are technological means which can be put in place to monitor this phenomenon and be preventive, if they are put in place by mutual agreement between the Government of India and Pakistan. This may not require the presence of external personnel physically on the Line of Control.

India should take note of assurance given by Pakistan about not supporting militant groups. India need not insist on a complete stoppage of all violent activities which may not be possible, if there is sufficient evidence on the ground substantiating Pakistan assurances, India should be responsive in conducting a dialogue.

Pakistan should take note of the fact that the new Government of the state of Jammu and Kashmir has been elected in a free and fair election in the presence of foreign observers. There was 65 to 75 per cent voting in the elections. The Government of Mr. Mufti Mohammed Sayeed is taking serious steps to gain the trust and confidence of people of J&K. This process should not be questioned or disrupted. The political stabilization of Jammu and Kashmir can become the basis for a reconciliation between India and Pakistan.

Apart from issues of Jammu and Kashmir and separatist violence, India and Pakistan should give particular attention to stabilizing nuclear weapons related security environment in the subcontinent. The agreement embodied in the Lahore Memorandum of February 1999 should be followed up as early as feasible.

As far as basic issue of Jammu and Kashmir goes, suggestions put forward by Mr. Pervez are worth examining at the Track II level of Indo-Pakistan interaction.

There should be conscious and assiduous attempts by Governments of India and Pakistan, to educate public opinion on the imperative need for normalisation of Indo-Pak relations.

Vajpayee and Jamali-Kamal in Indo- Pakistan Relations

Indo-Pakistan relations are again in a roller coaster ride following Vajpayee's speech in Srinager and Pakistan Prime Minister Jamali's telephone conversation with him. Jamali followed through his conversation with a television interview on the 6th of May in which he announced steps in normalization which Pakistan is willing to take. He said Pakistan is willing to restore surface transport in stages, restore civil aviation contacts, resume trade relations, and restore diplomatic relations at the High commissioners level, and so on.

There is a groundswell of optimism about new beginnings in the media and in the public. But there is need for a careful scrutiny of all the evolving policy stance of India and Pakistan. Two factors which should influence any prognosis of Indo-Pakistan relations are the substance of policy orientations and the ground realities in Jammu and Kashmir. The point to be noted is that there is nothing new in the suggestions made by Pakistan except Jamali's statement that both countries should act on the Memorandum of Understanding of Lahore for nuclear risk reduction. All other points have been operational in Indo-Pakistan relations for the last decade or more. The offer to restore civil aviation is only to restore air flights from India to Pakistan and from Pakistan to India. There is no offer to restore over-flight facilities to Pakistani airspace for Indian civilian aircraft because Pakistan wants to make India's civil aviation contacts westwards a costly phenomenon. The irony is that it is we who started this unnecessary game. One wishes we had not. As far as Jamali's offer of including 78 items in the trading list for import from India is concerned, it is a meaningless cosmetic offer. What needs to be done is a bold move to allow free exchange of goods between the two countries, bilaterally and under the SAARC arrangements. This Pakistan is not willing to do.

On the basic issue of Jammu and Kashmir, both Musharraf and Jamali have publicly stated that Pakistan would continue to support the cause of Jammu and Kashmir against alleged Indian oppression. Pakistan's Foreign Office spokesman Aziz Ahmed Khan repeated this policy assertion throughout the last week of April and first week of May. Pakistani statements that they are opposed to terrorism remains subject to their caveat that they have nothing to do with violence in Jammu and Kashmir. Two further tactical Pakistani nuances have to be kept in mind. First, Jamali rushing to send a formal invitation to Prime Minister Vajpayee to visit Islamabad despite the experience at Lahore and Agra, and secondly, his stating that the forthcoming round of Indo-Pak dialogue should commence from the point where matters rested at Agra (It is reasonable to assume that the point of starting a dialogue from Pakistani's point of view of the Agra summit is the suggestion). The aborted Agra Declaration in the drafting of which former Foreign Prime Minister Jaswant Singh got unnecessarily involved made the territorial solution of the Kashmir issue top item on the Agenda without any reference to cross-border terrorism. These two nuances in Pakistani policies clearly indicate Pakistan's limited objective of gaining publicity advantage at a point of time when US Deputy Secretary of State Richard Armitage and Assistant Secretary of State Christina Rocca are visiting Islamabad and New Delhi. There is no inclination to discuss matters seriously as far as one can discern.

While Vajpayee's offer to resume dialogue, there is no clarity regarding the conditionality related to terrorism which India has repeatedly spelt out over the last 18 months. Even his speech in Parliament did not clear up the extent to which this conditionality is absolute and non-negotiable. The other measures which he announced are on expected lines.

Moving on to ground realities levels of infiltration and cross-border terrorism have increased with the onset of summer. Pakistan sponsored terrorist groups are undertaking calibrated targeting against the individuals and entities working for peace and stability in the State of Jammu and Kashmir. This targeting also includes the objectives of ethnic cleansing. Targets of terrorist violence have been politicians and civil servants of the Mufti Government who are responsible for implementing this policy "the healing touch". The second category of targets are the security forces, particularly those managing external security in the state to bring about break down of law and order. The third category of targets is organizations involved with information, public services and developmental activities. The suicide attacks on the facilities of All India Radio and Television in Srinagar, exemplifies this approach. The fourth category of targets are Members of the Hindu community particularly those living in Muslim areas or in the border areas of Jammu. The attempt is to change the ethno-religious demography of the state. Levels of tension and insecurity remain high.

Chief Minister Mufti Mohammed Sayeed remains steadfast in his commitment to the policy of reconciliation. Even more significant is the fact that despite partisan political differences, both Prime Minister Vajpayee and Deputy Prime Minister Advani have extended support to this policy in their statements during their visits to Srinagar in April. The Government of India has appointed a new special representative to talk various political groups and parties in Jammu and Kashmir, to formulate a comprehensive political solution responsive to the aspirations of the people of Jammu and Kashmir and related to constitutional and political relations between state and the centre, the nature and extent of autonomy, and so on.

N.N. Vohra, a distinguished civil servant, former Principal Secretary to Prime Minister Gujral, former Home Secretary and Defence Secretary has been entrusted with this responsibility. He has been to Srinagar during the third or fourth week of April, commencing discussions with important parties and leaders. While Hurriyat and Mr. Shabir Shah's Democratic Front, have refused to talk with Vohra, insisting on a dialogue with the Prime Minister and senior political figures, Vohra in a press conference on the 29th of April in Srinagar stated that he is not only willing to talk to all separatist groups but that he considers interaction with these groups essential to forge a durable solution to the internal political parties of Jammu and Kashmir.

A concerted effort seems to be on to negotiate a practical and reasonable solution to the domestic aspects of the Jammu and Kashmir issue. While this is so, some basic terms of reference governing India's policies in this regard have not changed, and rightly so. The assessment and conviction that normalcy in Jammu and Kashmir is possible only after terrorist violence sponsored by Pakistan stops, remains. That a solution to the Kashmir issue should in no way compromise India's territorial unity and integrity remains affirmed. There is and there can be no role for Pakistan as a third party, in discussions remains part of the Indian policy. That the constitutional and political dispensation in Jammu and Kashmir should not erode the cohesion of Indian polity, remains a major consideration. That these initiatives require an atmosphere of peace and stability in relations between India and Pakistan was the logic of Prime Minister Atal Behari Vajpayee's statements in Sikkim and in Srinagar in April, that India is willing to resume dialogue with Pakistan provided Pakistan seriously help create such an atmosphere by abandoning cross-border terrorism as an instrument of its India policies.

The current offer of talks by Vajpayee was to project a moderate and reasonable image of India in relation to Pakistan. Secondly, as the war in Iraq wound down, a certain amount of American diplomatic pressure on Pakistan and India commenced from the middle of April. First, the initiative is tentative and Pakistan has responded more under coercive pressure of the USA than India in comparative terms. Secondly, neither Musharraf nor Jamali in their response to Vajpayee have expressed any commitment to change their intrusive policies on Jammu and Kashmir.

The process of resuming dialogue must be gradual and slow.

The Agra fiasco should not be repeated. In my view, if Indo-Pakistan talks commence at the level of joint secretaries some time in last quarter of this year at a mutually agreed place and time there is no need to be choosy about this. The dialogue should be carefully structured in terms of preparation of Agenda, prioritization of the items of the Agenda without any polemical pyrotechnics. Once this happens, both countries could move on to higher levels of talks first, on official and military level talks and then to political levels. Heads of government should only meet after there are clear indications of a successful outcome.

One point which needs to be made is that macro level political and strategic prospects are that within two to five years, the US will suggest a solution to India and Pakistan basically rooted in the present territorial dispensation of Jammu and Kashmir between Pakistan and India. It would be an offer which would be difficult to refuse. India's attempt should be to ensure that offer does not erode India's fundamental interests in Jammu and Kashmir.

Indo-Pak Relations - Post Vajpayee-Musharraf Summit in Islamabad 4th to 6th January, 2004

There is reason for satisfaction that Indo-Pak bilateral relations have moved in the right direction on the margins of the 12th SAARC summit in Islamabad between 4th and 6th January, 2004. In some respects, the outcome of discussions between Prime Minister Atal Bihari Vajpayee and General Pervez Musharraf went beyond expectations, especially because of not just caution but disturbing ambiguities which characterised our Government's public pronouncements on the possibilities of bilateral discussions with the leaders of Pakistan during the SAARC summit.

The Government of India began by stating there is no likelihood of any meeting between Vajpayee and Pakistani leaders. Then a month before the summit Vajpayee announced in Lucknow that he may be willing to meet Jamali. Then a deliberate negative nuance was introduced that if such a meeting takes place it would be a courtesy call. A week before the summit indications were given that Vajpayee may not have any objection to meeting General Musharraf but this also be a courtesy call and nothing more.

Ultimately, Vajpayee had separate meetings with Jamali and Musharraf of a substantive nature. The results of the discussions went beyond what was expected in the context of policy statements made by the Government of India before the SAARC summit took place. Not only were some significant decisions taken to move forward in the process of normalisation but a road map for further interaction was clearly stated at the end of the visit.

It was agreed that the present cease-fire will be extended indefinitely to maintain stability and tranquility on the Line of Control.

It was announced that the bilateral dialogue will be resumed by February, 2004 and that the dialogue will cover a composite Agenda of issues, including issues related to Jammu and Kashmir.

Both Vajpayee and Musharraf agreed that high level political contacts will be sustained regardless of the ups and downs, that occurred in Indo-Pak relations.

While the Indian side expressed its willingness to discuss issues related to Jammu and Kashmir, Pakistan pledged that it will not allow any terrorist activity against India from territories under its control.

There was also an agreement that within the framework of the additional protocol on countering terrorism, India and Pakistan will cooperate in combating terrorism.

It is worthwhile examining the progress made so far in Indo-Pak peace efforts since April 2003 and to speculate on what constructive steps can be taken to make substantial progress for normalising relations between India and Pakistan.

The suggestions and proposals made so far, some of which are in the process of being implemented are essentially confidence-building measures aimed at creating a positive atmosphere for restoring dialogue now scheduled for February.

India should move forward beyond these confidence building measures and address the substance of the issues affecting Indo-Pak relations. The official dialogue to be resumed from February 2004, could contain the following elements.

The Directors-General of Military Operations of both countries should meet once every three months to ensure a continuation of the cease-fire and to maintain peace and stability on the Line of Control. This arrangement should go beyond Hotline Telephone connections existing between the two DGMOs, and which hopefully now stand activated.

The meetings between DGMOs should continue regardless of marginal violence which occur in Jammu and Kashmir.

The official level bilateral dialogue when it commences in February should be at the Foreign Secretaries level. During this dialogue a signal should be given that India is willing to have exchange of views on Kashmir in a realistic and practical manner.

India could renew the offer to hold discussions on a No War Pact or an agreement on Peace and Cooperation with Pakistan, drafts of which have been in existence since 1983. The suggestions for such agreements which were made during the tenure of General Zia-ul-Haq and Mrs. Indira Gandhi did not work out because India wanted two elements in this agreement, first that India and Pakistan should not allow any foreign military bases in their respective territories and that the agreement should cover the territories of Jammu and Kashmir on both sides of the Line of Control.

The first condition was rooted in the Cold War situations which is no longer relevant as both India and Pakistan are involved in defence cooperation with the US and US military personnel have been functioning in collaboration with their Indian and Pakistani counter-parts in their respective countries.

The second condition on Kashmir can be met given the agreement between Vajpayee and Musharraf to discuss Kashmir and to cooperate in countering terrorist activities. India could make the suggestion that India and Pakistan should resume discussions on three draft agreements which already exist in draft form the period 1988 to 1996. These agreements deal with issues of redeployment of forces of both sides away from Siachen and agreement for completing Wullar or Tulbul project and an agreement on the boundary at Sir Creek between Gujarat and Sindh.

These agreements could be updated and finalised taking into account the developments which have occurred since 1986 affirming the basis for resolving these issues.

India could suggest that the proposals made in Lahore Memorandum for Nuclear Risk Reduction in February 1999 should be implemented.

A joint experts group of Indian and Pakistani representatives should discuss methods of nuclear risk reduction between the two countries in the context of their nuclear weaponisation.

The general agreement reached on finalising extradition treaty between the two countries should be pushed forward. Pakistan seems to be serious about this suggestion, given the fact that the Minister for Interior of Pakistan, Mr. Faisal Saleh Hayat has sent an invitation to Indian Deputy Prime Minister L.K. Advani to work out and finalise the modalities of this Extradition Treaty. This would be an important step forward in countering terrorist activities and other illegal and criminal activities across the India-Pakistan border.

India and Pakistan should move forward to liberalise and expand bilateral economic and commercial relations in the context of the agreement reached at the SAARC Summit meeting to move forward on the proposals for the creation of South Asia Free Trade Area, by the year 2006. That this proposal has the support of the business community of both the countries, is clear from the fact that the Confederation of Indian Industries and the Federation of Indian Chambers of Commerce and Industry of India, have been interacting with their Pakistani counterparts. These organisations have prepared position papers and policy advocacies for economic cooperation which should be taken note of, given governmental support, and implemented.

It is logical assessment that if these steps are taken by mutual consent, that would positively improve the environment for a serious dialogue on the Kashmir issue.

Much hype was given in the Media in Pakistan not having referred to the question of Jammu and Kashmir in its policy pronouncement at the SAARC Summit. This is nothing new and remarkable.

SAARC Charter specifically stipulate that no country would raise bilateral issues at dispute at the SAARC summit deliberations.

The Heads of State/Governments of Pakistan have abided by this stipulation in the formal proceedings of the SAARC. In fact, the Indian delegation had got an assurance in this respect from the Pakistani delegation at the SAARC summit in Kathmandu, Colombo and Islamabad in the 80s and early 90s of the last century.

What is important is that bilateral exchanges between Vajpayee and Pakistani leaders, the discussions on Kashmir and the issue of terrorism did not turn polemical and that an effort was there on the part of both Pakistan and India, to discuss these intractable issues in a constructive manner.

This outcome was not a result of any sudden surge of positivism. There are reports that the preparations for these discussions began in April or May with Back Channel diplomacy between the Government of India and Government of Pakistan. Unlike the period preceding the Agra summit, the officials of both sides painstakingly prepared the ground for these discussions which culminated in Principal Secretary to the Prime Minister Brajesh Mishra's interaction with his senior Pakistani counterparts between the 1st and the 4th of January. These discussions included interaction between Musharraf's Advisor Tariq Aziz and the Director General of the Inter-Services Intelligence Agency of Pakistan.

What then are the prospects of this normalisation process progressing on satisfactory lines. This hinges on two issues.

A tangible and qualitative reduction in cross-border infiltration and terrorism in Jammu and Kashmir with the onset of the summer in April, 2004.

Secondly, the attitude of both countries on dealing with the issue of Jammu and Kashmir, particularly the attitude of Pakistan. Though President Musharraf in an interview to Reuters at the end of December stated that he is willing to set aside Pakistan's insistence on UN resolutions being a basis for discussions on Kashmir and that he is willing to come down half way to find a solution. Reading the whole text of the interview he classifies that Pakistan will not be willing to give up its stipulation and views on Jammu and Kashmir. The questions requiring an answer are :

- Does Pakistan still consider the acquisition of Jammu and Kashmir as "the unfinished Agenda of the partition of India in 1947".

- Does or does not Pakistan recognises the legality of the Accession of Jammu and Kashmir to the Indian Republic at the time of the Partition, within the terms of India Independence Act passed by the British Parliament.
- Does or does not Pakistan recognises the legal and political validity and sanctity of the Line of Control within the framework of the Shimla Agreement.
- Is Pakistan agreeable or opposed to a solution based on existing ground realities in Jammu and Kashmir as they have evolved over the last fifty years or more.
- India has to respond to the following questions:
- Would India be agreeable to discuss the territorial status of Jammu and Kashmir.
- Would India be inclined to accept new territorial adjustments for resolving the Kashmir issue which have been advocated by Pakistan and some foreign think-tanks.
- Would India be willing to modify the ground realities rooted in the Line of Control, to come to an agreement with Pakistan on the Kashmir issue.
- Would India be willing to recognise the separatist organisations in Jammu and Kashmir as a separate negotiating partner in tripartite framework of negotiations with Pakistan on the issue.

These are hard and substantial questions which will have to be addressed by both governments, if they are serious about resolving related to Jammu and Kashmir.

The most important question that both sides would have to answer is whether they want the Kashmir issue to hold the well-being of nearly 1.3 billion people of India and Pakistan hostage.

On all counts, Kashmir issue is very intractable. So far India is concerned the bottomline is that there cannot be further partitions of the Indian Republic.

Governments of India and Pakistan have a daunting task ahead in structuring a durable peace in our region.

KASHMIR PROBLEM AND POLICY

11

Way to Solution

Third Party Intervention in Kashmir—Should it be Allowed ?

There has been intense diplomatic pressure on India and Pakistan since January this year to defuse high levels of tension generated by the attack on the Indian Parliament on December 13, 2001, and the earlier attack on the Jammu and Kashmir State Assembly building in October that year. Adversarial political rhetoric and military confrontation reached levels which are as critical, if not worse, than the build up of the 1997 Indo-Pakistan War. Major powers of the world and the international community in general are more actively interested in defusing Indo-Pakistan tensions and impelling them towards negotiating table on the Kashmir issue due to the following reasons:

First and foremost, apprehensions about an Indo-Pakistan military conflict spiralling into a nuclear confrontation. Second, the impact that such a conflict will have on the long-term plans of the ongoing campaign against international terrorism by the US-led coalition. Third, the impact that it will have on the stability of the Governments of India and Pakistan, particularly of Pakistan, and fourth, the ethnic and demographic ramifications of the conflict on the minorities, particularly in India, and to some extent in Pakistan and by implicating in Bangladesh.

It is in this context, that one examines third party involvement in the sub-continental political situation. One makes a distinction between involvement and intervention. Because involvement reflects concern and general political activities of important powers and the international community about the Kashmir issue. Intervention connotes direct participation, political, diplomatic and ultimately military, if necessary, in the processes of first defusing tensions, second, facilitating negotiations by one means or another for forging a solution and then assisting in the implementation of a solution. Once there is clarity about this definitional dimensions of third party involvement, one can examine the advisability of allowing such intervention objectively. India has been insistent since the mid-50s that it will not countenance third-party intervention in resolving the Kashmir issue, but the fact of the matter is that third party intervention has been a recurring phenomenon over the last 50 years. Whenever India was in a major conflict situation since 1948, right until now, the major powers of the world became active in focusing attention on the Kashmir issue and pressurising India and Pakistan to negotiate and find a solution to this issue. The Resolutions and Reports of the United Nations, the initiatives taken by UK and the USA (Averell Harriman and Duncan Sandys coming as special envoys during the 1962 Sino-Indian war, the combined initiative of the US and the then Soviet Union during the 1965 and 1971 wars confirm this reality. So there is a continuum in the important powers of the world getting involved in diplomatic and political initiatives to broker a solution between India and Pakistan. There is also a recurrence of dual objectives of these exercises. First, to defuse the military predicaments and then orchestrate negotiations between India and Pakistan in one form or the other.

In the current critical situation, external involvement is a reality, external intervention is more or less a fait accompli, if the Indo- Pakistan confrontation escalates into an actual conflict, especially due to its potential nuclear dimensions. Since external involvement in one form or the other is an inevitability, it is pertinent to examine the manner in which India should influence these processes of external involvement to safeguard its interests. There is no justification for direct physical political mediation by third parties in resolving the Kashmir issue. India's experience since 1947 -48 of such mediation clearly indicates that third party mediation or operational intervention has not been even-handed, objective or even impartial. Politically the proposals emerging from past mediatory efforts have invariably suggested the alienation of territories of the State of Jammu and Kashmir from India to Pakistan. Militarily, UN military observers' could not stop Pakistan's subversive activities in India right till 1965 after which India rejected the jurisdiction of this Military Observers Group. Not only this Observers Group was unable to prevent the subversive activities, even its reports on incidents and situations were obfuscatory and not ready to pin the responsibility on Pakistan. This is the rational of India's objections to direct mediation or any kind of military or para-military involvement by third parties in dealing with the Kashmir issue.

Having said this, one has to acknowledge that given the nuclear weaponisation of both countries and given Pakistan's deliberate inclination to indulge in nuclear blackmail to achieve its objective in Jammu and Kashmir. It would be practical for India to accept cooperation and general diplomatic efforts from major powers who have tangible influence with the Pakistan Government. This should be acceptable in the context of declared policies of the major powers on the following points:- There is a clear decision to oppose and eliminate all kinds of terrorism; secondly, an affirmation that established international frontiers—formal or temporary, should not be changed by violent means. (Clinton said this in March 2000, Bush has affirmed this); Third, the sanctity and the legitimacy of the Line of Control in Jammu and Kashmir has been accepted by all the major powers of the world. If important powers, led by the USA are willing to continue to undertake diplomatic and political efforts to persuade Pakistan to come to the negotiating table within the above policy framework, to solve the Kashmir problem, India should not have inhibitions about their playing such a role. This role should also be predicated on general understanding that their efforts should not lead to any suggestions which affect the territorial integrity of India, barring some minor adjustments, of the Line of Control.

As far as the more immediate operational requirements are concerned, that is of preventing infiltration, the stopping of logistic and operational support by Pakistan to separatist elements, US, UK and other countries could possibly assist India and Pakistan in monitoring and verifying ground realities on the Line of Control not by deployment of any troops by them but by providing technological assistance to both sides to ensure peace and tranquility and to prevent the violation of the Line of Control

I emphasise that the UN should not be involved in this process, nor should the important powers act as a collectivity in this matter. The efforts should be individual and in a bilateral framework. Political and diplomatic help undertaken collectively would be the thin edge for institutional intervention which will not serve Indian interests.

The external involvement should be first focussed on defusing tensions on the Line of Control and the international border between India and Pakistan. The next stage, the third party involvement, should be limited to the role of facilitation and encouragement for a focussed bilateral dialogue between India and Pakistan to resolve the Kashmir issue.

Indo-US Relations –Through the Prism of Issues of Kashmir and Terrorism

US Secretary of State Colin Powell completed his last round of discussions in Islamabad and New Delhi and over the week-end between the 27th and 28th July. His visit was preceded by the visit of British Foreign Secretary Jack Straw in mid-July. Both the USA and UK are of the view that the subcontinental situation remains tense despite a partial reduction in prospects of any immediate military conflict between India and Pakistan. Consequently they have decided to continue high-level political and diplomatic pressure on both countries to move towards a dialogue. The declared rationale of this policy appears unexceptionable, which is (a) Indo-Pakistan tension on the Kashmir issue should not escalate into a military conflict leading to a nuclear war; (b) The Indo-Pakistan stand off should not disrupt the USA's anti-terrorism campaign being carried out with active collaboration of President Musharraf of Pakistan; (c) the resolution of the Kashmir issue through political dialogue is essential for long-term stability in South Asia which is an active objective of US security and economic politics related to this region; (d) While the US accepts that the resolution of this problem is to be achieved primarily by bilateral interaction between India and Pakistan , USA is increasingly of the view that this bilateral process has to be actively facilitated by third parties led by the United States.

It is in this context that one assesses the discussions of General Powell with his Indian and Pakistani counterparts in July. The manner in which India and Pakistan indicated their responses through political atmospherics is interesting. The British Foreign Secretary Jack Straw was not received by General Pervez Musharraf because perhaps of a number of public pronouncements by Jack Straw criticising Pakistan's support for terrorism in India. General Powell was received by Prime Minister Vajpayee cursorily during his visit for any detailed exchange of officially acknowledging the links between Pakistan authorities and cross-border terrorist activities in Jammu and Kashmir. The substance of General Powell's discussions both in Islamabad and New Delhi were on expected lines. Musharraf was urged to take additional measures to the extent feasible to prevent terrorist infiltration into Jammu and Kashmir. India was told to step down from its absolute pre-conditions about complete and permanent cessation of terrorist activities for entering into a dialogue with Pakistan. India was also advised that holding free and fair elections in Jammu and Kashmir, withdrawal of Indian forces from their massive deployment postures, are necessary along with some movement forward on the part of India towards holding direct discussions with Pakistan on all pending issues particularly the Kashmir issue.

Indian and Pakistani response to the Powell visit were comparatively assertive. Musharraf told Powell that Pakistan has done enough to de-escalate tensions, that there is no infiltration from the Pakistan side into India and that it is now India's turn to take substantive initiatives in terms of withdrawal of troops, and holding a dialogue, if India is really interested in easing tensions. Deputy Prime Minister L.K. Advani and External Affairs Minister Yashwant Sinha, were equally assertive regarding Pakistan-sponsored terrorism being stopped visibly and permanently which is not the case despite the assurances contained in General Musharraf's speeches of January 12 and May 27, 2002. Terrorist violence in Kashmir continues. India's continuing restraint is proof of its commitment to peace, and willingness to listen to advice for moderation given by major powers of the world.

The more important aspects of General Powell's visit to be taken note of by India, is his public proceeding at a press conference in New Delhi before proceeding to Brunei for the Asian Security Conference (THE ARE) meeting of the ASEAN. Three significant points were made by General Powell which question India's policy stance on the Kashmir issue and Indo-Pakistan relations. General Powell categorically stated that Kashmir is on the international agenda and that USA is deeply interested in resolving the problem. Second, that the Government of India should ensure free and fair elections in Jammu and Kashmir and that this can be established on the basis of India allowing foreign observers to monitor the elections. Third that India should free all political prisoners of Jammu and Kashmir to facilitate free and fair elections in Jammu and Kashmir . One cannot make allowance for the first point in the statement by the explanation that General Powell was merely stating the reality that Kashmir is a matter of international concern. His saying that it is on the international agenda implies that the US will be active politically and diplomatically in pressurising India and Pakistan to resolve the Kashmir issue.

His advocacy for international observers for the scheduled elections in Jammu and Kashmir despite being fully aware of India's objections to the suggestion, shows a certain assertive stance in USA's policies on the Kashmir issue. His suggestions that India should free political prisoners, apart from being assertive is an intrusive statement questioning the legitimacy of Government of India's preventive actions against political figures involved in subversion, terrorism and separatism. While acknowledging that cross border terrorism in Jammu Kashmir has not stopped and that something more should be done, he did not accept the link between Pakistani power structure and terrorist groups. He added the palliative advice that Pakistan should not interfere with the electoral process.

These policy pronouncements of General Powell have to be taken note of in the context of the policy statements by official spokesman of the State Department Richard Boucher on the 17th of July, about ten days before Powell's visit to Islamabad and New Delhi. Instead of squarely addressing the issue of Pakistan-sponsored terrorism, Mr. Boucher declared : "We have condemned the continuing violence. It is vital to all sides in Kashmir to exercise restraint, to take steps to reduce the violence and to create an environment for a political process to resolve the conflict. The United States and the international community are continuing diplomatic efforts to encourage India and Pakistan to move away from armed conflict. President Musharraf has assured us that infiltration across the Line of Control has ended continues to be highest priority for Pakistan. We will continue to follow that issue closely" Boucher then added for good measure : "Since September 11, Pakistan has been and continues to be one of our foremost and indispensable allies in the war against terrorism. President Musharraf has pointed out that Pakistan has also been the victim of terrorism and extremism. And together we were working on fighting this scourge". Boucher also complimented President Musharraf for having taken bold decisions to counter terrorism.

What is one to make of current trends in US policies towards India in the light of these policy statements. The conclusions though unpalatable have to be accepted. Despite India's complete support to the US in its anti-terrorism campaign and its general policies of trying to establish a close relationship with the US, the US is not fully responsive to the realities on the ground in Jammu and Kashmir or India's related concerns, particularly regarding Pakistan's policies.

The United States will not move beyond exerting general political and diplomatic pressure on Pakistan to reduce its support to terrorist violence in Jammu and Kashmir. In fact, Musharraf is considered an important and reliable ally in USA's anti-terrorism and Asian policies, safeguarding USA's political, strategic and economic interests in the Gulf, in Central Asia and South Asia. There is a likelihood of an incremental intrusive pressure and involvement by the US in the Kashmir issue and Indo-Pakistan relations with the slant being to pressurise India to give more compromises on internal issues of Jammu and Kashmir and to the Pakistani stand on Kashmir issue. Though this latter point is not openly stated by the USA.

The United States will be firmly opposed to any punitive action that India may be compelled to take against continuing external terrorist subversion in Jammu and Kashmir. India should be prepared for not just political but economic and other counter-measures from the US if India reaches a threshold where it is to take punitive action against Pakistan-sponsored terrorism outside Indian territory.

Indian political circles and public opinion have been progressively disappointed by US policy stances on Jammu and Kashmir and Pakistan's interventionist involvement in the state. This is partially due to excessive expectations following India's declaration of full support to the US after the September 11, 2001. But at a deeper level it is time for the US to realize that an important ingredient in the rationale and logic of India's pro-US policies since 1999, is now subject to questions and apprehensions, viz. that despite the decade-long efforts of establishing a closer Indo-US equations, US still remains inhibited about giving full support to Indian interests and concerns. This is so because objectively speaking Indian policy-makers ignored the fundamental reality that foreign policies of other countries, particularly of great powers, are primarily structured with the framework of their own perceived interests. These policies become supportive of concerns and interests of other countries only to the extent that there is a convergence between these concerns and interests and the policy objectives of major powers like the USA. Perhaps it is necessary to nuance our foreign policy taking this elemental reality into account.

Emerging Prospects in Kashmir– An Assessment

Elections for the new Legislative Assembly in Jammu and Kashmir were complete on the 8th of October, despite terrorist violence aimed at disrupting the process. About eight hundred civilians including senior political leaders were killed during the run upto, and at the time of elections. Nearly four hundred terrorists were killed, indicating the intensity of effort by Pakistan and its supporters to subvert the political process and the territorial integrity of India.

There is general acknowledgement at home and abroad (except Pakistan) that elections were held smoothly and fairly and that a new Legislative Assembly and new Government in Jammu and Kashmir could initiate the process for a political solution to the issues related to Jammu and Kashmir, if the Government of India engages them in serious discussion.

What then are the immediate prospects about normalization of the situation in Jammu and Kashmir? The National Conference though capturing the largest number of seats (28) in the 87- member Assembly has been clearly voted out of power with the politically significant defeat of the President of the Party Omar Abdullah. The Indian National Congress with 20 seats and the People's Democratic Party of Mufti Mohammed with 16 seats have emerged as new factors in the political dispensation in the state. Independents, and members of smaller parties like Panthers Party hold the balance of power in the new Coalition Government which would have emerged by the time this article is published.

The Congress's victory has to be attributed to the following factors. Mrs. Sonia Gandhi personally campaigning in the elections in Srinagar and Jammu. She was the only leader of national party who proceeded to campaign in the state despite serious security threats. By campaigning, she emphasized three factors. First her affirmation of the Indian identity by participating in the political processes in this highly violent and dangerous election state. She successfully revived the position of the Congress party in the politics of the strategically important state of Jammu and Kashmir where the centre-stage was being incrementally taken over by local political parties. Third, she affirmed the traditions of the emotional and political involvement of congress leadership, specially the Nehruvian leadership in Jammu and Kashmir.

Ghulam Nabi Azad's organizational skills produced results, despite his lack of political roots in Jammu and Kashmir in recent years. Most importantly, the state cadres of the Congress party made a purposeful effort with deep conviction and commitment.

Regardless of which political party emerges as the leading partner in the Government, it is clear that there is going to be across the board political consensus in the new Legislative Assembly about state autonomy being their major advocacy for the future political dispensation in Jammu and Kashmir.

There would be differences of opinion about the details of the autonomy package being sought by different political parties of Jammu and Kashmir. The National Conference has been asking for autonomy as it existed in the early 50s. There are other political parties which want a more confederal arrangement. Parties representing Ladakh and Jammu are more keen on getting delegated powers for administrative and economic management from Srinagar. They would also desire separate package of social and developmental assistance for each region of Jammu and Kashmir (the Valley, Jammu and Ladakh).

There could also be some demand for a separate status for Jammu and Kashmir with complete autonomy based on joint guarantees from India and Pakistan. This proposition is non-negotiable and would not be accepted by any Government of India. There is a genuine and deeply felt desire for economic, social and developmental assistance from the Central Government amongst the people of Jammu and Kashmir. In recent months, there have been public pronouncements by political figures of Jammu and Kashmir appealing to focus on spheres of education, health, roads, communications, restoration of irrigation works and local crafts. These pronouncements significantly do not make any reference to the desirability of excessive autonomy or separation from India.

The Government of India is likely to commence negotiations with representatives of the State Government of Jammu and Kashmir about the future dispensation in the State, some time by December 2002 or January 2003. The terms of reference and objectives of these negotiations are still ambiguous and subject to uncertainties because the political parties in Jammu and Kashmir themselves do not have an agreed framework objectives on the basis of which to negotiate with the Government of India.

On the other hand, the Government of India should be clear about only one basic objective, that Kashmir should not be politically and territorially alienated from the Indian Republic. But there is ambiguity about the extent of autonomy which the Government of India would be willing to grant to the State of Jammu and Kashmir. This is a matter still under discussion within the Government of India. So one should expect a complex and prolonged period of negotiations between the Government of India and the State Government of Jammu and Kashmir.

Equally important is the fact that there is a definite likelihood of not just continuing but increased terrorist violence in Jammu and Kashmir sponsored from Pakistan. This will vitiate the processes of negotiations which is the objective of Pakistan. The only counter-measure to Pakistan-sponsored disruptions and the internal frustrations in the State of Jammu and Kashmir is to undertake a purposeful, detailed and clearly prioritized programme of developmental work and economic assistance to the people of Jammu and Kashmir responsive to their basis concerns and aspirations. This is the only means by which the people of Jammu and Kashmir can become part of the mainstream of Indian democracy.

The Government of India should therefore enter into negotiation with the new State Government of Jammu and Kashmir as early as possible, to evolve a package of political measures which would conform to the requirements mentioned above. It is also important that the Government of India evolves its negotiating stances with the Government of Jammu and

Kashmir on the basis of consultations in the Indian Parliament and backed up by a national consensus.

The external dimensions of managing the emerging prospects in Jammu and Kashmir are equally important. Pakistan-sponsored terrorism will continue, perhaps at a higher scale because Pakistan failed to disrupt the democratic political processes in Jammu and Kashmir. This has to be countered effectively not only within Jammu and Kashmir, but where necessary India should not hesitate from taking preemptive and preventive action across the Line of Control. India has shown sufficient restraint and patience. Such preventive action should be measured and carefully calibrated to avoid any full-scale conflict with Pakistan which is not necessary or desirable.

The successful holding of Jammu and Kashmir elections, if followed through by discussions with the State Government would increase India's credibility on issues related to Kashmir in the international community. There would be increased pressure from the international community, particularly, the major powers led by the United States on India and Pakistan to enter into a bilateral dialogue to resolve those aspects of Kashmir problem which affect Indo-Pakistan relations. US Secretary of State Colin Powell in a press interview on the 9th of October welcomed the successful holding of elections in Jammu and Kashmir as a major step which would contribute to the restoration of normalcy in the subcontinent. He has urged India and Pakistan to commence bilateral dialogue early. The orchestrated elections in Pakistan are also over. There is little doubt that General Pervez Musharraf will continue in power in Pakistan in the foreseeable future. Regardless of our reservations about him and his adversarial policies towards India, India has to deal with him and his Government.

Keeping in mind the three objectives of normalizing the situation in Jammu and Kashmir, reducing the high levels of Indo-Pak tensions, and augmenting international support for Indian concerns about terrorism in Jammu and Kashmir, it is time for us to move out of the somewhat static negotiating position that we have adopted for Pakistan since December 2001. We should move towards a dialogue with Pakistan by early next year. The preparatory steps that we should take, in my assessment are: to repeat the offers which we have made to Pakistan about restoring overflights, and raising diplomatic relations back to full Ambassadorial or High Commissioner's levels. We must also gradually reduce the massive deployment of our forces on the Line of Control and international border. We could perhaps begin by moving back some of our troops from the international frontiers first. We can also reduce the size on our deployment on the Line of Control depending on the levels of terrorist intrusions across the Line, and terrorist activities in Jammu and Kashmir. This process could be initiated by suggesting discussions between Directors-General, Military Operations, of the two countries to work out details on this matter.

Parallely, Pakistan should be given clear signals that if terrorist activities increased backed up by intrusive support; India will be more decisive and preemptive than ever before; even if it slows down the plans for resuming a dialogue with Pakistan. India should take the major powers and members of the UN Security Council into confidence about these initiatives which we it may take in relation to Pakistan. If we do not move out of strait jacket of Rejectionism, about a dialogue with Pakistan, we will be isolated in the international community.

India's policies in Kashmir must have two ingredients: a purposive approach to evolve a political formula responsive to the aspirations of the people of Jammu and Kashmir, and measured mix of military decisiveness and politico-strategic flexibility in reviving the dialogue with Pakistan.

Trial Balloons on the Line of Control being Basis of Solution to Kashmir Dispute between India and Pakistan

The third phase of the Legislative Assembly elections in Jammu and Kashmir would be over by first week of October. Two exercises which the Government of India has to undertake somewhat inevitably are: first, to commence a dialogue with the newly elected members of the J&K Legislative Assembly about future political dispensation in Jammu and Kashmir. The second, even if the process gets delayed, to engage Pakistan in a dialogue to resolve the Indo-Pak dimension of the Kashmir issue. It is in this context that one takes note of media reports in Pakistan and abroad about the possibility of Pakistan willy-nilly agreeing to the resolution of the Kashmir issue on the basis of the Line of Control.

The Pakistan newspaper *NEWS* published a news item in the last week of August that converting the Line of Control as the international border between India and Pakistan, could be the basis for a solution to the Kashmir problem and that the idea was gathering momentum. There was speculation that the United States is supportive of the idea and would persuade President Musharraf to accept this compromise. Media both India and abroad, indulged in much optimistic and excessive speculation that President Musharraf would discuss this proposal with President Bush, which would be followed by discussions between Mr. Bush and Prime Minister Vajpayee when both Musharraf and Vajpayee would be in New York for the UN General Assembly session.

A number of political and strategic analysts contributed to this misplaced optimism by talking about another breakthrough resulting from the impulses generated by the terrorist attacks on the USA on 11th September 11, 2001.

President Musharraf when questioned about these reports about the Line of Control providing the basis for a solution of the Kashmir issue, at a press conference on the 11th of September in New York, indulged in a curt and abrasive counter question: "Do you think I am a fool to think about such a solution." He added for good measure that his policy on Kashmir has not changed and that he will raise the issue in every forum and every occasion available. Prime Minister Vajpayee was equally categorical in refusing to the idea of the Line of Control as a solution three days later at a press conference in New York.

It is worthwhile examining why this suggestion regarding the LOC propped up again and also about historical background about the Line of Control being possible basis for a solution. First the history:

The origin of the Line of Control in Kashmir lies in the Karachi Agreement of July 17, 1949, in which the ceasefire line was drawn up between Indian and Pakistani forces in Jammu and Kashmir at the end of the Indo-Pakistan war, on Kashmir in 1948. This agreement demarcating the ceasefire line was signed by Indian and Pakistani military commanders as well as representatives at the UN Commission on India and Pakistan.

The ceasefire line commenced from Manawar in the south (south-west Jammu) to "Khot" in the north upto a map grid reference point NJ 9842 from where it lies (in the language of the ceasefire line agreement "thence North to the Glaciers)".

During the 1965 war the ceasefire line was violated but at the end of the war, India and Pakistan agreed to exchange territories captured by either side across the ceasefire line, restoring the ceasefire line to status quo before 1965 war.

At the end of 1971 war, however, both sides decided to keep the minor territorial gains that they had made across the ceasefire line under the Simla Agreement. So Prime Minister Indira Gandhi and Zulfiqar Ali Bhutto decided to re-delineate the ceasefire line and to re-delineate it as "Line of

Control". This was agreed upon in accordance with paragraph 4 (ii) of the Simla Agreement. Their re-delineation and the change in the nomenclature of the line signified an important political transition from the ceasefire line being a military line separating the two armies, to a line demarcating a political divide which was to evolve into an international boundary in Jammu and Kashmir between India and Pakistan. Zulfiqar Ali Bhutto had agreed to this arrangement. Lt. General P.S. Bhagat of India and Lt General Abdul Hamid Khan signed the agreement confirming the Line of Control at Suchetgarh on December 11, 1972. This new Line of Control defined in December, 1972 was cartographically demarcated in detail in two sets of maps each containing 25 map sheets formed into 17 Mosaics.

The present Line of Control has a length about 740 kilometres from International Border in the south upto the Grid Reference NJ 9842 in the north mentioned above.

The legality of this Line was accepted by Pakistan for nearly 28 years, till 1999. It is only when Pakistan invasion across the Line of Control in Kargil was in progress that the Pakistani army headquarters and the Pakistan Foreign Office started indulging in the patently mendacious argument that the Line of Control was not fully demarcated, that it's delineation was ambiguous in some sectors etc. In substance, Pakistan wanted to regress from the political legitimacy of the Line of Control to make it a temporary ceasefire line, the validity of which could be challenged by Pakistan. This was necessary for Pakistan to push forward its claim to the whole of Jammu and Kashmir as "the unfinished part of the Partition"

It is keeping this background in mind that Mrs. Indira Gandhi advocated a permanent settlement of the Kashmir issue on the basis of the Line of Control to Zulfiqar Ali Bhutto in 1972 in Shimla. Bhutto agreed to the suggestion but pleaded for time to make a formal announcement on the subject requesting that the suggestion should not be incorporated in the Simla agreement. That Bhutto was serious about implementation of this suggestion is indicated by the fact that he merged the northern areas and made them a centrally administered territory of Pakistan, soon after the Simla Agreement. He only resiled from assurances to Mrs. Gandhi in this regard when he found Mrs. Gandhi enmeshed in domestic crisits in 1974-75. The Indian side has informally raised the question of the territorial dimension of the Kashmir dispute along the Line of Control more than once between 1983 and 1991. Pakistan consistently refused the suggestion stating that even if Bhutto had agreed to any such idea, changed circumstances in Jammu and Kashmir preclude the LOC being accepted as the international border. Consequently, the Indian response has been to revert back to the original legal and political position that the whole State of Jammu and Kashmir, including areas now under the control of Pakistan, are an integral part of India. The Indian Parliament passed a resolution to this effect in 1995. Prime Minister Vajpayee only reiterated this position in New York this September.

President Musharraf is not likely to accept the proposal regarding the Line of Control as a permanent solution because Pakistan is convinced that the people of Jammu and Kashmir are alienated from India to an extent where they will ultimately choose to become part of Pakistan. Secondly, he is convinced that the Indian armed forces would not be able to hold on to Kashmir in face of the continuing battle of attrition which he has waged and which he plans to continue. He also has the compulsion of placating the Islamic and theocratic elements in Pakistani politics who are upset with him for having fallen in line with the Americans to fight the Taliban and Al-Qaeda. He cannot afford to move to any rational and practical solution to the Kashmir issue.

Given this situation there is no need for India to suggest a solution on the basis of the Line of Control. While this is the short-term prospect, it is clear that ultimately the solution to the Indo- Pakistani dimensions of the Kashmir issue will have to be on the basis of the Line of Control, getting converted into international border with some adjustments. It is not well known but the fact of the matter is that important think-tanks in the western democracies, particularly in the United States as well as policy planners in these countries are getting increasingly convinced about the validity and logic of a durable solution on the basis of the Line of Control.

The trial balloons in the US and Pakistani media could have been generated by these think-tanks and back channels in the policy planning staff of important powers. While there is no need to be in a hurry to advocate proposals regarding the LOC, in the long run that is the objective towards which India and Pakistan should work, even if the process is gradual. Other alternative solutions to the Kashmir issue would be too drastic affecting the interests either of India or of Pakistan.

12

Regional Tension

Kashmir – Danger of Disllusionment and Regional Tension

Expressions of satisfaction at the completion of the Legislative Assembly elections in Jammu and Kashmir and the consequential expectations about some kind of sub-continental normalcy seem to be stuck in the doldrums of narrow political interests and factious political prospects in Pakistan. Before commenting on the actual developments, it is pertinent to recall the logical objectives which India had in mind or atleast India should have had in mind. The elections in Jammu and Kashmir were supposed to result in the establishment of a newly elected Government, more representative of the people of Jammu and Kashmir regardless of the nature of the Government, whether it was a one-party Government or a coalition Government. The Government of India was to enter into substantive discussions with the new Government of Jammu and Kashmir to discuss and finalise a political dispensation dealing with the problems of the people of Jammu and Kashmir and responsive to their legitimate aspirations.

Parallely, the Government of India was to assist the new Government of Jammu and Kashmir in meeting the urgent developmental needs of the State in all respects. Once this process started, possibilities were to be considered for gradually moving towards a dialogue with Pakistan to deal with those dimensions of the Kashmir issue which are a result of Pakistan's illegal violent and intrusive involvement in Jammu and Kashmir. Anybody who had the basic understanding of the problems related to Jammu and Kashmir was aware that a successful holding of elections was but only the first very initial step in dealing with the complex issues related to Jammu and Kashmir.

Ground realities as they have emerged after the elections need to be understood in as objective a manner as possible. The National Conference has been voted out of power in the State and specially in the Kashmir valley. In a 87-member house the National Conference has won 28 seats. People's Democratic Party has 16 seats while the Indian National Congress has 21 seats. (Most of which were won in Jammu). Independents have 22 seats. Whatever the political clout or lack of it of all the organized parties, none of them can singly form a Government. Each one of them would have to either get into a coalition with other political parties or gain sufficient support from the independent members to have a majority in the State Assembly.

Two macro-level political factors to be taken note of are, first, that there was sufficient spontaneous and genuinely free involvement of the voters in the elections. Second, that the people of Jammu and Kashmir desired a change from the National Conference Government. These two factors would inhibit at least for a short period, the inclination of the PDP or the Congress coming into a coalition arrangement with the National Conference. (Though Farooq Abdullah has said that his party has not given up hope, one does not know precisely about what). Ghulam Nabi Azad, the leader of the Congress Legislative Party has claimed the support of 41 members of the Legislative Assembly at the time of writing this article. He also expressed the optimism about getting support of three or four more Legislators from the group of independents. There were even unconfirmed reports of some PDP legislators being persuaded to support the Congress. Then there have been reports about monetary incentives being offered by political parties to get the support of legislators not averse to such persuasions.

Nearly a fortnight has passed since Jammu and Kashmir elections were completed. But no Government could be established because of the insistant claims of the Congress and the People's Democratic Party on the post of the Chief Minister. Had the leadership of the Congress and the PDP in Jammu and Kashmir being imbued with a broader vision of establishing stable democratic Government in Kashmir, thereby creating circumstances of discussions with the Government of India for a practical political dispensation in the State, the uncertainties afflicting the State would not have occurred. The reasoning of the People's Democratic Party has been that it has emerged as a major political force in the Valley, the most sensitive and problematic part of the State of Jammu and Kashmir. Since PDP is a regional party of the state and since it has replaced the National Conference, it should have the post of Chief Minister and the highest responsibility of managing the State. The PDP also claims its manifesto is the most responsive to the people of Jammu and Kashmir. Therefore, it should be allowed to lead the Government. The counter rationale of the Congress Party is that it has the larger number of seats in the Legislative Assembly than the PDP. That it has a larger support from the independent MLA's who have given their support on the condition that the Congress will lead the State Government. That Congress being the national party, its assuming the Chief Ministership of the State on the basis of the most recent public mandate would be a more effective counter to separatist elements in the State. That the leadership of the PDP cannot provide a stable Government to Jammu and Kashmir on its own. In contrast, the Congress has the experience of governing the terrorist and secessionist infected States bringing them back to the mainstream national politics. That the Congress party can focus more effectively on developmental activities in the State, which would remedy the frustrations of the people. That if the Congress does not take over the Chief Ministership, the independents will not support any PDP-led Government and that National Conference may come to power through back door, negating the verdict of the people of Jammu and Kashmir.

Whatever interpretive value judgments, one may have about these claims to the Chief Ministership, objectively speaking, the delay in the formation of the Government has generated disappointment in public and political uncertainty in the State which could have been avoided.

The aspirations and expectations of Congress workers in Jammu and Kashmir for office after their having successfully achieved the electoral victory is logical. The Chief Ministership in a coalition Government where Congress will have decisive voice seems to have been the criteria for power or a critical objective. One must also remember that without the establishment of a democratic Government, discussions between Central and State Governments for devolution of power or autonomy cannot be held in a meaningful manner. If this process gets scuttled or delayed because of the competition for political power, it will qualitatively diminish the objectives of the elections just completed and will profoundly disappoint the people of Jammu and Kashmir.

Pakistan's policies of continuing terrorist subversion will be fuelled further if this political process gets delayed. India's ability to deal with incremental international pressure on issues relating to Kashmir and of resuming a dialogue with Pakistan and a position of strength and political self-assurance will also diminish if a government is not established in

Jammu and Kashmir on the basis of elections. It must be realised that the stakes are too high in terms of India's national interests.

Kashmir—Emerging Political Dynamics

The problems related to Kashmir are mostly viewed through the prisms of Pakistan's sustained subversive activities over the last decade and a half or of ongoing internal security operations undertaken by the Government of India amd State Government of Jammu and Kashmir. There is also a segment of Indian political circles which advocates either an absolutist jingoistic stance of laying claims to all the territories which belong to the old State of Jammu and Kashmir or advocating the trifurcation of the areas of Jammu and Kashmir now part of India on religious lines in terms of the demography in Ladakh, in the Valley, and in Jammu.

Assessments through the prisms mentioned and the advocacies referred to above result in opaque and confused perceptions on the Kashmir issue. It is time to move beyond events and developments to analyse the roots of the problem as we face it today and to understand the reality of political dynamics affecting Jammu and Kashmir.

First and foremost, India must consciously accept the fact that the old princely State of Jammu and Kashmir which came into being in the mid-19th century was an artificial creation of the Dogra Imperium. The collective political entity of Jammu and Kashmir as a plural multi-ethnic, multi-linguistic united territorial entity based on the feeling of the people of Jammu and Kashmir in only post –independence phenomenon which was being consolidated since 1947. Secondly, this process of consolidation and the affiliations of Jammu and Kashmir to India stands disrupted because large segments of people in the Kashmir valley, are alienated from the present power structure in Jammu and Kashmir and have lost their convictions about the logic of the State's affiliation to India (which most of them believed in till the Seventies).

The reasons for this disaffection are well known and have been the subject-matter of much analysis and cogitation in the Indian media as well as scholarly circles here. It must also be noted that in a recent public opinion poll, The Mori Report, only 6.2 per cent of the people of Jammu and Kashmir favoured the State's becoming part of Pakistan. Most of them indicated a desire for independence or extensive autonomy.

One cannot gainsay the fact that this sense of separateness in the State of Jammu and Kashmir, when compared with the other States constituting the Indian Union, is partially the result of the separate status and jurisdictional arrangements given to Jammu and Kashmir when it acceded to India. A political post mortem of the manner in which India handled the Kashmir issue, politically and military over the years, has only limited relevance to the complex predicaments which we face today. It would be more pertinent to squarely perceive the current situation and then to examine what can be done to overcome the present impasse: One has to accept that the State Government of the National Conference does not have much credibility among the people of Jammu and Kashmir. It is equally true that the political groups constituting the Hurriyat do not really represent the board cross-section of the people of Jammu and Kashmir: Ladakh and Jammu remain unrepresented in the Hurriyat. So do sections of the population in the Valley. Infiltration and terrorism continue, which though sponsored and supported by Pakistan cannot be sustained unless there is some residual support from local disaffected youth and other cadre who participate in this violence either out of political conviction or under the threat of violence by foreign-based terrorist groups.

The outright rejection of the resolution on autonomy passed by the State Assembly of Jammu and Kashmir, nearly an year and a half ago by the Government of India, without even an offer to discuss it, has generated an undercurrent of resentment in political circles. There is also the profound contradiction on this issue between the Hindu and Buddhist populations of Jammu and Ladakh, on the one hand and disaffected political groups in the Kashmir valley, on the other. So developing a consensus on possible political solutions amongst the people of Jammu and Kashmir would be a complex and difficult task, this is made more difficult because externally sponsored violence continues to disrupt a rational dialogue amongst political parties of Jammu and Kashmir as well as between them and the representatives of the Government of India.

It is equally important to note that the discussions between political parties themselves in Jammu and Kashmir on this issue are practically non-existent. The gulf between them is wide; no meaningful efforts have been undertaken to bridge this gulf. The number of special envoys or representatives who are entrusted with the task of interacting with political groups in Jammu and Kashmir by the Government of India, have not so far been able to enter a substantive and meaningful discussion with Kashmiri political parties (not even with the National Conference).

There is also disillusionment among the separatist groups in Jammu and Kashmir about terrorist groups operating from foreign bases with foreign mercenaries who are operating in the State under the guidance of

Pakistan and other extremist Islamic groups. It is taking note of this disillusionment that the Government of India has entered into dialogue with various dissident groups in Jammu and Kashmir to wean them away from terrorist violence and persuade them to join the political processes. K.C. Pant, Ram Jethmalani, A.S. Dulat, former chief of the Research and Analysis Wing of the Cabinet Secretariat and Arun Jaitley are engaged in this exercise, now perhaps with some urgency to ensure their participation in the scheduled State Legislative Assembly elections in September.

The expectation is that if elections are held with the participation of dissident groups, the political democratic processes in Jammu and Kashmir could be brought back on the rails. Though this effort is on, there are still uncertainties about the dissident political groups joining the electoral process.

The assassination of moderate leaders like Abdul Ghani Lone and the Government of India's decision to take drastic action against hardcore anti- Indian leaders like Syed Ali Gilani have only increased this uncertainty.

India, however, is keen about holding the election and reviving the democratic process which it hopes would become a springboard for a long-term political solution to the internal problems of Jammu and Kashmir. Ensuring that elections are manifestly free and fair, is also subject into differences of opinion between Farooq Abdullah and the Government of India about holding the elections under President's rule. This is apart from India's reluctance to allow institutional foreign observers for the proposed elections. It is clear that Pakistan would try to disrupt the electoral process. It is this consideration which made the Government of India reticent about squarely blaming Pakistan for the Qasim Nagar massacre (near Jammu) of civilians of July14.

Accusing Pakistan would have clearly involved an operational response against Pakistan which in turn would have delayed the elections. A military operation with prospects of escalation would inevitably delay the poll. Internal discussions on the Jammu and Kashmir issue are at a crucial stage at present. It is clear that holding the elections with participation by all political groups is imperative. So is the requirement of elections being manifestly free and fair.

More important, the Government of India should repackaged containing maximum autonomy the only solution to separatism. Dilatory tactics on this issue would be counter-productive, even dangerous to the unity of India. The other suggestions from the Rashtriya Swayamsevak

Sangh and other quarters about trifurcation of Jammu and Kashmir on ethno-religious lines reflects desperation and exhaustion, apart from striking at the pluralistic terms of refrence of the Indian polity.

The most important consideration which should underpin our policies is that unless it finds a practical solution regarding the internal political dispensation of Jammu and Kashmir acceptable to the people of the State, the external dimension of the problem that is coming to terms with Pakistan, cannot be achieved. Resolving the internal contradictions of the political dynamics of Jammu and Kashmir is the litmus test for India's commitment to democracy.

Normalisation in Jammu and Kashmir - A Tenuous Beginning

Expressions of satisfaction about the completion of the Legislative Assembly elections in Jammu and Kashmir were subjected to some uncertainties because of the competing claims for the Chief Ministership between the Indian National Congress and the People's Democratic Party of Jammu and Kashmir. The reasoning of the People's Democratic Party for claiming the Chief Ministership was that it has emerged as a major political force in the Valley, as an alternative to the National Conference which stood rejected at the polls in public perceptions. The PDP is a regional party of the state and therefore it is leading the Government both inside Jammu and Kashmir and outside. The PDP also claimed that its manifesto was the most responsive to the aspirations of the people of Jammu and Kashmir.

The counter rationale of the Congress Party was that it had a larger number of seats in the Legislative Assembly than the PDP and most of the independent groups. That the Congress has greater support from independent MLAs than the PDP, and that Congress being the national party, its assuming the Chief Ministership of the State on the basis of the most recent public mandate would be a more effective counter to the separatist elements in the State. The leadership of the PDP does not have sufficient appeal in Jammu and in Ladakh. In addition Congress legitimately claimed that it has greater experience in governance and in dealing with terrorist and secessionist infected areas and therefore would be more capable of bringing Jammu and Kashmir back to the mainstream of democratic national politics in India. Ultimately the Congress showed a greater sensitivity to the more pertinent considerations of national interests and of the wellbeing of the people of Jammu and Kashmir, rising above considerations of party aspirations and agreed to the PDP led by Mufti Mohammed Sayeed, leading the new State Government of Jammu and

Kashmir. General information available about discussions relating to this compromise was that Mrs. Sonia Gandhi and her principal emissary Man Mohan Singh were instinctively in favour of the ultimate decision taken of letting the PDP lead the Government. But the delay in finalizing this compromise was a number of senior figures in the Congress Party and party leaders in Jammu and Kashmir, insisting on the Chief Ministership on the basis of the rationale which has been summarized above.

The compulsions of carrying the party cadres of Jammu and Kashmir in the final decision to be taken and requirements of an amount of inner party democracy, resulted in the cogitations and discussions for little more than a fortnight before a final logical compromise is arrived at. It is clear while taking the decision to let the PDP lead the new Government in Jammu and Kashmir, Sonia Gandhi has conveyed timely and important signals about the Congress Party's approach to significant issues affecting national politics. First, she has emphasised that the party's overall credibility and its commitment to the wellbeing of people is more important than any individual. Second, that national interests are a matter of higher priority than the interests of the Congress party even if those interests were based on logical and rational considerations. That the party should be imbued and motivated by a larger vision.

On all counts, this will increase the credibility of the Congress not only amongst the people of Jammu and Kashmir but also the Indian public opinion in general.

Having said this, it must be emphasised that it was a difficult decision to take, given that a fair segment of Congress leaders, including leaders in Jammu and Kashmir aired different views. The new Government being sworn in on Saturday, the 2nd of November. A common minimum programme has been agreed upon and the broad structure of the new Government is available in advance, with a deputy Chief Minister from the Congress and from the Jammu region. At the organizational level there is bound to be difficult negotiations about the distribution of portfolios. Having conceded the Chief Ministership, the Congress would be right in demanding some of the important portfolios. Mufti Mohammed Sayeed would do well not to indulge in too much bargaining on this subject. His party should be deeply conscious that the successful holding of the elections and his assuming the Chief Ministership is but only the first initial step in dealing with the complex issues related to Jammu and Kashmir. PDP should also rise above partisan considerations to move forward to deal with these issues.

While the common minimum programme has been agreed upon between the Congress and the PDP, one cannot shy away from the differences of approach on various issues inherent in the election manifestos of the PDP and the Congress. A fundamental factor underpinning these differences is that while the PDP's concerns and objectives are limited to its constituency in Jammu and Kashmir, particularly in the valley, the Congress Party's concerns and objectives have broader and deeper national dimensions. The manner in which Congress participants in the Government deal with the issues of Jammu and Kashmir, have nation-wide implications because Congress is a national party. Issues related to the dialogue with secessionist groups (of all categories) will have to be dealt with in a manner where those committed to secessionism and violent means should not be allowed to utilize the proposed dialogue as only a tactical move to further their objectives. The problem of releasing political prisoners will have to be resolved with the law and order agencies of Jammu and Kashmir in a manner where the operational efficiency of this specially trained force does not diminish, given the prospects that Pakistan will continue its intrusive violent activities in Jammu and Kashmir. The new Government of Jammu and Kashmir has already declared its intention to seek an early dialogue with the Central Government in India, for the future political dispensation in Jammu and Kashmir in terms of autonomy or devolution of power. One hopes that the BJP-led Government does not undertake the dialogue with partisan objectives and that the Central Government will deal with the dialogue in a manner which will convey the clear message that the aim is to be responsive to the interests and aspirations of people of Jammu and Kashmir. The three objectives on which this dialogue should focus and on which the new Government of Jammu and Kashmir should concentrate are: First, to forge an autonomy or devolution package which should politically assuage the expectations of the people of Jammu Kashmir, secondly, to give serious and continued attention to the social and economic development of the State in all dimensions with a careful prioritization of projects and programmes, and thirdly, to ensure that the devolution package also provides for the delegation of power and responsibilities internally within Jammu and Kashmir from Srinagar to Ladakh and Jammu. That the dialogue between the State Government and the Central Government should be the first item on the Agenda of the new Government. Priority should also be given to deal with political groups in Jammu and Kashmir who did not participate in the elections, but who may be willing to have a discussion with the newly elected Government, barring those amongst them who remained committeed to violent disruption of unity of India.

It must also be kept in mind that satisfactory and positive progress in these discussions will have implications for future dialogues between India and Pakistan on the Pakistani dimensions of the Kashmir issue. The more the successes in these dialogues the lesser would be the credibility of Pakistan's spurious claims about speaking on behalf of the Muslim citizens of India in Jammu and Kashmir. Meaningful progress in this respect would help India in curbing Pakistan-sponsored terrorism both politically and in operational terms.

All elements in the power structure which would be involved in the dialogue should remember the basic and important message which the people of Jammu and Kashmir have given by participating in the Legislative Assembly elections despite the threat of violence. They have rejected the Pakistani advocacy of separation of Jammu and Kashmir from India. They have affirmed not only the willingness but a conviction that a solution to the issues related to Jammu and Kashmir can be fashioned within the mainstream of democratic processes of India and thirdly, they have clearly rejected terrorist violence both externally and internally, as means to resolve their problems. More importantly, they have rejected externally-sponsored terrorist secessionism. It is imperative that the Central Government, the State Government and the political parties perceive the significance of this message and respond to it to free the people of Jammu and Kashmir from the thrall of violence and socio-political angst to which they have been subjected for more than a decade.

13
Fear and Hope

Through a Looking Glass

The European Union has been incrementally concerned about the India-Pakistan stand-off since December last. Despite the existing direct access to subcontinent developments, Europeans still look to Britain officials for their action on this account. High level officials have visited India since the beginning of the year and there is a perception that Britain's experience and knowledge about India endows them with some special capacity to influence India. Therefore, the British representatives in the various fora of the EC are an influential voice about India and Pakistan.

The British members of the European Parliament convened a special meeting of the foreign affairs committee to hold a hearing on the current Indo-Pakistan confrontation and the Kashmir issue on June 20 in Brussels. I participated in this meeting on behalf of India and in this hearing as the keynote speaker. The other speakers were Pakistan's ambassador in Brussels, Shaukat Umar and two professors Vernon Hewitt from Britain and Jean-Luc Racine from France.

The Pakistani presentation was a historical justification of Pakistan's claim on Jammu and Kashmir and the manner in which India had obstinately rejected these claim. Professors Hewitt and Racine, while deliberately providing a detached and impartial analysis emphasized that the current troubles between India and Pakistan originated in Pakistan which was the base from which terrorist subversion is launched against India. Both these speakers also emphasised that India has to overcome the alienation of a segment of the people in 'Indian Jammu and Kashmir' by providing them a political solution responsive to their aspirations.

My perceptions about the reactions of the members of the European Parliament are as follows:

- There is a general appreciation for the political and military restraint with which India has reacted to Pakistan-sponsored terrorism during the last seven months.
- It is accepted that it is primarily Indian restraint which prevented a war in the subcontinent and a nuclear confrontation.
- There is also the view that war has been averted partially due to Pervez Musharraf declaring his intention to stop supporting cross-border terrorism.
- It was felt that Indian restraint and Musharraf's speeches on January 12 and May 27 were a result of international political and diplomatic pressure generated particularly by the US and western democracies in Europe.
- The advocacy was that India should continue to remain restrained in the large interest of stability and peace not only in Asia but also in the world.

These reactions were on expected lines. But the comments and questions on the presentation reflected certain nuances which we in India should take note of while there was acceptance that terrorism originated in Pakistan and terrorists were under the control of Pakistan there is still a great amount of hesitation in acknowledging direct links between Musharraf and the Pakistani Government, on the one hand and across the border in India, on the other. The theory is that Musharraf is trying to do his best but he cannot completely control extremist Islamic terrorism on three fronts: in Afghanistan, against India and in his own country.

The view was expressed that India should give Musharrf some time to implement the promises which he has made in his policy pronouncements since January. Moreover, India should strengthen firmly against terrorist organization by making more substantial concessions in terms of moving back our security forces and agreeing to a dialogue at the political level as early as possible.

There was agreement that cross-border terrorism should be stopped and that the sanctity of the LoC should be respected. There was, however, a consensus that Pakistan has a legitimate *locus standi* on the Kashmir issue. While India's policy stance that the issue should be resolved through bilateral negotiations is respected, there is an incremental feeling that India should not remain negative about external mediation or facilitation by friendly Governments. Members of the European Parliament had no reticence about proposing some kind of a referendum, joint Indo-Pakistan sovereignty over Kashmir or creation of an independent State of Jammu and Kashmir.

When I firmly pointed out the impracticability of all these suggestions the response was that India should not be hesitant to explore all possibilities of this type. And when I emphasised that Kashmir is more than a territorial dispute—that it affects the very plural democratic ideologies, the response I got was that Indian democracy is strong and stable enough not to be destabilized by territorial and political concessions on J&K. Ultimately, I had to categorically emphasise that the question of territorial alienation of J&K from the Indian Republic just does not arise whatever its cost. My audience was not pleased with this affirmation but I think there was some realization that half backed suggestions without any comprehension of the subcontinental realities would not be accepted by India.

All my European interlocutors accepted the high priority and importance that the Indian Government attaches to the holding of legislative assembly election in J&K without any disruption by Pakistan sponsored terrorist groups. Some suggested package in keeping with the people's aspirations to the maximum extent possible. Officials of the council of Europe and the EC were more inclined to accept the practicality of fashioning a solution to the J&K issue on the basis of the LoC with some adjustments. I told them that while the Indian Government cannot examine this proposal – given Pakistan's continuing subversive activities – I personally felt that a solution could be sought with some adjustment in the delineation of the LoC combined with a political package for the people of J&K.

There was not much enthusiasm to refer back to the UN resolutions on this issue. Nor was there any great enthusiasm for the UN to play any role. There was concern about the spread of Islamic extremist terrorism and Islamic orthodoxy in Central and South Asia. There was special concern about the states of women the role of madrasas and prospects of violation of human rights if lslamic orthodoxy finds a place in the power structure of Asian countries. There was also an assessment that Musharraf is the only safeguard between moderation and there resurgence of highly assertive Islamic forces in Pakistan.

Western democracies are not interested in the internal dynamics affecting the Kashmir issue. Their concerns are : one, that the Kashmir dispute should not lead to a nuclear war; two, that Indo-Pak confrontation should not disrupt their campaign against international terrorism which affects their regional security interests; three, there is a concern about human rights and good governance in general terms but not in terms of any passionate commitment. It would be unrealistic to expect any substantive support from Europe or western democracies on our concerns about J&K. India has to deal with this struggle on its own.

Valley of Fear and Hope

The problems related to Kashmir are mostly viewed through the prisms of Pakistan's sustained subversive activities over the last decade and a half or of ongoing internal security operations undertaken by the Government of India and State Government of Jammu and Kashmir. There is also a segment of Indian political circles which advocates either an absolutist jingoistic stance of laying claim to all the territories which belong to the old state of Jammu and Kashmir or advocating the trifurcation of the areas of Jammu and Kashmir now part of India on religious lines in terms of the demography in Ladakh in the valley and in Jammu.

Assessments through the prisms mentioned and the advocacies referred to above result in opaque and confused perceptions on the Kashmir issue. It is time to move beyond events and developments to analyse the roots of the problem as we face it today and to understand the reality of political dynamics affecting Jammu and Kashmir.

First and foremost, India must consciously accept the fact that the old princely State of Jammu and Kashmir which came into being in the mid-19th century was an artificial creation of the Dogra Imperium. The collective political entity of Jammu and Kashmir as a plural multi-ethnic, multi-linguistic united territorial entity based on the feeling of the people of Jammu and Kashmir is only a post-independence phenomenon which was being consolidated since 1947. Second, this process of consolidation and the affiliations, of Jammu and Kashmir to India stands disrupted because large segments of people in the Kashmir valley alienated from the present power structure in Jammu and Kashmir and have lost their convictions about the logic of the state's affiliation to India (which most of them believed in till the Seventies).

The reasons for this disaffection are well known and have been the subject-matter of much analysis and cogitation in the Indian media as well as scholarly circles here. It must also be noted that in a recent public opinion poll, the Mori report, only 6.2 per cent of the people of Jammu and Kashmir favoured the state's becoming part of Pakistan. Most of them indicated a desire for independence or extensive autonomy.

One cannot gainsay the fact that this sense of separateness in the State of Jammu and Kashmir, when compared with the other states constituting the Indian Union, is partially the result of the separate status and jurisdictional arrangements given to Jammu and Kashmir when it acceded to India. A political post mortem of the manner in which India handled the Kashmir issue, politically and military over the years, has only limited relevance to the complex predicaments which we face today. It would be more pertinent to squarely perceive the current situation and then to examine what can be done to overcome the present impasse: One has to accept that the State Government of the National Conference does not have much credibility among the people of Jammu and Kashmir. It is equally true that the political groups constituting the Hurriyat do not really represent the broad cross-section of the people of Jammu and Kashmir: Ladakh and Jammu remain unrepresented in the Hurriyat. So are sections of the population in the valley. Infiltration and terrorism continue, which, though sponsored and supported by Pakistan, cannot be sustained unless there is some residual support from local disaffected youth and other cadre who participate in this violence either out of political conviction or under the threat of violence by foreign-based terrorist groups.

The outright rejection of the resolution on autonomy passed by the state assembly of Jammu and Kashmir nearly an year and a half ago by the Government of India, without even an offer to discuss it, has generated an undercurrent of resentment in political circles. There is also the profound contradiction on this issue between the Hindu and Buddhist populations of Jammu and Ladakh, on the one hand and disaffected political group in the Kashmir valley, on the other. So developing a consensus on possible political solutions among the people of Jammu and Kashmir would be a complex and difficult task. This is made more difficult because externally sponsored violence continues to disrupt a rational dialogue among political parties of Jammu and Kashmir as well as between them and the representatives of the Government of India.

It is equally important to note that the discussions between political parties themselves in Jammu and Kashmir on this issue are practically non-existent. The gulf between them is wide; no meaningful efforts have been undertaken to bridge this gulf. The number of special envoys or representatives who are entrusted with the task of interacting with political groups in Jammu and Kashmir by the Government of India have not so far been able to enter a substantive and meaningful discussion with Kashmiri political parties (not even with the National Conference).

There is also disillusionment among the separatist groups in Jammu and Kashmir about terrorist groups operating from foreign bases with foreign mercenaries who are operating in the state under the guidance of Pakistan and other extremist Islamic groups. It is by taking note of this disillusionment that the Government of India has entered into dialogue with various dissident groups in Jammu and Kashmir to wean them away from terrorist violence and persuade them to join the political processes. K.C. Pant, Ram Jethmalani, A.S. Dulat, the former chief of the Research and Analysis Wing of the cabinet secretariat and Arun Jaitley are engaged in this exercise, now perhaps with some urgency to ensure their participation in the scheduled state legislative assembly elections in September.

The expectation is that if elections are held with the participation of dissident groups, the political democratic processes in Jammu and Kashmir could be brought back on the rails. Although this effort is on, there are still uncertainties about the dissident political groups joining the electoral process.

The assassination of moderate leaders like Abdul Ghani Lone and the Government of India's decision to take drastic action against hardcore anti-India leaders like Syed Ali Geelani have only increased this uncertainty.

India however is keen about holding the election and reviving the democratic process which it hopes would become a springboard for a long-term political solution to the internal problems of Jammu and Kashmir. Ensuring that elections are manifestly free and fair is also subject to differences of opinion between Farooq Abdullah and the Government of India about holding the elections under President's rule. This is a part from India's reluctance to allow institutional foreign observers for the proposed elections. It is clear that Pakistan would try to disrupt the electoral process. It is this consideration which made the Government of India reticent about squarely blaming Pakistan for the Qasim Nagar massacre (near Jammu) of civilians of July14.

Accusing Pakistan would have clearly involved an operational response against Pakistan which in turn would have deluged the elections. A military operation with prospects of escalation would inevitably delay the poles. Internal discussions on the Jammu and Kashmir issue are at a crucial stage at present. It is clear that holding the elections with participation by all political groups is imperative. So is the requirement of elections being manifestly free and fair.

More important, the Government of India should realize that a political repackage containing maximum autonomy is the only solution to separatism. Delivery tactics on this issue would be counter productive, even dangerous to the unity of India. The other suggestions from the Rashtriya Swayamsevak Sangh and other quarters about trifurcation of Jammu and Kashmir on ethno-religious lines reflects desperation and exhaustion, apart from stringent pluralistic terms of reference of the Indian policy.

The most important consideration which should underpin policies is that unless it finds a practical solution regarding the internal political dispensation of Jammu and Kashmir acceptable to the people of the state, the external discussions of the problem, that is, come to terms with Pakistan, cannot be evolved. Resolving the internal jurisdictions of the political dynamics of Jammu and Kashmir is the life of India's commitment today.

The Challenge of Peace

There is general acknowledgement at home and abroad, except in Pakistan that elections were held smoothly and fairly in Jammu and Kashmir and that a new legislative assembly and Government in the state could initiate the process for a political solution to the problem. What, then, are the immediate prospects of normalization in J&K?.

Though it has captured the largest number of seats in the 87-member assembly, the National Conference has been clearly voted out of power, party president Omar Abdullah's defeat is especially significant. Congress with 20 seats and Mufti Mohammed Sayeed's People's Democratic Party with 16 seats, have emerged as the new actors while independents, and members of smaller parties like the Panther's Party, hold the balance of power.

Sonia Gandhi personally campaigned in the elections in Srinagar and Jammu. She was the only leader of a national party who campaigned despite the serious security threats. By campaigning she emphasised three factors. One, affirmation of the Indian identity. Two, she successfully revived the position of the Congress in the state where the centrestage was being incrementally taken over by local political parties. Three, she reaffirmed the tradition of emotional and political involvement of the Congress, especially Nehruvian leadership, in J&K. Ghulam Nabi Azad's organizational skills produced results, despite his lack of political roots in J&K in recent years. Most importantly, the state cadres of the Congress made a purposeful effort with deep conviction and commitment.

There is going to be political consensus in the new assembly about state autonomy being the major advocacy for the future. There would be differences of opinion about the details of the autonomy package. The NC has been asking for autonomy as it existed in the early 50s. Other parties want a more confederal arrangement. Parties representing Ladakh and Jammu are more keen on getting delegated powers for administrative and economic management from Srinagar. They would also desire a separate package of assistance for each region – the Valley, Jammu and Ladakh. There could also be some demand for a separate status for J&K with complete autonomy based on joint guarantees from India and Pakistan. This proposition would not be accepted by any Government of India.

There is a genuine and deeply felt desire for economic, social and developmental assistance from the Central Government among the people of J&K. In recent months, there have been pronouncements by political figures of the state appealing for a focus on the spheres of education, health, roads, communications, restoration of irrigation works and local crafts.

The Government of India is likely to commence negotiations with representatives of the State Government by December 2002 or January 2003. The terms of reference and objectives are still ambiguous because the political parties in J&K themselves do not have an agreed framework of objectives. The Indian Government should be clear about only one basic objective that Kashmir should not be politically and territorially alienated from the republic.

Equally important is the fact that there is a definite likelihood of not just continuing but increased terrorist violence sponsored from Pakistan. The only counter-measure to Pakistan-sponsored disruptions and the internal frustration in the state is to undertake a purposeful programme of developmental work that is responsive to the people's aspirations. It is also important that the Government of India evolves its negotiating stances on the basis of consultations in parliament backed by a national consensus.

The external dimensions of managing the emerging situation in J&K are equally important. Pakistan-sponsored terrorism will continue because it failed to disrupt the democratic processes in the state. This has to be countered within J&K and where necessary, India should not hesitate from taking pre-emptive action across the LoC. Such preventive action should be carefully calibrated to avoid full-scale conflict with Pakistan which is neither necessary nor desirable.

The successful holding of J&K elections, if following through by discussions with the State Government, would enhance India's credibility on issues related to Kashmir in the international community. There would be increased community presssure from the international community on India and Pakistan to enter into a bilateral dialogue. There is little doubt General Pervez Musharaf will continue in power in Pakistan in the foreseeable future. Regardless of our reservations about him, India must deal with him.

Keeping in mind the three objectives of normalizing the situation in J & K, reducing the high levels of Indo-Pak tensions and augmenting international support for Indian concerns about terrorism in J & K, it is time for us to move out of the somewhat static negotiating position we have adopted vis a vis Pakistan since December 2001. We should move towards a dialogue with Pakistan by early next year. The preparatory steps are: to repeat the offers which we have made to Pakistan about restoring overflights and raising diplimatic relations. We must also gradually reduce the massive deployment of our forces on the LoC and the international border. We could begin by moving back some of our troops from the international frontiers. We can also reduce the size of our deployment on the LoC depending on the levels of terrorist intrusions and activities in J&K.

On a parallel track, Pakistan should be given clear signals that if terrorist activities increased, India will be more decisive and pre-emptive than ever before. India should take the major powers and members of the UN Security Council into confidence. If we do not move out of the straitjacket of rejectionism about a dialogue with Pakistan, we will be isolated in the international community.

India's policies in Kashmir must have two ingredients: a purposive approach to evolve a political formula responsive to the aspirations of the people of the state, and a measured mix of military decisiveness and politico-strategic flexibility in reviving the dialogue with Pakistan.

A Tenuous Beginning

Expressions of satisfaction about the completion of the legislative assembly elections in Jammu and Kashmir were subjected to some uncertainties because of the competing claims for the chief ministership between the Congress and the People's Democratic Party of Jammu and Kashmir. The reasoning of the PDP for claiming the chief ministership was that it has emerged as a major political force in the valley as an alternative to the National Conference which stood rejected at the polls in public perception. The PDP is a regional party of the state and therefore its leading the Government would increase the credibility of the Government both inside Jammu and Kashmir and outside. The PDP also claimed that its manifesto was the most responsive to the aspirations of the people of the State.

The counter-rationale of the Congress was that it had a larger number of seats in the legislative assembly than the PDP, and most of the independent groups, that the Congress has greater support from independent members of the legislative assembly than the PDP, and that the Congress being the national party, its assuming the chief ministership of the state on the basis of the most recent public mandate would be a more effective counter to the separatist elements in the State. The leadership of the PDP does not have sufficient appeal in Jammu and in Ladakh.

In addition, the Congress legitimately claimed that it has greater experience in governance and in dealing with terrorist and succession-infested areas and therefore would be more capable of bringing Jammu and Kashmir back to the mainstream of democratic national politics in India. Ultimately, the Congress showed a greater sensitivity to the more pertinent considerations of national interests and of the well-being of the people of Jammu and Kashmir, rising above considerations of party aspirations and agreed to the PDP, led by Mufti Mohammed Sayeed, leading the new state government of Jammu and Kashmir.

General information available about discussions relating to this compromise was that Sonia Gandhi and her, principal emissary. Manmohan Singh, were instinctively in favour of the ultimate decision taken of letting the PDP lead the Government. But the delay in finalizing this compromise was because of senior figures in the Congress and party leaders in Jammu and Kashmir insisting on the chief ministership on the basis of the rationale which has been summarized above.

It is clear while taking the decision to let the PDP lead the new Government in Jammu and Kashmir, Sonia Gandhi has conveyed timely and important signals about the Congress's approach to significant issues affecting national politics. First, she has emphasized that the party's overall credibility and its commitment to the well-being of people are more important than any individual. Second, that national interests are a matter of higher priority than the interests of the Congress even if those interests were based on logical and rational considerations. On all counts, this will increase the credibility of the Congress not only amongst the people of Jammu and Kashmir but also in the Indian public opinion in general.

It was a difficult decision to take, given that a fair segment of Congress leaders, including leaders in Jammu and Kashmir had different views. The new Government was sworn in on November 2. A common minimum programme has been agreed upon and the broad structure of the new Government is available in advance, with a deputy chief minister from the Congress and from the Jammu region. At the organizational level, there is bound to be difficult negotiations about the distribution of portfolios.

Having conceded the chief ministership the Congress was right in demanding some of the important portfolios. Sayeed would do well not to indulge in too much bargaining on this subject. His party should be deeply conscious that the successful holding of the elections and his assuming the chief ministership are but only the initial step in dealing with the complex issues related to Jammu and Kashmir. The PDP should also rise above partisan considerations to move forward to deal with these issues.

While the common minimum programme has been agreed upon between the Congress and the PDP, one cannot shy away from the differences of approach on various issues inherent in the election manifestoes of the PDP and the Congress. A fundamental factor underpinning these differences is that while the PDP's concerns and objectives are limited to its constituency Jammu and Kashmir, particularly in the valley, the Congress's concerns and objectives have a broader and deeper national dimension.

The manner in which Congress participants in the Government deal with the issues of Jammu and Kashmir has nation wide implications because the Congress is a national party. Issues related to the dialogue with secessionist groups will have to be dealt with in a manner where those committed to secessionism and violent means should not be allowed to utilize the proposed dialogue as only a tactical move to further their objectives. Although Yasin Malik and several others have been released, the problem of releasing political prisoners will have to be resolved with great care. The issue of merging the special task force with the law and order agencies of Jammu and Kashmir should be resolved in a manner where the operational efficiency of this specially trained force does not diminish, given the prospects that Pakistan will continue its intrusive activities in Jammu and Kashmir.

The new Government of Jammu and Kashmir has already declared its intention to seek an early dialogue with the Centre for the future political dispensation in Jammu and Kashmir in terms of autonomy or devolution of power. One hopes that the Bharatiya Janata Party-led Government does not undertake the dialogue with partisan objectives, and that the Centre will deal with the dialogue in a manner which will convey the clear message that the aim is to be responsive to the interests and aspirations of the people of Jammu and Kashmir.

The three objectives on which this dialogue should focus and on which the new Government of Jammu and Kashmir should concentrate are: first, to forge an autonomy or devolution package which would politically assuage the expectations of the people of Jammu and Kashmir. Second, to give serious and continued attention to the social and economic development of the state in all dimensions with careful prioritization of projects and programmes, and to ensure that the devolution package also provides for the delegation of power and responsibilities internally within Jammu and Kashmir from Srinagar to Ladakh and Jammu.

The dialogue between the State Government and the Centre should be first on the agenda of new government. Priority should also be given to deal with political groups in Jammu and Kashmir who did not participate in the elections but who may be willing to have a discussion with the newly elected Government barring those amongst them who remained committed to the violent disruption of unity of India. Satisfactory progress in these discussions will have implications for future dialogue between India and Pakistan on the Pakistani dimensions of the Kashmir issue. The more the successes in these dialogues, the lesser would be the credibility of Pakistan's spurious claims about speaking on behalf of the Muslim citizens of India in Jammu and Kashmir. Meaningful progress in this respect would help India in curbing Pakistan-sponsored terrorism.

All elements in the power structure involved in the dialogue should remember the basic and important message which the people of Jammu and Kashmir have given by participating in the legislative assembly elections despite the threat of violence. They have rejected Pakistan's advocacy of the separation of Jammu and Kashmir from India. They are convinced that a solution to the issues related to Jammu and Kashmir can be fashioned within the mainstream of the Indian democratic processes. They have clearly rejected terrorist violence both externally and internally as a means to resolve their problems. More important, they have rejected externally-sponsored terrorist secessionism.

The Centre, the State Government and the political parties should see the significance of this message and respond to it to free the people of Jammu and Kashmir from the thrall of violence and socio-political anxiety to which they have been subjected for more than a decade.

Kashmir Scenario in the Iraqi Context and Internal Developments

I was in Jammu and Kashmir for three days from the 24th to the 26th of March. The massacre of Hindus at Nandigram occurred the day I arrived. A number of us who had gone for a conference at the University of Jammu, had the privilege of meeting Chief Minister Mufti Mohammed Sayeed on the 25th. As expected he was deeply distressed at the massacre of Kashmir Pandits. He emphasised the obvious motive behind continuing and incremental acts of terrorism in Jammu and Kashmir –that of scuttling the efforts at restoring stability and harmony in the State which he initiated since coming to power nearly four months ago.

It is relevant, therefore, to examine the developing situation in Jammu and Kashmir, particularly in the context of the USA's military operations against Iraq and continuing civil strife in Afghanisten. One also has to take note of the contradiction in the Pakistani polity in undertaking this examination.

First, the internal political realities in Jammu and Kashmir. The assurance given by the Mufti Government to resume a purposeful dialogue with dissidents in Jammu and Kashmir, is still to gain substance because both the State Government and separatist groups have not been able to formulate an innovative and constructive Agenda for the dialogue.

Chief Minister Mufti Mohammed Sayeed's handicap is that the Central Government has not given him an indication of what the Centre's framework is for such a dialogue. Government in New Delhi has appointed a new Chief Negotiator to deal with issues related to Jammu and Kashmir. N.N. Vohra, former Defence Secretary, Home Secretary and Principal Secretary to the Prime Minister has been designated as Government of India's representative. He has had preliminary discussions with Deputy Prime Minister L. K. Advani, Chief Minister Mufti Mohammed Sayeed and some Kashmiri leaders. But two points have been made by political circles in Jammu and Kashmir. First that the Central Government has not undertaken any consultations with other political parties, particularly political leaders of Jammu and Kashmir to evolve a consensual brief for Mr. Vohra's negotiations. Second, that Mr. Vohra is being left out on a limbo because the Deputy Prime Minister Advani has not given him any clear idea so far about the broad framework for his project, leaving aside the lack of consultations mentioned above.

- Separatist groups have always been divided but contradictions have emerged even within each group, whether it is Hurriyat or Hizbul Mujahiddin or other important dissidents.

- Steps taken to moderate the punitive role of the security forces are being viewed with mixed feeling, particularly in Jammu and Ladakh. The assassination of leaders like Abdul Ghani Lone and Abdul Majid Dar, have intensified fear and inhibitions in separatist groups about entering into a meaningful discussion with Government representatives.
- Terrorist acts are on the increase due to Islamist parties in Pakistan being in power in the North West Frontier Province and Baluchistan.

Significant and pernicious changes have occurred in General Musharraf's Kashmiri policies. Leaving aside the cosmetic arguments about operation self-determination etc, the substantive ingredients in this policy now are to sustain and increase terrorist violence against minorities and against the para-military forces; at the same time eliminating leaders of the separatist movement who may have an inclination to negotiate with Mufti Mohammed Sayeed and the Central Government. Secondly, the structured ethno-religious cleansing in Jammu and Kashmir to compel the minorities to migrate from the valley and on the other hand, to change the demography of Jammu by increasing the influx of Muslims from other parts of the State into Jammu. The consequence is increasing hostility between Muslims and other religious groups in the population of the State.

With the onset of summer anticipations are that military pressure on the Line of Control would be increased by Pakistan. The US-led Coalition's operations in Iraq will have longer term ramifications for Jammu and Kashmir in terms of cross-border terrorism. While the outcome of the US military operations seems more or less inevitable the critical consequence would be the rise and expansion of Islamic extremist terrorism from Algeria in the North-west to the Philippines in the East and in all the countries in between. This time the phenomenon will have the support of Muslim populations who are full of resentment against the U.S. military action in Iraq.

With prospects of political uncertainty in Iraq in the aftermath of war and the Afghanistan situation continuing to be on the boil, the fall out on the Gulf, and on Afghanistan would generate violent and destabilising influences in the South Asian region, particularly in India. Whatever admonitions and pressures that USA may generate on Pakistan, there is not going to be any qualitative or positive change in Pakistan policies towards Jammu and Kashmir. What is important to keep in mind is that Pakistani's objective of alienating Jammu and Kashmir from India is not a limited one-issue objective. The objective is the long-term strategic objective of the Pakistani power structure to de-stabilise India by generating violence and communal divisiveness and then fragmentation of India on the basis of centrifugal, ethno-religious forces which it seeks to create, sustain and encourage. As a parallel priority in this exercise, attempts would continue to be made to prevent restoration of democracy, harmony and normalcy in Jammu and Kashmir. In fact, Pakistani's rhetonic by insisting on a dialogue will be cover for these policy objective and will also be an exercise in preventing important world powers from understanding the substance of Pakistani machinations and intentions.

It is necessary that India projects this assessment both diplomatically and in terms of media projections to the world at large. It must also be mentioned that our advocacy on these points can be effective and credible only if domestic politics in India exercise itself from narrow communal agendas which have become instrumentalities for electoral victories, particularly over the last two or three years. If communal disharmony becomes significant characteristic of civil society and power structure in India, our efforts at projecting our cause in Jammu and Kashmir through the prism of democracy, secularism, will not succeed.

POLICY IN AFGHANISTAN

14

New Predicaments

USA's Anti-Terrorist Campaign in Afghanistan Predicaments and Long Term Strategic Implications

Analyses and assessment regarding the anti-terrorist military campaign being carried out by the US-led coalition in Afghanistan has been mostly focused on the military operations and interim political arrangements which were put in place late in December 2001 under head of Government Hamid Karzai. While such a limited analysis is topically relevant, it is more important and pertinent to look at the longer term implication of the developing phenomenon of the USA involvement in this region, and its impact on the strategic and security environment in the coming years, say atleast for a decade or two. The over-arching phenomenon to take note of is that since October 7, 2001 (when the United States led coalition launched anti-terrorist military campaign) there has been an incremental US military presence not only in Afghanistan but in Uzbekistan, in Azerbaijan and Pakistan. The United States is assured of operational and logistical support and facilities in India and in Bangladesh. The elements of the Central Command of the US stands augmented in the Gulf and in the northern reaches of the Indian Ocean, including in the Arabian Sea.

Objectively speaking, the United States military presence and political interaction in Central, Western, South Asia is at bigger levels even beyond what they were during the Cold War and during the Gulf War. It is obvious therefore that the security, political and economic objective of this incremental US presence go beyond eroding and then eliminating the Taliban and Al-Qaeda Movement.

In terms of inter se priorities, the more immediate objective of the US presence is to mop up remnants of Taliban and Al-Qaeda forces in

Afghanistan and in North-Western parts of Pakistan, to the extent possible. That this campaign still continues, is clarified by a Commanding General of the Central Command of the US Lt. General Tomy Franks in the second week of March. The US bombing and ground action in Eastern Afghanistan throughout the first half of March confirms this situation.

The second objective is to stabilize Afghanistan which is subjected to contradictory pulls and pressures. Given the absence of any cohesive Pushtoon military force in Afghanistan, Hamid Karzai has had to accept troops of the Northern Alliance as the main instrumentality for defence and security of the interim administration which he heads. He has also had to give a number of important portfolios to leaders from the Northern Alliance (Uzbeks and Tadjiks) in the interim cabinet to ensure that the coalition holds together in this initial stage till the Loya Jirga or the Grand Assembly meets and finalises future political dispensation in Afghanistan.

The writ of the Karzai government does not run effectively outside Kabul. Local warlords supported by cadres following their own Agenda have been functioning in defiance of the central authority of the interim government. This interim government has to cope not only with the Pushtoon/non-Pushtoon politico-ethnic divide but it has also to face internecine factionalism and violence within different Pushtoon factions, between the components of the Northern Alliance political groups. The Tadjik and Uzbek cadres of the Northern Alliance are subjected to simmering tensions pregnant with prospects of violence. The assassination of Karzai's Minister for Civil Aviation in early February and the refusal of regional tribal leaders in southern and south-eastern Afghanistan remain hurdles in the way of a movement forward towards political stabilization of the country.

Another factor which compounds the negative situation is that large numbers of Taliban and Al Qaeda cadres who had escaped from the US-led military campaign with their arms intact, and they have merged with the local population. Latest reports indicate that these cadres, some of whom are also based in North-western parts of Pakistan, have regrouped and have commenced guerilla warfare to which the United States is reacting.

It is important to note that the major powers led by the United States envisage two distinctive roles, one for the US-led coalition military force who would be concentrating on the anti-terrorist war. The second is a combined military force led by Britain consisting of troops from Western democracies who would function as peace-keeping and internal security force for the stabilization of Afghanistan. It is, logical, therefore to conclude that the US-led anti-terrorist force would play a strategic role in Afghanistan while the other coalition members led by Britain would play the role of stabilizing the politics of the country supporting the interim Afghan government till such time as it is needed.

It is the broader objective of US military presence in different parts of Pakistan (Peshawar, Quetta, Pesni,Gwador, and Karachi), in Uzbekistan, in Azerbaijan and in the Gulf which merit a rational speculative prognosis the extent. US political and military leaders led by President Bush, as well as Prime Minister Tony Blair of the UK have publicly stated that the war against terrorism would be a long-struggle. President Bush has been more specific, talking about "Axis of Evil", mentioning North Korea, Iran and Iraq, indicating that these countries could be the next target of US military operations. There are currently 7 countries on the USA's list of state sponsoring terrorism, namely, Cuba, Iran, Libya, Iraq, North Korea, Sudan and Syria. Out of these 7 countries only Cuba and Libya lie outside the geographical limits of Central and West Asia. The augmented US military presence from Turkey in the North to the Philippines in South East Asia, is clearly a physical manifestation of strategic and security understanding which the US has reached with various countries in this region, to contain religious extremism and violence as well as to stabilize the region with a view to ensuring long-term energy and economic security for the international community, particularly, the security of western democracies and their allies. It must also be realized that 3 out of 5 Central Asian countries are also Members of the Partnership for Peace arrangements for NATO. The twin macro-level strategic objectives of American politico-strategic presence in the region (it is indicated that this would be a long-term presence) are in a manner an exercise to balance off, or prevent any excessive domination or influence by China and Russia, on the countries of the region. The second objective is to secure the energy resources of the Gulf and to have long-term access to the proven hydro-carbons and mineral resources of the Central Asian countries. This is apart from the attraction of investment opportunities and the markets of Central Asia. Equally relevant is US objective of stabilizing the nuclear weapons and missiles security environment in the region. The presence of the US troops and creation of a pattern of political and security concentrations, positions the US to effectively intervene in any nuclear confrontation between India and Pakistan. Such an exercise could contribute to gradual capping of nuclear weapons and missiles capacities of these two countries and to persuade them to an effective arms control measures within the framework of the international Non-Proliferation Agenda determined by the Five Permanent Members of the UN Security Council. The Cordon Sanitairre or the structuring the politico-military stabilization of the security environment being put in place by the US would also be a more direct instrumentality in preventing the horizontal proliferation of weapons of mass destruction in countries stretching from North Korea to Iran. This assessment is not purely speculative. This message has been inherent indirectly in public pronouncement of President Bush, US Defence Secretary Donald Rumsfeld and by testimonies given by senior officials of the US Government to various committees of the US Congress. More recent report of the Congressional Research Service on Terrorism and Non-violence, implies these underlying objectives of the US policies.

In the short term, the two major powers of the region, Russia and China seem to have reconciled themselves to these new equations being forged under the leadership of the United States. It is also obvious that these policy orientations will face resentment and dissent not only from these major powers and to some extent from India, but there may be reservations regarding this assertive US posture from important European powers like Germany and France.

Developments since September 11, 2001 are not limited to international consensus about fighting terrorism. They also signal critical changes in the strategic and security environment in the Asian region and in the new global order which is being aimed at by the United States. The major task of Indian foreign and strategic policies is to carefully assess the extent to which these new arrangements would benefit India or militate against India's substantive security interests and freedom of options. It is obvious that in the short and medium terms, positive equation with the US is the practical option.

Coping with Terrorism Affecting India—Our Dilemmas

Our attention is so focused on the anti-terrorist campaign being led by the US against Afghanistan that we seem to be unaware of consequences of this campaign in terms of our struggle against terrorism; terrorism of which India has been a victim specially over the last 11 years since 1989. Our government in its initial reactions to terrorist attack on the US conveyed full and unreserved support to the US in its anti-terrorist campaign. In retrospect, we seem to have predicated our policy on the assumption that the campaign of the United States against international terrorism would automatically cover within its ambit terrorism perpetrated against us by Pakistan-sponsored extremist Islamic mercenaries. This was an optimistic and unrealistic prediction. There were speedy signals within a week after the catastrophic violence in New York and Washington that Pakistan was going to be the main operational and logistical instrumentality in the USA's anti-terrorism campaign. Musharraf's first message of support to the US clearly stipulated two pre-conditions for Pakistan joining the counter-terrorist coalition. First that India and Israel should be kept out of the coalition with the rider that India should not have any say in the future political dispensation in the post-Taliban Afghanistan. The second pre-condition was that the United States should not include the violence in Jammu and Kashmir in its anti-terrorist campaign. Pakistan's advocacy being that the violence in Jammu and Kashmir is an indigenous freedom struggle to which Pakistan only extends political, moral and diplomatic support, and nothing more.

(an unvarnished lie which the Americans are fully aware of).

Though the United States has not made any policy pronouncements responding to these two Pakistan pre-conditions, they seem to have been accepted de facto for the present by the United States Government. Responding to Indian concerns in this regard the US has given the general assurances, both in Washington and New Delhi during high level governmental discussions over the last three weeks. One has to relate policy pronouncements with ground realities which India has to face since September 11. These realities instead of signifying any general sense of security in India against terrorism only indicate serious dilemmas which India is likely to face. One has to recall the public memory to policy statements of substance distinguishing them from statements regarding general intentions and then give attention to the emerging ground realities. The US gave specific advice to India not to take any action against Government of Pakistan in response to violence occurring in Jammu and Kashmir within the first ten days after the terrorist attacks in USA in September. While the US condemned the Jaish-e-Mohammed attack on State Assembly building in Jammu and Kashmir in which nearly 40 people died, the US has not acknowledged Jaish-e-Mohammed being an organization sponsored by Pakistan and which is based in Pakistan.

Responding to Prime Minister Vajpayee's communication on this incident in which Vajpayee stated that India's patience is running out, President Bush advised restraint and caution in terse language asking both India and Pakistan to "stand down". Perhaps taking longer strategic and political interest into account India has abided by Bush's advice so far. But Pakistan has not. The bomb attack on the Jammu and Kashmir State Assembly was preceded by series of terrorist attacks on civilians and security personnel in Jammu and Kashmir disregarding the advice given by President Bush and Secretary of State Colin Powell, Pakistan continues its terrorist campaign in India. The last important violent incident was terrorist attack on the Awantipur airbase near Srinagar in India.

Earlier, when Indian armed forces undertook some operations to thwart an attempted large-scale infiltration of mercenaries, India was again admonished not to upset the apple cart of Musharraf's support to the US military campaign against Afghanistan. General Musharraf, however, seems to be confident that as far as he gives useful support to the United States military operations, he would be immune from any US pressures to restrain himself against India.

In an interview given to the Pakistan Television on Monday the 22nd of October, Musharraf made the following remarks "The Pakistani forces are fully prepared not only defensively but to teach a lesson to New Delhi if it tried any adventurism. The threats on the Line of Control must be stopped. Pakistan is not a Chhota Mota country. We are not wearing Chudian (bangles). They (India) will be paid back in the same coin. Advani and George Fernandes are stepping up anti-Pakistan rhetoric. The events in Jammu and Kashmir are part of a freedom struggle. The Indian army is indulging in state terrorism. Pakistan is fully capable of defending itself. India should not be under the misconception that they can take advantage of the turmoil in Afghanistan. We will not be intimidated by India. We have our own means to defend ourselves. The Kashmir cause would have been a different story had Pakistan not joined the international coalition. Pakistanis should think of the scenario when international coalition would be against us, with India on their side. But now we have no threat to our strategic assets. And they are safe."

While making these bellicose statements he indulged in the strategum of wanting to resume dialogue with Prime Minister Vajpayee, to tell the US and other powers that Pakistan is still willing to have a dialogue. The factual implication of Musharraf's evolving India policy post-September 11 are:

- Pakistan will continue to sponsor terrorist violence in Jammu and Kashmir.

- Musharraf seems to be sanguine that US will not take any action against Pakistan in this respect.

- While repeatedly referring to the safety of his strategic assets, namely, his nuclear weapons and missile capacities and then going on to warn India that he will teach India a lesson, he is sending a signal that he will not hesitate to use weapons of mass destruction against India if India takes any effective action against terrorist violence organized by his government against Indian targets. A parallel motive is to convey the impression to the US and other major powers that if India is not kept under restraint there are possibilities of a nuclear confrontation between India and Pakistan and therefore these powers should actively intervene to resolve the Kashmir issue within the framework of Pakistani demand.

We would only know how objective and impartial the US would be in relation to India, in the context of the threats inherent in Musharraf's statement after the US completes the current phase of its operations against Afghanistan. It is however logical to anticipate that the US would not be inclined to take any strong position on Pakistani activities against India's security and territorial integrity. The USA's approach would be to generate pressure both on India and Pakistan to resume dialogue with greater pressure on India not to react operationally against Pakistan-sponsored terrorism. Musharraf on his part is certain to demand that US does not cover Pakistani terrorist activities in the ambit of its general campaign against international terrorism. This scenario is the most important macro-level strategic and political problem which India would face in structuring relations with the US in the short and medium term.

India should also expect a continuation of terrorist violence in Jammu and Kashmir, particularly, during the period when US is engaged against Afghanistan and some other countries because of Pakistani's confidence that the US would generate effective pressure on India not to act against Pakistan as the US campaign progresses.

Another dilemma which the Government of India faces and will continue to face is the groundswell of public opinion within the country in support of India taking decisive punitive action against Pakistani terrorism, particularly large-scale and blatant terrorist violence sponsored by Pakistan-based terrorist mercenary groups. This view is shared by segments of the Indian political and security establishment. Defense Minister Fernandes and Home Minister Advani's pronouncements should be perceived in this context. It must also be clearly acknowledged by the government and people of India that there is little likelihood of the US politically or operationally supporting any anti-terrorist campaign undertaken by India against Pakistan. This is a campaign which we will have to undertake on our own wherever and whenever it becomes necessary.

We have been fighting terrorism so far within our own territorial limits. The question is can we or should we take the battle across the Line of Control to strike at the roots of Pakistan-sponsored terrorism. If we undertake such a fight it again will be an exercise which we would have to undertake alone. The best scenario one can visualise of the international community not taking action against us as far as these operations do not deteriorate into a nuclear confrontation with Pakistan.

The four consideration which should influence our decision in this regard are: First, we must be prepared for Pakistan threatening nuclear and missile retaliation against punitive action by India in its territory. Secondly, any effective action by India be in response to a manifestly serious terrorist incident against India which could justify our action in the eyes of the international community. Thirdly, we must carefully examine whether we have the operational capacity to undertake such action atleast for proportionate retaliation. (There is no guarantee that Pakistan will re-concile itself to the concept of proportionate retaliation; or it would want to expand the conflict). Do we have the political will to undertake such punitive action and more importantly the mind-set to cope with the military consequences of our taking such an initiative.

It is obvious any decision that we take in these matters would require deep thought and careful political and strategic calculations. The more important point is that patience and restraint beyond a certain threshold becomes appeasement which may lead to long-term threats to India's security and territorial integrity.

The Anti-terrorist War—Afghan Predicaments

The current episodic attention of the media and political analysts is on Prime Minister Vajpayee's visits to Russia, the United States and UK. This is natural in terms of projecting Indian concerns and interests to the Governments of these countries and assessing responses from them. More important, however, is to ruminate on developments inside Afghanistan and the future prospects of the people of that country in the context of the ongoing military campaign being carried out in Afghanistan under the leadership of the United States. It is now a little over eight weeks since the military campaign was launch against the Taliban and the Al Qaeda cadres led by Osama bin Laden.

Leaving aside the claims and counter-claims about the impact of this military operation by the US and allies on the one hand, and the Taliban on the other, a conscious effort merits being undertaken to understand not just the physical but the political realities on the grounds, comprehending the evolving political realities of Afghanistan, should not be limited to what is happening to the Taliban or to Osama bin Laden and his followers. The processes of our analyses and assessments must take into account the impact of military campaign on Afghan civil society and on social and economic foundations of Afghan society.

First the military ambivalances. There is a massive and continuous use of overwhelming air power against Taliban. While this has eroded the weapons systems and logistical facilities of the Taliban considerably, Taliban's political will to carry on the fight does not seem to be diminished. They also remain adamant about not handing over to Osama bin Laden, or his cadres located inside Afghanistan. Though the United States has deployed ground troops in southern, south-western and Northern Afghanistan, they have not been able to locate Osama bin Laden. While remaining elusive, bin Laden seems to remain confident about his chances of survival and his political objectives as manifested in his periodical television interviews on the Arab TV network, Al Jazeera, even after the US military campaign commenced. Then there is the inner contradiction in US political objectives. On the one hand, Bush and Rumsfeld have declared that their objective is to remove the Taliban from the power structure of Afghanistan and to obliterate them to the extent possible as they are participants in international terrorism, on the other the US is not giving sufficient operational and logistical military support to the forces of Northern Alliance to capture the major urban centres of Afghanistan, particularly Kabul.

First the delay and then the gradualness in attacking the Taliban forces deployed north of Kabul and Kabul-Herat Axis is interpreted as USA's responding to Pakistani sensitivities in the matter because General Pervez Musharraf does not want the Northern Alliance emerging as clearly victorious or the dominant factor in future political arrangements in Afghanistan. In fact, the US and its Western allies are still uncertain about how to create an effective enough Pashtun and Pathan political front in

Afghanistan which can function in tandem with the Northern Alliance to ultimately forge the necessary multi-ethnic representative coalition to govern Afghanistan after the campaign is over, when it comes to an end.

Representatives of ex-King Zahir Shah with whom authorities from the US and the United Nations have been in touch, are not proving to be an effective instrumentality to isolate and senitise the Taliban cadres. Those who have made these attempts have either been captured or killed or have been arrested by the Taliban cadres, which to some extent implies that the Pashtun population is not as yet sufficiently aliented from Taliban. There have been reports of desertions from Taliban forces but this has not resulted in tangible and visible impact on the Taliban's unity and purposiveness. It must also be noted that large numbers of Pathans from Pakistan's North-West Frontier Province and Northern Baluchistan are infiltrating ınto Afghanistan to support the Taliban despite the Afghan-Pakistan border being formally closed. It must be realized that in any case this border cannot be sealed, both due to geographic and ethnic reasons. The previous attempts stretching over nearly a thousand years in this respect have not succeeded. It is also curious that despite full declaratory support given by Russian Federation to this military campaign against the Taliban, the Putin Government seems to be playing only a marginal operational role in the campaign.

Iran which would have been willing to be a more active partner in this exercise seems to remain unacceptable to the Bush Government despite British Foreign Secretary Jack Straw's visit to Teheran and his discussions with President Khatemi. Keeping Iran isolated from this campaign is a singular example of political and strategic inaptitude. (There is of course the argument that Iran supports certain terrorist organizations in West Asia and the Middle East). The point to remember is that no durable political settlement in Afghanistan can take place without the cooperation of Iran and Uzbekistan. The most significant impact of the military operations has not been on the Taliban forces or the Al Qaeda, the main negative/destructive impact has been on the people of Afghanistan, the non-combatant civilians. Afghanistan, in any case has become devastated and bleak country due to the continuous military conflict which it has gone through and is going through over the last 22 years. The responsibility for the violence in Afghanistan has to be shared incontrovertibly by the former Soviet Union, the United States, Pakistan, Saudi Arabia and their allies.

Apart from the 3 million to 4 million refugees who went out of Afghanistan, another eight hundred thousand to one million refugees are escaping into neighbouring countries. The entire infrastructure of the Afghan economy stands completely destroyed. In addition to large number of Afghans seeking refuge in neighbouring countries, there are large numbers of people in that country who are internally displaced without any basic life support systems to sustain them on minimal levels of survival in terms of food, drinking water and essential health facilities. This last requirement is particularly important in the conflict situation affecting Afghanistan.

At the fundamental, human and sociological levels, the Taliban, the Al Qaeda movement, the USA, Pakistan and Saudi Arabia have to share responsibility and acknowledge the fact that their policies over the last decade have only heightened the adversarial attitudes between different ethnic groups, constituting the Afghan nation.

This phenomenon of animosity and suspicion has only been heightened by the present military campaign. Conceptual policy statements about the desirability and objective of establishing a new government in Afghanistan, representing all ethnic groups which can safeguard their respective concerns and interests, is not enough to transcend the negative chemistry of inter-ethnic apprehensions in Afghanistan. All this apart, an insipient civil war and simmering terrorist activities generated from Afghanistan, are the likely prospects in the near future. This perhaps is the reason why the Chief of General Staff of the British Armed Forces gave the assessment late in October that the campaign in Afghanistan will last not just for two, but four years.

All this is happening in the context of the macro-level internal geo-political situation where neither the Northern Alliance nor the Taliban are any longer in control of Afghan provinces in the countryside. Nor have US forces undertaken any effort to control the major urban centres of the country viz. Mazar-e-Sharif, Kabul, Jalalabad, Ghazni, Kandahar and Herat.

Given this scenario, it would be unrealistic to suggest any prescriptive solutions. One foresees a period of instability and uncertainty in Afghanistan, while focusing attention on the elimination of terrorism and its perpetrators, is the legitimate short-term objective in the context of international consensus about this objective, it must be noted that a large number of Islamic countries and other developing countries are incrementally doubtful about the usefulness of long military campaign against Afghanistan.

The campaign is also willy-nilly being perceived as an anti-Islamic exercise among Muslims all over the world. The long-term political attention should be to undertake serious efforts to bring security, stability and economic succour to the people of Afghanistan. Such an effort would be credible only if the endeavour is catalysed through the UN and by active participation by the neighbours of Afghanistan who have tangible and long-term interest in the welfare of the Afghan people rooted in history. The economic dimensions of this endeavour should become as much a responsibility of the US and the major powers of the world, as the responsibility to eradicate terrorism has been assumed as an imperative necessity by these powers.

15

The Next Phase

Stabilisation in Afghanistan – Factors Afftecting the Next Phase

Political stabilization of Afghanistan and starting the programme of its development and reconstruction has to be evaluated in the context of the initiative which had been taken in early December. The instititional framework and the terms of reference for the political dispensation in Afghanistan now stands concretised with the formation of the interim government of Afghanistan. Mr. Hamid Karzai, a Popalzai Pushtoon has been designed the Prime Minister of the new government. A 29-member Interim Council stands nominated. The Northern Alliance representative have taken the lion's share of portfolios in this interim Afghan cabinet. Alliance's representatives have taken over 19 of the 30 cabinet portfolios including Ministers of Interior, Foreign Affairs, and Defence.

Former King Zahir Shah's faction called the Rome Group has assumed charge of finance, public works, education and reconstruction. Afghan representative of the Cyprus group representing interests of Hazaras and Iran did not participate in the final stages of the Bonn Conference. They have no representatives in the interim cabinet of Afghanistan.

Some socio-ethnic factors of political relevance to the prospects of this dispensation have to be taken note of.

Afghanistan's population could be anywhere between 19 to 20 million people at present. Of this about 40 to 42 per cent are Pushtoons. Tadjiks constitute between 30 to 35 per cent. The Uzbeks about seven percent and Hazaras about eight per cent. The remaining miniscule ethnic minorities consist of Turkmen, Persians, Hindus and Sikhs. Some are Qizalbashis.

The interim government as constituted, and especially the distribution of portfolios is characterized by manifest ethnic imbalances and distribution of political power. With the Northern Alliance the Tadjiks seem to have taken charge of most powerful departments in the interim government. Though a Pushtoon, Mr. Hamid Karzai is the Prime Minister but he does not represent the majority of Pushtoons of Afghanistan who inhabit in eastern Afghanistan and south-central Afghanistan. Karzai represents the Kandhari Pushtoons, consisting of the Beragzai, Saddozai and Popalzai tribal groups.

Pushtoon representatives from ex-King Zahir Shah's factions are also mostly from this group. The majority of Pushtoons are perhaps under-representated. The Hazaras are not represented and Uzbeks seem to have under-represented, in the interim government. There are therefore undercurrents of dissention in the interim government rooted in ethnic tribal representation in the cabinet as well as in the distribution of portfolios. There were reports that Pushtoon leader Haji Qadir threatened to walk out of the Bonn Conference due to the reasons mentioned above, and was persuaded with difficulty to remain a participant.

Former President of Northern Alliance Government Burhanuddin Rabbani and Uzbek General Abdul Rashid Dostum announced non, acceptance of the decisions taken at Bonn soon after the decisions were made public. Former Mujahideen leader Mujaddadi convened a meeting of Pushtoon leaders in Jalalabad and Peshawar to voice opposition to the decisions taken and to announce non-cooperation with the interim government because of its not being truly representative of Pushtoons in Afghanistan.

The last phase of the military campaign in Kandahar in the second week of December brought factional strife and competition between the Kandahar Pushtoons to the fore with warlord Maqbool and the Governor of Kandahar conflicting with each other over jurisdiction over Kandahar and its surroundings. The situation on the ground is fraught with jurisdictional confusion, local military commanders and warlords are in de facto control of the important urban centres all over Afghanistan with their respective militias still not confirming their allegiance to the interim government of Afghanistan. The interim government is to formally assume charge on 22nd of December. Its effectiveness even as a short-term controlling authority will depend on several factors and trends.

Will the interim cabinet be able to function in unity and harmony, given the tensions and frustrations mentioned above?

Though the Northern Alliance claims to be a united military force, it is not because of the rivalries between Dostum and the Tadjik military leader, the new Defence Minister of Afghanistan General Mohammed Fahim whose rivalry is underpinned by their respective ethnicity. The former is an Uzbek, the latter a Tadjik. There have been reports of skirmishes between groups of Northern Alliance militia in Northern and North-central Afghanistan. The Pushtoon militias in the West, in south and east of Afghanistan, are functioning under different tribal leaders and warlords. Their cadres may include Taliban elements who have changed sides over the last two months. Simmering antagonism and dissidence between the Pushtoons and non-Pushtoons and factionalism between each of these groups remain a disturbing possibility. Forging a unified and disciplined military force as a coercive instrumentality of the interim government is going to be one of the most difficult tasks faced by Prime Minister Hamid Karzai and his interim government. Consequently, the maintenance of law and order throughout Afghanistan till the proposed Loya Jirga (Grand National Assembly of Tribal leaders) is assembled is going to be a dicy proposition.

Political frustrations and disappointments regarding the constitution of the interim government will come to the fore whenever Loya Jirga meets which in turn would make the task of drawing up the new constitution and a long-term political arrangement a complex and difficult task.

It is obvious, therefore, the presence of an international military force in Afghanistan a year or two may be necessary to pre-empt and prevent the possibility or re-emerging of fractiousness in Afghan politics degenerating into a new cycle of violent conflict in the country. It is important to note that the United States is not inclined to have a long-term presence of its military forces in Afghanistan. Their present policy stance seems to be move out of Afghanistan after the capture and elimination of Osama bin Laden and Mulla Mohammed Omar, and destroy all Al Qaeda and Taliban organisations inside Afghanistan.

The prospects are the US pulling out support, the deployment of an international force led by the US and other members of NATO along with troops from some Muslim countries like Turkey, Bangladesh, Jordan and perhaps Egypt. The government of Islamic countries do not seem to be very enthusiastic about participating in such a peace-keeping or peace-making force. The project for deploying an international force is complicated by two additional factors. The Northern Alliance has already expressed reservations about any foreign force being deployed in Afghanistan after the interim government takes charge and Loya Jirga commences consultations. In general political terms, Afghans regardless of ethno-tribal identities would be opposed to presence of foreign forces particularly of NATO or Russian Federation in Afghanistan. Indications from the Bonn Conference as well as other multilateral consultations were that the proposed international force will not be a United Nations force but it will be a separate entity within the framework of the US-led international coalition against terrorism. Though this force will have the general sanction of the UN Security Council resolutions on the Afghanistan situation passed so far, its operational and jurisdictional mandate would be based on the international coalition arrangements.

Structuring of political, jurisdictional and operational equations between the force and the interim government of Afghanistan this international force will be a sensitive exercise requiring highest level of tact and adjustment between interim government of Afghanistan and US-led coalition.

Given these uncertainties and undercurrents of traditional rivalries, doubts and suspicions in Afghan civil society, it is clear that the flow of external development and reconstruction assistance could be delayed despite the anxiety and willingness of the international community to go to the assistance of Afghan people as early as possible.

What then could be India's role in the stabilization and reconstruction of Afghanistan. The Indian special envoy on Afghanistan S.K. Lambah reportedly played an important behind the scene role in facilitating the compromises and decisions taken at the Bonn conference. The Indian diplomatic mission will start functioning in Kabul from the 22nd of December. An interim Indian diplomatic mission is already functioning in Kabul. Indian developmental and medical assistance has already started flowing into Afghanistan. The Minister of Interior of the Interim government of Afghanistan Qanooni has already been in Delhi. His visit is to be followed by visits of foreign minister Abdullah Abdullah and the Defence Minister General Fahim by the third week of December. Indian Ambassadors in Tashkent and Teheran have been in touch with leaders of the Northern Alliance at Mazar-e-Shrif and Hazara leaders from Herat like Mir Waiz Sadiq and Ismail Khan.

The objective is to emphasise Indian commitment to the stabilization and re-construction of Afghanistan. Ambassador Lambah and External Affairs Minister Jaswant Singh are likely to have discussions with Prime Minister Hamid Karzai in Kabul towards the end of December.

These Indian initiatives have the general support of neighbouring countries like Uzbekistan and Iran as well as the United States of America.

Taliban's destruction and departure from the scene as well as the neutralization of Al Qaeda are positive developments in terms of Indian interests and objectives in relation to Afghanistan as well as Central Asia. Indian policies should assiduously avoid getting enmeshed in the internal political rivalries and factionalism of the Afghan people in the coming days. It should focus on encouraging the forces of moderation and stabilisation in Afghanistan accepting Afghanistan's Islamic identity and the ethno-tribal foundation of Afghan civil society. There should be no advocacies on our part about new Afghan government being secular, non-aligned, etc. Our primary aim should be to gain the confidence of common people of Afghanistan through active participation in reconstruction and development of that country. We have made good beginnings over the last two months.

Stabilisation of Afghanistan—Post Loya Jirga Prospects

The Loya Jirga or the Grand National Assembly of Afghanistan concluded its session in Kabul in the third week of June as scheduled by the United Nations sponsored International Conference on Afghanistan at Bonn in October, 2001. The Loya Jirga was to designate an interim government which is to remain in power till the year 2003. The Jirga also had to determine the membership of the new National Parliament of Afghanistan which was to consist of 111 members representing all segments and sections of civil society of Afghanistan. This Parliament is to draft a new constitution of Afghanistan on which the long-term political structure of Afghanistan will be established.

The Loya Jirga designated former King Zahir Shah as Baba-e-Millat (Father of the Nation). This was a compromise because King Zahir Shah's supporters were initially keen on assigning a role to him as Head of State and Chief of Interim Government. In the event, Hamid Karzai was confirmed as the Executive President of the Interim Government. The political, administrative and National Security decisions taken by him from October 2001 to June 2002 were endorsed by the National Assembly.

There was some controversy about the formation of new Cabinet. Pushtoon (Pathan) Members of the Loya Jirga asserted that the initial cabinet constituted in the autumn of 2001 was ethnically and politically asymmetrical and unbalanced with non-Pushtuns dominating the cabinet and practically (Members of the non-Pushtun Northern Alliance being in charge of all the significant portfolios, Home, Defence, External Affairs, and so on). Ultimately, the Tadjik Home Minister Yunus Qanuni gave up his portfolio reluctantly and accepted the post of Education Minister with additional responsibility of being adviser on Natioanl Security to Hamid Karzai. The Northern Alliance, however, refused to relinquish the portfolios of defence and external affairs. Mr. Fahim and Mr. Abdullah followers of the Tadjik leader Ahmed Shah Masood remain incharge of these portfolios. These decisions were not easily reached but they are a remarkable achievement coming in the context of the ground realities in which the political situation in Afghanistan is evolving. It is pertinent to draw attention to these realities.

The writ of the Karzai Government still does not run all over Afghanistan effectively. Local Pushtun warlords, with their own militia still dominate most of southern and eastern Afghanistan, including important urban centres of Kandahar, Ghazni and Jalalabad. In the North, General Dostum (an Uzbek) and the successor military leaders of Ahmed Shah Masood (Tadjik) still retain their military clout and a fair amount of territorial jurisdiction. The Shias of Northern Afghanistan are similarly endowed and not yet fully reconciled to trusting the new political structures being sought to be put in place. These political trends have been finding expression in military skirmishes and refusal to implement political directives issued from Kabul off and on, over the last eight months. That the Loya Jirga was successfully convened is an achievement in itself because the processes of sending representatives to this Assembly were subject to contradictory and competitive political trends described above.

Deputy Defence Minister Dostum had laid claim to higher responsibilities and a more prominent role in the new Government. So have leaders of the Masood faction. There was high controversy about designation/election of the new members of the 111 member Parliament. The 1500 or so Members of the Loya Jirga were supposed to elect these 111 members. There were not only debates but even physical disturbances about the basis on which representation should be ensured in the Parliament. It is not the major ethnic communities, the Pushtoons, Tadjiks, the Hazaras and Uzbeks who demanded representation as collectivities, there were claims and assertions demanding representation for sub-groups of these major ethnic groups on the principals of tribal representation as well as sub-regional representations from the 29 different Provinces of Afghanistan. There was a major controversy about the representation of women in the Parliament. Initially thirteen seats were allocated for women. But there were demands that this number should be doubled. The problem was not fully solved towards the end of the formal discussions of the Loya Jirga.

Older political leaders involved in the anti-Soviet campaign between 1979 and 1990, like Burhannudin Rabbani and Gulbuddin Hekmatyar are still active and ambitious about resuming some role in the emerging new dispensation. They are firmly opposed by the younger political and military leaders as well as leading ethnic and tribal figures, who were more active in the struggle against the Taliban since 1996 and particularly since October, 2001. Karzai still has to create a unified Afghan army, establish a national administrative system and re-start the process of economic re-construction, apart from the Macro-level institutional tasks of establishing and re-activating new Parliament and appointing a new Cabinet.

International involvement in Afghanistan to eradicate the remnants of terrorism, to provide security to the new Afghanistan government and to participate in the economic reconstruction is also facing problems. While the top leaders of the Interim Authority of Afghanistan led by Hamid Karzai feel the need to continue the presence of both the anti-terrorist military units led by the USA, and the Coalition troops led by the UK, tasked with providing security for the new government, a major segment of the Loya Jirga wanted these troops to move out in conformity with the traditional Afghan opposition to foreign forces operating in their country. While international aid agencies and bilateral aid have increased and are gradually making their presence felt, they are functioning in difficult political circumstances and potentially volatile internal conflict situation. There have been clashes between Afghan military groups and the foreign security forces led by the United Kingdom, the focus of the US anti-terrorist campaign has shifted to Pakistan. While Al-Qaeda in Afghanistan and from Pakistan remain active in fomenting trouble in the country.

Though the government of Pakistan is officially supportive of the initiatives for stabilization of Afghanistan, there are segments of the Pakistan Government which still continue covert support to the disruptive activities of the Taliban and Al-Qaeda cadres.

Three latest developments signal the shape of things to come. Mr. Karzai announced on the 30th of June that his government will act in a planned and purposive manner to eliminate the role of warlords and regional military groups engaged in questioning the authority of the Karzai Government and disrupting the administration. Secondly, Mr. Yunus Qanuni has announced plans for organizing a new political party in Afghanistan called Mehez-e-Milli, the Afghan National Party. Indications are that this political party world try to organize mostly non-Pushtun ethnic groups into a political force. Third, there are some unconfirmed reports about General Dostum remaining disaffected because of not getting a prominent portfolio in the Cabinet. The coming 18 months will therefore be characterised by complex political activities and competition for spaces in the emerging power structure of Afghanistan.

In overall terms, the results of discussions at the Loya Jirga can at best be considered as a very tentative beginning of political stabilization of Afghanistan. President Karzai has a highly difficult and complex task ahead, in which he needs international support. India has been incrementally active in assisting Afghanistan in its programme of economic revival, reconstruction, infrastructure improvement and in providing training facilities for its administration, in all aspects. It is for the people of Afghanistan to decide how to resolve their contradictions but it is important that India joins in any effort that will prevent external involvement or intrigues aimed at distrupting the gradual stabilization of the country after a gap of nearly 29 years.

16

The Reconstruction

War and Reconstruction in Afghanistan- parallel Exercises in Stabilising the Country

Hamid Karzai , the Chairman of the Interim Government of Afghanistan announced on the 30th of March that the Loya Jirga (the Grand Tribal Assembly) to determine the future political dispensation in Afghanistan has been summoned to meet in Kabul around the 10th of June. Over 1400 delegates representing the major ehtnic components of Afghan civil society are expected to participate in this conference. Discussions at this Jirga would be aimed at creating the new power structure for Afghnistan and the institutional framework of its government. The exercise will be carried out in a competitive, even fractious atmosphere rooted in ethnic, regional and even religious adversarial relationships between different sections of the Afghanistan population.

One does not have to go into great detail about the suspicions and rivalries between the Pushtuns, Hazaras, Tadjiks and Uzbeks. Nor does one have to over-emphasise the internal dichotomies between the Pushtuns of Western Afghanistan and south-eastern Afghanistan or the internecine conflicts between the Hazaras and the Uzbeks and Tadjiks who constituted the Northern Alliance. This situation has been compounded by local tribal leaders and warlords questioning the authority of the Interim Karzai Government and reports about Taliban and Al-Qaeda cadres re-grouping and initiating military operations against both the US troops and the forces of the Afghanistan Government. The operation "ANACONDA" undertaken by the US forces in the Shahkot mountains in South-eastern and eastern Afghanistan, and the tenuous truce between troops constituting the Northern Alliance confirm this critical reality. It is in this uncertain context that the Afghan government has to initiate its reconstruction and stabilisation programme. Nearly 2000 kilometres of roads and practically every primary and secondary school in Afghanistan has to be re-built. Hospitals and medical clinics not only in Kabul, but in all the major urban centres of Afghanistan have to be re-established from scratch. Practically all the power projects, particularly the hydel power projects based on the Helmand and Kabul Rivers systems have to be revived after a gap of nearly 25 years. This is apart from keeping the Afghan people supplied with essential medicines and all basic foodstuffs. The depredations of the Taliban followed by the anti-terrorist campaign has been topped by a massive earthquake in the fourth week of March in which nearly 3000 Afghans have died. Some reports say there have been five thousand deaths and extensive dislocation of population from the rural areas.

Leaving aside the macro-level political and institutional stabilisation of Afghanistan, the task of reconstruction of Afghanistan is going to be a risky and difficult process despite the availability of pledged funds. It is in this context that one has to assess not only the internal but the broader geo- strategic implications of the ongoing anti-terrorist campaign led by the United States.

The over-arching phenomenon to take note of is that since 7 October, 2001 (when the United States led coalition launched its anti-terrorist military campaign), there has been an incremental US military presence not only in Afghanistan but in Uzbekistan, in Azerbaijan and Pakistan. The United States is assured of operational and logistical support and facilities in India and in Bangladesh. The elements of the central command of the USA stands augmented in the Gulf and in the northern reaches of the Indian Ocean, including in the Arabian sea.

Objectively speaking, the United States military presence and political interaction in Central, Western South Asia is at bigger levels even beyond what they were during the Cold War and during the Gulf War. It is obvious therefore that the security, political and economic objectives of this incremental US presence go beyond eroding and then eliminating the Taliban and Al-Qaeda Movement.

In terms of inter se priorities, the more immediate objective of the United States presence is to mop up remnants of Taliban and Al-Qaeda forces in Afghnistan and in North-western parts of Pakistan, to the extent possible. That this campaign still continues, is clarified by a Commanding General of the US Central Command of the US Lt. General Tomy Franks in the second week of March.

The second objective is to stabilise Afghanistan which is subjected to contradictory pulls and pressures. Given the absence of any cohesive Pushtoon military force in Afghanistan, Hamid Karzai has had to accept troops of the Northern Alliance as the main instrumentality for defence and security of the interim administration which it heads. He has also had to give a number of important portfolios to leaders from the Northern Alliance (Uzbeks and Tadjiks) in the interim cabinet to ensure that the coalition holds together in this initial stage till the Loya Jirga or the Grand Assembly meets and finalises future political dispensation, in Afghanistan.

It is important to note that the major powers led by the United States envisage two distinctive roles, one for the US-led coalition military force who would be concentrating on the anti-terrorist war, and the second is a combined military force led by Britain consisting of troops from Western democracies who would function as peace-keeping and internal security force for the stabilisation of Afghanistan. It is, logical, therefore to conclude that the US-led anti-terrorist force would play a strategic role in Afghanistan while the other coalition members led by Britain would play the role of stabilising the politics of the country supporting the interim Afghan government. Till such time as it is needed.

It is the broader objectives of the US military presence in different parts of Pakistan (Peshawar, Quetta, esni, Gwadar and Karachi), in Uzbekistan, in Azerbaijan and in the Gulf which merit a rational specultative prognosis to the extent possible. US political and military leaders led by President Bush, as well as Prime Minister Tony Blair of the UK have publicly stated that the war against terrorism would be a long struggle. President Bush has been more specific, talking about "Axis of Evil", mentioning North Korea, Iran and Iraq, indicating that these countries could be the next target of US military operations. There are currently seven countries on the USA's list of states sponsoring terrorism, namely, Cuba, Iran, Iraq, Libya, North Korea, Sudan and Syria, Out of these 7 countries only Cuba and Libya lie outside the geographical limits of Central and West Asia. The augmented US military presence from Turkey in the north to the Philippines in South East Asia, is clearly a physical manifestation of strategic and security understandings which the US has reached with various countries in this region, to contain religious extremism and violence as well as to stabilise the region with a view to ensuring long-term energy and economic security for the international community, particularly the security of western democracies and their allies. It must also be realised that 3 out of 5 Central Asian countries are also Members of the Partnership for peace arrangements of NATO. The twin macro-level strategic objectives of the American politico-strategic presence in the region (it is indicated that this would be a longer presence) are in a manner an exercise to balance off, or prevent any excessive domination or influence by China and Russia on the countries of the region. The second objective is to secure the energy resources of the Gulf and to have long-term access to the proven hydro-carbons and mineral resources of the Central Asian countries. This is apart from the attraction of investment opportunities and the markets of Central Asia. Equally relevant is US objectives of stabilising the nuclear weapons and missiles security environment in the region.

The presence of US troops and creation of a pattern of political and security confrontations positions the US to effectively intervene in any nuclear confrontation between India and Pakistan. Such an exercise could contribute to gradual capping of nuclear weapons and missile capacities of these two countries and to persuade them to an effective arms control measures within the framework of the international Non- Proliferation Agenda determined by the Five Permanent Members of the UN Security Council. The Cordon Sanitaire or the structuring the politico-military stabilization of the security environment being put in place by the US would also be a more direct instrumentality in preventing the horizontal proliferation of weapons of mass destruction in countries stretching from North Korea to Iran.

Developments since September 11, 2001, are not limited to international consensus about fighting terrorism. They also signal critical changes in the strategic and security environment in the Asian region and in the new global order which is being aimed at by the United States. The major task of Indian foreign and strategic policies is to carefully assess the extent to which these new arrangements would benefit India or militate against India's substantive security interests and freedom of options. It is obvious that in the short and medium terms, positive equations with the US is the practical option.

External Affairs Minister Yashwant Sinha's Visit to Afghanistan—An Assessment

Foreign Minister Yashwant Sinha rounded off his South Asian diplomatic tour by visiting Kabul during the second week of August. The immediate occasion for the visit was India's decision to present three airbus aircraft to the Government of Afghanistan to build up its civil airlines, ARIANA. Sinha travelled in the first of these aircrafts and presented them to the Afghan government.. The deeper and longer term purpose of

Yashwant Sinha's visit was to maintain continuity in India's high-level contacts with the present power structure of the Afghan Government which commenced as the Taliban was being ousted from power. Factual details of India's engagement with Afghanistan since October 2001 are well known and this is a matter of public knowledge. What is important is to analyse India's interests and motivations related to Afghanistan.

Regardless of the passage of time and the political upheavals which Afghanistan has gone through since India's independence, the conceptual framework of India's Afghanistan policy is the following :

India's primary interest is to ensure continuity in relations between the peoples of Afghanistan and India. India firmly believes that these relations to be mutually beneficial can be sustained only if India supports trends and policies in Afghanistan which would make the Afghan people prosperous and the Afghan polity stable. The establishment of a political dispensation which is moderate, representative of all the ethnic segments composing Afghan civil society and which would not be unfriendly towards India, is the first necessary step to meet the above objective. India has no desire to interfere in the internal affairs of Afghanistan and would deal with whichever government is in effective authority.

India's Afghan experience of recent years has resulted in India being quite clear in its stand that Afghanistan dominated by extremist Islamic forces or having a government which is not representative of the multi-ethnic, pluralistive nature of Afghan civil society would not serve Afghanistan's interests or India's political or geo-strategic interests in the current security environment.

India will not take sides in any manner in the conflicts and controversies attendant upon the evolving events in Afghnistan at present. India's primary focus is to structure cooperation in substance in the social, economic infrastructural and health sectors.

India's active participation in the Bonn, Tokyo and Geneva conferences on stabilisation of Afghanistan and its economic reconstruction over the last ten months reflect these policy objectives. While nearly 1.8 million dollars have been pledged by the international community to Afghanistan for economic and social development, the Indian segment of the assistance has been most operational since January, while all the other assistance remained only pledged. India has translated its pledges valued at about a hundred million dollars into concrete action, in the spheres of health, civil aviation, training facilities for Afghan diplomatic, administrative and police personnel, as well as food assistance.

Leaving aside the important aim of maintaining continuity in high level interaction, Sinha's visit to Kabul had in my opinion more substantive objectives. Despite the successful completion of the Loya Jirga meeting and the establishment of a government under Hamid Karzai, the Government of Afghanistan continues to suffer from internecine competition and controversies. The Pushtoons, the Tadjiks, the Uzbek antagonisms have surfaced in Afghan politics again. The differences of opinion between President Hamid Karzai and the Tadjik leader Fahim are out in the open, the latter remaining resentful for his being deprived of defence portfolio. The regional warlords remain unamendable to the authority of the Central Government at Kabul. Uzbek leader General Dostum and Shia leader Ismail Khan remain alienated. Taliban cadres and other recalcitrant elements merging with various groups of warlords have vitiated the security environment by perpetration violence to a level where President Karzai has entrusted his personal security to foreign troops of the International Security Force now under the command of Turkish officers. Not only are there dissensions between Pushtoons and former constituents of the Northern Alliance, but there are bickerings within each of these groups. Foreign Minister Sinha's visit had the purpose of making a personal assessment about the current situation and the prospects of political stabilisation of Afghanistan. More than undertaking an assessment, Sinha's Kabul trip had the objective of encouraging the processes of harmony and unity in the Afghan power structure. Sinha's visit also had the aim of consolidating India's connectivity with the Pushtoon leadership in Afghanistan. This second purpose is of importance because between 1979 and 2001, India's interaction with the Pushtoon leadership was minimal. Pushtoons who constituted the main opposition to the Soviet intervention Afghanistan were alienated from India despite the traditional equations which Indian political leadership had with Pushtoon leadership since the beginning of the 20th century.

During the last two decades, India had closer connections with Northern Alliance leaders which became more substantial during the Taliban regime's tenure. The balance in India's relationships with leaders of all ethnic groups had to be restored. Sinha's visit was an important initiative in this respect. He not only met Fahim but also met General Dostum and Shia leader Ismail Khan during his visit. No excessive speculation is required about his exchange of views with these leaders. His meetings were aimed at emphasising to these leaders the importance of transcending suspicions and competition and come to agreements with the Pushtoon leaders who constitute the majority of people of Afghanistan to ensure that the difficult processes of political stabilisation and economic reconstruction are not disrupted. If these processes fail, Afghanistan's unity itself may be in danger.

India's more specific interests in Afghanistan are to have a strong relationship with Afghanistan so that it becomes a contributory factor in expanding India's relations with Central Asian Republics. Such a relationship is also important to counter Pakistani hostilities towards India. If by some miracle India's relations with Pakistan also get normalised, then a positive equation with Pakistan and Afghanistan will expand the horizons for political stability and security and for economic, technological and socio-cultural cooperation between India and the entire Central Asian and South West Asian regions.

Yashwant Sinha's meeting leaders like Dostum and Ismail Khan who are outside the power structure, contain the message that India is keen to help all segments of Afghan political leadership to join the mainstream of Afghan democratic politics.

Iranian President Khatemi visited Kabul within days of Sinha's visit. The views expressed by him and the objective of Iranian policies articulated by him during the visit indicated a clear convergence of interests and views between Iran and India on Afghan issues. It is necessary that India and Iran work together in stabilising Afghanistan regardless of misplaced antagonisms of the US against Iran, an antagonism which can be a hurdle against the stabilisation of Afghanistan, if the US does not become more objective and practical.

If friendly and practical suggestions given by Sinha and Khatemi to the Afghan leadership is not heeded, then the likelihood would be of Southern and Western Afghanistan emerging as a Pushtoon territorial entity. The remaining part of Afghanistan getting linked to Iran on the one hand and Uzbekistan on the other. Such a break up would have dangerous implications, particularly for Pakistan. It would also generate demographic and ethnic pressures in Central Asia which would not serve India's specific interests or the interests of security and stability in the region. This was the logic and impulse of Sinha's visit.

17

Socio-Economic Implications

Keynote Address by the Author at the Seminar on Geo-political and Socio-Economic Implications of USA's Involvement in Afghanistan Organised by the Academy of Third World Studies : Jamia Millia Islamia

Mr. Mahdi, Distinguished Members of the audience. I thank the Academy of Third World Studies for inviting me to participate in its seminar on the Geo-political and socio-economic implications of USA's involvement in Afghanistan. I feel specially privileged about being asked to deliver the Keynote Address at this Seminar.

Under the Umberella of the overall theme, this session is to be devoted to the impact of external forces on the nation-building processes in Afghanistan after 1970. The early 70s were a watershed in Afghanistan's history. The overthrow of King Zahir Shah by his cousin Mohammed Daud in a bloodless military coup in 1973 should be considered the beginning point of the traumatic and violent experiences of the Afghan people and of the Afghan state which are culminating in the present developments in that country. If one deliberately compartmentalises trends of international politics and Afghanistan's foreign relations as separate from the socio-economic and political developments in Afghanistan, one would not be wrong in concluding that the history of Afghanistan since the middle of the 19th century has been chequered and continuing attempt at nation- building specially equally continuously to impact of external forces involved in Afghanistan due to the geo-strategic considerations. Some fundamental facts, even elemental factors about the emergence of Afghanistan as a nation-state must be kept in mind.

Afghanistan emerged as a unified nation-state as the Persian and Mughal Empires declined in mid-18th century. The Afghans under the

Pushtoon domination with contours of its current territorial identity and the rule of Ahmed Shah Abdali. Territories which previously were under the jurisdiction of the Persian Empire, the Mughal Empire and later on the Khanats to the north from roughly the 15th century were merging into a single geo-political unit under Duranni Empire. Even before this phase of national consolidation could be completed the advent of European colonial powers in Central Asia, South Asia and the Gulf impinged on Afghanistan.

I do not have to dilate on the competition between the Czarist Russia and the British Empire for strategic domination and economic objectives in the Central Asian and South Asian regions from the mid 19th century onwards to this knowledgable audience. Suffice it to say that what is known as the Great Game was not the Great Game as far as Afghan people were concerned. The acquisitive confrontation between imperial/colonial powers disrupted the tenuous process of the consolidation of new Afghan state as multi-ethnic, multi-lingual, pluralistic political entity. Despite the feudal and monarchical power structure of Afghanistan from the times of Emir Dost Mohammed to King Amanullah and later up to the reign of King Zahir Shah, efforts at creating a composite national identity continued though the exercise remained asymmetrical with the Pushtoons remaining a dominant factor.

The most radical and vibrant phase of national consolidation in Afghan history during the last century was the political, social and economic reforms undertaken by King Amanullah (1919-1929). Amanullah tried to resolve the internal contradictions between the forces of modernisation and forces of Orthodox Islam and tribalism by initiating extensive reforms in the spheres of education, women's literacy, abolition of Purdah, land reforms, etc. He failed because he could not carry the Afghan people with him. His vision was far in advance of the political orientations and social mores of Afghanistan. He faced tribal opposition which evolved into military conflict ultimately resulting in his exile to Italy. History repeated itself after 44 years when King Zahir Shah also went into exile in Italy when his cousin Mohammed Daud expelled him from power.

Zahir Shah perhaps should be considered the most practical and rational leader of the Afghans in the 20th century. Learning from King Amanullah's experience, he opted for gradualness in modernising Afghanistan and in consolidating its identity transcending ethnic and tribal components of Afghan civil society. Realising that he did not have the resources or the power to exclude external influences on Afghanistan politics and on the Afghanistan economy, he opted for allocating different parts of his kingdom as areas of political influence and economic activity to the major powers desiring a foothold in his country. The northern half of Afghanistan was allowed to be the region of primary influence and activities of the former Soviet Union and the Socialist camp. The southern areas were allowed to be the arena of influence of the Western powers. King Zahir Shah adopted an approach of non-involvement and neutrality in the substance of his policies throughout his 40 year regime. Even during major upheavals like the Second World War and subsequent trends of the Cold War impacting on Central Asia and South Asia. It is the insistence on remaining a minimalist in the social and economic which ultimately resulted in his overthrow because he did not anticipate the challenge that he was about to face from the inter-play between impulses of rivalry for power in his family and the incremental political modernisation of an emerging middle class of professionals and military officers trained abroad. Daud Khan exploited this political impulses to overthrow Zahir Shah promising political modernisation and socio-economic reforms in Afghanistan.

This brings me to the 1970s, the point of time mentioned as the basic term of reference for examining developments in Afghanistan within the framework of the subject-matter of today's Seminar.

When Daud captured power in 1973, he inherited an atmosphere of bitterness and economic confusion. Parliamentary elections which were due in August-September 1973 ran into difficulties because of the difference of opinion between the judiciary and the cabinet on the Supreme Court's role as the watch-dog of parliamentary elections. The judiciary felt that over-seeing elections should be done by a separate and independent body and not the Supreme Court whereas the executive Branch as well as several legal experts felt that the Supreme Court itself should play such a role. A joint committee of representatives of the Cabinet and the Supreme Court could not come to any agreed conclusion. So the elections were delayed. Though Afghanistan's export performance had improved, many western sponsored banking and industrial projects got stuck in procedural wrangles. The increase in foreign loans to Afghanistan during the period 1969-73 had increased Afghanistan's total foreign indebtedness. The situation was compounded by the lack of infrastructural institutions in the country to manage finances or to deal with its emerging industrialisation. The armed forces and the small urbanised middle class were getting impatient with the role of the feudal and Royal power structure and the very gradual approach to modernisation, spread of education and reform.

The army and the middle class expected Daud to restructure the Afghan polity with the following objectives :

- Making the elected Parliament a centre of power structure.
- Ensuring that the executive branch of the Government should have greater representation from the media, academia and the middle class combined with the removal of members of the Royal family and related feudal order from the Cabinet and senior positions in the government.
- For Afghanistan to move away from the greater pro-western tilt in foreign and economic policies which had characterised the last years of the Zahir Shah regime so that a more equal relationship could be revived with the Soviet Union and Iran. Daud was expected to keep the Pushtoonishtan claim alive.

Daud however failed to meet any of the above objectives which had impelled those who supported him to replace King Zahir Shah. He failed to manage the economy well ; he was not inclined to assert Afghan nationalism and nationalistic position vis-a-vis Afghanistan' immediate neighbours and important powers interested in Afghanistan on the lines on which his revolutionary supporters desired. The most serious mistake he made was to exclude the officers of the armed forces and intellectuals of the Parcham and Khalq movements from power sharing when he consolidated his position by 1973-76.

From the middle of 1976 onwards the alienation between Daud and those who had supported him to come to power was more or less complete. This ultimately resulted in the army-led coup in 1978. Daud and members of his family were killed in the basement of the Royal Palace in downtown Kabul. The attack on the Presidential residence was led by a young armoured corps officer of the Afghanistan Army, Khan Aslam Watanjar. The rule of Afghanistan's Royal family of the Durrani descent came to an end in 1978 with Mr. Taraqi and the People's Democratic Party of Afghanistan coming to power.

The objective of this prologue is not to give a chronologically detailed description of the events which led to the Soviet intrusion into Afghanistan in support of the PDPA rule, or the Saur Revolution as it was called. The attempt would only be to describe the broad trends and events which led to the Soviet military intrusion towards the end of 1979. The Taraqi regime which came to power had left-of-centre ideological orientations. Throughout the year that Taraqi ruled Afghanistan, the country's relations with Pakistan, and Iran deteriorated. The Taraqi regime also did not keep equidistance from the USA and the Soviet Union in its foreign policy. Policies were initiated which could only have expanded the Soviet economic, technological and military presence in Afghanistan.

Compared to the modernisation and gradualness which characterised the Afghan regime from 1933 to 1978, the PDPA regime decided to launch radical programmes of literacy, women's education, modernisation of the economy and improving infrastructural facilities of transport and communications. The Taraqi regime also moved to create institutions of government with the representation from the various tribal and ethnic groups which constituted the Afghan nation. The domination of Pushtoon in Afghan politics was questioned and sought to be modified. The role of the orthodox clergy was also challenged under the new scheme of things.

The government now was manned by increasing numbers of PDPA cadres mostly trained in the Soviet Union and East Europe. These cadres replaced a majority of the public servants of the old school. A whole segment of vested interests in the traditional Afghan power structure was challenged and destroyed in the short span of a few months by the end of 1978. Those from the old Afghan elite who could afford to, left the country for North America and Europe. The others started migrating to Pakistan, India and the Gulf. These vested interests with linkages in Pakistan and Iran (the Iranian revolution was still a year away and took place in 1979) generated apprehensions about the likely results of the anti-Daud coup and the PDPA revolution. The simple argument of Taraqi's detractors was that Afghanistan, a non-aligned Muslim country was being forcibly turned into a communist country. Also that the Soviet Union will find a permanent foothold in Afghanistan, which will be a challenge to American, Pakistani and Iranian interests, as well as the interests of the countries of the Gulf.

President Daud's pro-western tilt from the end of 1975 onwards had resulted in Soviet resentment against his regime. The Soviet Union's contact with and support for the PDPA increased proportionately. So, when the Afghan army which was considerably dependent on the Soviet supplies and the large number of its cadres who were trained in the Soviet Union conducted a coup against Daud, the Coup had covert Soviet backing. Once Taraqi took over Soviet advisers started working in different departments of the Afghan Government. Both the People's Democratic Party of Afghanistan and the Government patterned themselves on the Soviet Communist Party and governmental systems. The Royal family, the Muslim clergy and the old elite stood excluded from the new arrangements.

This gave these elements an opportunity to argue that the Taraqi regime supported by the Soviet Union was challenging the traditional Afghan national identity and, more importantly, was hurting the religious feelings and the collective Islamic faith of the people of Afghanistan.

Taraqi was in power for a little less than one year. His hold over the government remained tenuous. His major problem was to keep PDPA united, given the intense rivalry and undercurrent of antagonism between Pushtoon-dominated Khalq faction and non-Pushtoon cadres belonging to the Parcham faction of the PDPA.

One is conscious that this can be seen as and over simplification of the Afghan situation and politics but these are the broad paradigms within which events developed in the country in 1978-79.

The period between 1979 and 1989 was in a sense a sort of Great Leap Forward aimed at national consolidation and modernisation. The Soviet backed Saur Revolution had three purposes. To dismantle permanently the feudal and tribal elite power structure of Afghanistan, to re-structure Afghanistan into a modern, secular nation-state and third to balance off the traditional Pushtoon ethnic domination of Afghan politics through constitutional and political means aimed at giving due representation to other major ethnic groups of Afghanistan, namely , the Tadjiks, the Hazaras, Uzbeks and other smaller ethnic communities.

The Saur Revolution of Afghanistan failed due to the following reasons : The programme of modernisation and reforms and the move towards the creation of a secular state did not have the support of the Afghan people. The opposition to these programmes was not limited to Pushtoons. Most of the population belonging to all ethnic groups felt threatened by and suspicious of the reforms. Secondly, the conflict between Pushtoon and non-Pushtoon in the People's Democratic Party of Afghanistan(Khalq and Parcham) prevented unity within the ruling party and there was no unity of purpose. Third, the Saur Revolution lost credibility because it was perceived as a revolution artificially foisted on Afghans with Soviet Support, even if the objectives of the revolution were legitimate or necessary. Fourth, the major western powers perceived the revolution as a strategic threat to their interests in the Gulf. The Afghan revolution was perceived just as an instrumentality in Soviet Strategic expansion beyond Central Asia to South Asia and the Gulf. Equally important was the apprehensions of governments of the Muslim countries neighbouring Afghanistan that the ideological fall-out of the Afghan revolution following soon after the Iranian Revolution would threaten their stability and security. This is apart from Members of the old power structure at the feudal and tribal levels, seeing the Saur Revolution as dangerous to their vested interests.

So this last effort at national consolidation also failed not only because of inner contradictions of internal politics of Afghanistan but also because of direct tangible external intrusive involvement. This phenomenon took the form of international problem and political campaign against the Afghan revolution and the systematic and fullscale organisation of military resistance to Afghan and Soviet troops backing them.

Agreements signed in Saudi Arabia and in Geneva marked the end of this phase of Afghan politics with the withdrawal of Soviet forces and at unsuccessful attempts at establishing a new Government in Afghanistan by the various Mujahideen groups and the remnants of the People's Democratic Party of Afghanistan.

The Soviet withdrawals instead of leading to the establishment of stable national government, resulted in a civil war situation during the period 1990-96. Mujadidi and Rabanni formed tenuous governments, after Najib stepped down. The conflict between Hekmatyar and Masood and then General Dostum created levels of conflict and political instability where no meaningful efforts could be undertaken for the stabilisation of the country or national consolidation. Out of this, it is this anarchic situation which led to the creation of the Taliban and its ultimately capturing power over most of Afghanistan between August 1996 and October 2001. It is worthwhile noting that the US and other powers withdrew support from various Mujahideen groups when they felt that these groups cannot establish Government in Afghanistan. Afghanistan was left to its devices in 1992-1996 with Pakistan, Saudi Arabia and Iran, being the only countries actively interested in Afghanistan developments. Their purpose was to establish a stable Islamic Government in Afghanistan which would not succumb to any form of Soviet and later on Russian influence. The Shia-Sunni divide manifested itself in the undercurrents of competition and confrontation in Afghanistan between Iran, on the one hand and Pakistan, Turkey and Saudi Arabia, on the other. The fact should not be ignored that these latter three are close allies of the United States.

Taliban came to power and consolidated its position in Afghanistan between 1996-1999, primarily with the support of Saudi Arabia and Pakistan and to some extent from Turkey. Whatever one's criticism of Taliban, they had a philosophy and approach towards national consolidation and reforms. Their aim was to create a strong orthodox Afghan Islamic nation-state. They also believed and wisely so, that the stability of Afghanistan can be guaranteed only after Afghan politics is dominated by Pushtoons, who constitute majority of population of Afghanistan. Neither the Taliban leadership nor the Taliban cadres had any interest in or knowledge about national consolidation and reconstruction in modern terms. They did not have any interest in evolving a composite national identity cutting across the ethnic and subordinate national identities of different sections of Afghan civil society. While the Taliban brought some stability and law and order inside Afghanistan, there was no attempt at social reforms or developmental work to remedy the results of the destructive war of the previous 17 years. In fact, the Taliban was purposefully opposed to the creation of a modern civil society or nation state. They had no commitment to international norms of human rights. They were officially discriminatory against women in aspects of their existence. They were determined to establish an Islamic state on the basis of their warped antediluvian interpretation of Islam. Taliban's ideology and intellectual orientations was in tune with violent and orthodox Islamic extremist movements in different parts of the world. In consequence while consolidation itself in power in Afghanistan, Taliban also developed close contacts with extremist Islamic militant groups who were operating from Afghanistan in the West and to the Philippines in the East. It is in this process that the Taliban Government provided bases to Osama bin Laden and forged links with the Al Qaeda movements. Spreading the message of Islam through violent and aggressive mean became a matter of greater attention than dealing with problems and processes of Afghanistan's national consolidation.

The western democracies particularly, the US had no interest in the political destiny of the Afghanistan people during this period. Their only concern was that Taliban or whichever government is in Afghanistan is not allowed in revival of Russian strategic influence in Afghanistan and south-west towards the Gulf. A more important interest of the western democracies was to have a friendly regime in Afghanistan which would be sufficiently stable to support US policies of outsourcing oil and hydro-carbons energy resources from Turkmenistan, Uzbekistan, and Kazakhstan. They wanted a friendly and cooperative Afghanistan through which oil and natural gas could be supplied by American multinationals to the vast markets in South Asia. This pipeline had to come through Afghanistan. So the limited purpose logic of the interests of the western countries in Afghanistan was obvious. There were not even formal advocacies to Taliban Government to mend its ways and to allow the Afghan civil society to function normally. In fact, the US State Department and some US multinational corporations had initiated contacts with the Taliban Government for this purpose between 1996-1997. The approach could not take off the ground because of continuous civil war situation in Afghanistan and incremental worries about Extremist Islam being based in Afghanistan on the part of the US.

Disappointed at USA's withdrawing support from the Taliban, Taliban proceeded to generate financial resources for itself by entering into the world drug market. Afghanistan became the second largest producer of opium poppy crop after India. But unlike the controlled production in India, the Taliban Government openly utilised the poppy crop to generate cash flows through manufacture and trading of Narcotics. This money was also made available to extremist Islamic militant groups operating from bases in Afghanistan and in other countries of West Asia. Irrationally fanatical Islamisation, active involvement in terrorist movements and conscious rejection of modern norms of building up of a civil society characterised the Taliban regime.

The terrorist attacks in New York and Washington on September 11, 2001 was the culmination of Taliban's involvement in terrorist activities in Kenya, Uganda, in the Muslim countries of Maghrab and West Asia. This is apart from logistical and training support for violent Muslim mercenaries who operate against India in Jammu and Kashmir. The political conundrum was that while in the late 70s and 80s and till 1996, external involvement in Afghanistan derailed national consolidation, from 1996 till October 2001, it is the engagement of western democracies which isolated the Taliban regime, making it follow insular and antediluvian policies leaving all processes of national consolidation in a disarray, neglect and total confusion.

This brings us to the latest stage in Afghanistan developments spreading over the last ten months or so. The international antiterrorist military campaign led by the US has ousted the Taliban from Power. There is intensely active external involvement in Afghanistan with three dimensions; First, the continuing campaign against Al-Qaeda and Taliban cadres. Second, that of providing internal security to the Afghan government and the Afghan state and third, to stabilise new Afghanistan political dispensation and parallely to provide across the board assistance for national reconstruction, economic development and the creation of a stable democratic institutions.

Another exercise in national consolidation commenced after the Bonn conference on Afghanistan in October last. The Loya Jirga or the National

Assembly session which concluded on June 18 last, have made some very tenuous beginnings to move forward down this path of stabilising Afghanistan.

The ground realities in Afghanistan remain volatile. Though the Loya Jirga took decisions about convening the Parliament, creating of Government, etc, factional contradictions remain rampant in Afghanistan. Afghan Minister for Civil Aviation and Vice President of the Government has been killed over the last two months. Important political leaders like Rashid Dostum, Gulbuddin Hikmatyar, Barhanuddin Rabanni remain disaffected. The revelries and suspicions between Pushtoon and non-Pushtoon ethnic power structures remain a pernicious influence against political consolidation. Afghan Government's writ does not run beyond Kabul and its surroundings. The large amount of economic aid promised at the Tokyo conference cannot be effectively utilised in these circumstances. Though some projects have been initiated. Tensions have emerged between common Afghans and the foreign forces operating under US and British command in the country. Programmes for training and creation of a new police and military force and administrative cadres are facing problems of ethnic tension and divided loyalties of the trainees belonging to different factions.

It is in this context that one assesses the impact of external forces on the nation-building processes in Afghanistan. The most important external entity involved in this process is the US. Keeping in mind developments and ingredients of US policies so far, the presence of US and other allied foreign entities in Afghanistan could be analysed in terms of discernible objectives on the following lines :

In terms of inter se priorities, the more immediate objective of the US presence is to mop up remnants of Taliban and Al Qaeda forces in Afghanistan and in North-western parts of Pakistan, to the extent possible. That this campaign still continues, is clarified by a Commanding General of the Central Command of the US Lt General Tomy Franks in the second week of March. The US bombing and ground action in Eastern Afghanistan throughout the first half of March confirms this situation.

Another factor which compounds the negative situation is that large numbers of Taliban and Al-Qaeda cadres who had escaped from the US-led military campaign with their arms intact and have merged with the local population. Latest reports indicate that these cadres, some of whom are also based in North-western parts of Pakistan have regrouped and have commenced guerilla warfare to which the United States is reacting.

It is important to note that the major powers led by the United States envisage two distinctive roles, one for the US-led coalition military force who would be concentrating on the anti-terrorist war. The second is a combined military force led by Britain consisting of troops from western democracies who would function as peace-keeping and internal security force for the stabilisation of Afghanistan. It is, logical therefore to conclude that the US-led anti-terrorist force would play a strategic role in Afghanistan while the other coalition members led by Britain would play the role of stabilising the politics of the country supporting the interim Afghan government till such time as it is needed.

It is the broader objectives of US military presence in different parts of Pakistan (Peshawar, Quetta, Pesni, Gwador, and Karachi), in Uzbekistan in Azerbaijan and in the Gulf countries which merit a rational speculative prognosis to the extent possible. US political and military leaders led by president Bush, as well as Prime Minister Tony Blair of the UK have publicly stated that the war against terrorism would be a long-struggle. President Bush has been more specific, talking about "Axis of Evil" mentioning North Korea, Iran and Iraq, indicating that these countries could be the next target of US military operations. There are currently 7 countries in the USA's list of states sponsoring terrorism, namely, Cuba, Iran, Iraq, Libya, North Korea, Sudan and Syria. Out of these 7 countries only Cuba and Libya lie outside the geographical limits of Central and West Asia. The augmented US military presence from Turkey in the North to the Philippines in South East Asia, is clearly a physical manifestation of strategic and security understandings which the US has reached with various countries of this region, to contain religious extremism and violence as well as to stabilise the region with a view to ensuring long-term energy and economic security for the international community, particularly, the security of western democracies and their allies. It must also be realised that 3 out of 5 Central Asian countries are also Members of the partnership for peace arrangements of NATO. The twin macro-level strategic objectives of the American politico-strategic presence in the region (It is indicated that this would be a long-term presence) are in a manner an exercise to balance off, or prevent any excessive domination or influence by China and Russia, on the countries of the region. The second objective is to secure the energy resources of the Gulf and to have long-term access to the proven hydro-carbons and mineral resources of the Central Asian countries. This is apart from the attraction of investment opportunities and the markets of Central Asia. Equally relevant is US objective of stabilising the nuclear weapons and missiles security environment in the region. The presence of US troops and creation of a pattern of political and security concentrations, positions the US to effectively intervene in any nuclear confrontation between India and Pakistan. Such an exercise could contribute to gradual capping of nuclear weapons and missile capacities of these two countries and to persuade them to effective arms control measures within the framework of the International Non-proliferation Agenda determined by the Five Permanent members of the UN Security Council. The Cordon Sanitaire or the structuring the politico-military stabilisation of the security environment being put in place by the US would also be a more direct instrumentality in preventing the horizontal proliferation of weapons of mass destruction in countries stretching from North Korea to Iran, This assessment is not purely speculative. This message has been inherent in public pronouncements of President Bush, US Defence Secretary Donald Rumsfeld and the testimonies given by the senior officials of the US Government to various committees of the US Congress. More recent report of the Congressional Research Service on Terrorism and Non-violence, implies these underlying objectives of the US policies.

In short term, the major powers of the region, Russia, and China seem to have reconciled themselves to these new equations being forged under the leadership of the United States. It is also obvious that these policy orientations will face resentment and dissent not only from these major powers and to some extent from India, but there may be reservations regarding this assertive US posture from important European powers like Germany and France.

Developments since September 11, 2001, are not limited to international consensus about fighting terrorism. They also signal critical changes in the strategic and security environment in the Asian region and in the new global order which is being aimed at by the United States. The major task of Indian foreign and strategic policies is to carefully assess the extent to which these new arrangements would benefit India or militate against India's substantive security interests and freedom of options. It is obvious that in the short and medium term, positive equation with the US is the practical option.

I am conscious that I have not been able to cover many important and detailed aspects of the manner in which external entities would influence the dynamics of nation-building in Afghanistan underway. The most important point to remember, however is that the fractious politics of Afghanistan cannot be overcome by imposed prescriptions or political or organisational steps emanating from foreign powers or external entities. It should also be remembered beyond certain threshold leaving aside Afghanistan's immediate neighbours the other external entities would not be over-interested or over-involved in the difficult task of Afghanistan's national consolidation. The responsibility for national consolidation rests primarily with the emerging Afghan leadership at present. There is no doubt that overcoming their inner contradictions is going to be a daunting task which involves the setting aside of historical memories and burdens and purposefully transcending current contradictions and narrower vested interests. The role of foreign powers, however, remains significant in one respect. They have an interest in a stable Afghanistan in the context of their immediate and long-term objectives. Karzai and other leaders of Afghanistan should take full advantage of this factor to further the processes of national consolidation by ensuring external support to policies of national re-construction which should be national, practical, properly prioritised and responsive to the aspirations and needs of Afghanistan people as a whole.

Index

V

W

Y

Z